West from Shenandoah

West from Shenandoah

A Scotch-Irish Family Fights for America
1729–1781

A Journal of Discovery

THOMAS A. LEWIS

WILEY

John Wiley & Sons, Inc.

Cartography by Mike Kirchoff (cartographer-online.com)

Published by John Wiley & Sons, Inc., Hoboken, New Jersey
Published simultaneously in Canada

Library of Congress Cataloging-in-Publication Data:

Lewis, Thomas A., 1942–
    West from Shenandoah : a Scoth-Irish family fights for America,
  1729–1781 : a journal of discovery / Thomas A. Lewis.
      p. cm.
    Includes bibliographical references (p. 243) and index.
    ISBN 0-471-31578-8 (acid-free paper)
    1. Lewis family. 2. Scots-Irish—Shenandoah River Valley (Va. and
W. Va.)—Biography. 3. Pioneers—Shenandoah River Valley (Va. and
W. Va.)—Biography. 4. Frontier and pioneer life—Shenandoah River
Valley (Va. and W. Va.) 5. Scots-Irish—Shenandoah River Valley (Va. and
W. Va.)—History—18th century. 6. Shenandoah River Valley (Va. and
W. Va.)—History. 7. Indians of North America—Shenandoah River Valley
(Va. and W. Va.)—History. 8. Culture conflict—Shenandoah River Valley
(Va. and W. Va.)—History—18th century. 9. Shenandoah River Valley
(Va. and W. Va.)—Race relations. 10. Land settlement—Shenandoah
River Valley (Va. and W. Va.)—History—18th century. I. Title.

  F232.S5L49 2004
  975.5'902—dc21

                             2003006651

Printed in the United States of America

10 9 8 7 6 5 4 3 2 1

This book is dedicated to the memory of

Fred Painter
Garland Hutchinson
Stewart Bell Jr.

You have become
the heritage that you loved.

Contents

Acknowledgments

For their unselfish help during the long gestation of this work, I would like to express my profound gratitude to the following people:

Hana Lane, my editor at John Wiley & Sons, for her undaunted patience, unflagging grace, and unerring advice;

Russ Adams, whose friendship and feral eye for infelicities have, as always, been invaluable to me;

Dr. Bill Gardner, who, contrary to his reputation, suffered this fool gladly, and ushered him into the world of twelve thousand years ago, and whose knowledge I can only hope to have approximated in translation;

My many mentors in the lore of the Shenandoah, including especially the three men to whom this book is dedicated: Fred Painter of Woodstock, who showed me the wagon road over the Massanutten and explained how to shoe a turkey; Garland Hutchinson of Toms Brook, who knew the historical provenance of every structure in Shenandoah County; and Stewart Bell Jr., who loved George Washington like a brother; and the many others who have over the years shared their love and knowledge of our valley without reservation;

All research librarians everywhere, without whose service such projects as this would founder, especially those of the libraries of Shenandoah, Augusta, and Frederick counties and the Lloyd House annex of the Alexandria, Virginia, library;

And my children, Jason, Kimberly, and Andrew, who have ever been the sources of light and warmth in my life and who continue to teach me the abiding pleasures of being family.

List of Maps

Introduction

A few dozen feet from the northwest corner of the Virginia state capitol building in Richmond, on the edge of a tiny parking lot for the highly privileged, a marble pedestal bears aloft a bronze statue of George Washington astride a prancing horse. The monument was raised in the 1850s by the sons and grandsons of the men who had fought the Indians and the British with Washington. Their reverence for his likeness was such that when the casting arrived from Munich, they would not allow horses to cart it from the docks, apparently thinking that to do so would be somehow undignified. They hauled it to its place of honor themselves.

The monument was conceived as a tribute not to Washington alone, but to Virginia's participation in the American Revolution. Around the base of the pedestal are arrayed sculptures of seven sons of Virginia, each representing a critical element of the struggle. Most are familiar to every American; Thomas Jefferson is there, representing "Independence"; as is Patrick Henry ("Revolution"); the first Chief Justice of the United States, John Marshall ("Justice"); and George Mason, representing the Bill of Rights of which he was a principal author. Less familiar is the figure of Thomas Nelson ("Finance"), who was a relatively minor character in the political and military story of the Revolution—circumstances made him briefly governor of Virginia at the time of the surrender of Cornwallis—but a major financier of Virginia's military efforts who freely dispensed his vast fortune in support of the cause.

The seventh figure stands to Washington's right front. He wears a caped hunting shirt and grasps with his left hand the muzzle of a grounded musket. In the ideology of the monument, he represents something called "Colonial Times." Of the people who pass the monument today, not one in a hundred will know who he is, or why he stands as an equal among this glittering company of patriots.

His name is Andrew Lewis, and one purpose of this book is to explain what he is doing there.

———

Had I written this story thirty years ago, when I first delved into it, I would have presented a straightforward tribute to the American pioneers who were driven westward by forces that could have destroyed them, but instead prepared them to assist in the difficult birth of the American Republic. It would have made an excellent action movie ("inspired by true events"), with a dramatic beginning as the boy Andrew Lewis sees his family's life in Ireland destroyed in a spasm of violence; then a tense interlude as they make a perilous sea crossing to America and an arduous new beginning in the wilderness; followed by more violence as they come in conflict with the native inhabitants; building to a crescendo—the full-scale battles of the Revolution—ending in bittersweet victory for the unsung hero.

It would have been a celebration of the dynastic family of John Lewis (Andrew's father) and the ethnic group to which they belonged—the Scotch-Irish, now largely forgotten even by their descendants, although they played a central role in our country's struggle with its western wilderness, native inhabitants, and English king. Written thirty years ago, my story would have run smoothly in the well-worn tracks of the distinguished chroniclers of Virginia and the Shenandoah Valley, refining the historical ore provided by the written recollections of elderly, respectable (that is to say, wealthy) Christian men.

But the story, like the Scotch-Irish who are its subject, proved to be unruly. As my movie-script story bustled along its well-worn path, questions and anomalies welled up underneath it like eruptions of lava, obstructing my course and burning down quite a number of my neat constructions. Such questions turned my attention to the dark side of history, which, like the dark side of the moon, can be made out when you look away from the parts that are shining brightly. Writers about history of necessity leave out most things that happen, choosing and portraying epochal events and people in accordance with a body of assumptions shared with their readers. These core beliefs about what is good, what is progress, what is estimable in people and societies are so basic and unquestioned that they dictate not only what we record, but also what we see. The unthinkable is invisible. That which contradicts our basic assumptions simply goes without saying.

Yet what we do not tell each other plays a role in our lives. As biological systems evolve by weeding out inadequate organisms, so history is shaped by the things it discards. What an observer of events omits from a diary or letter, whether because of modesty or shame, diffidence or repugnance, cultural or personal bias, is not available to the later chronicler. On the other hand, the historian, given a choice of sources, of which some are unconventional, will usually find credible the accounts that reflect his own assumptions. As generations pass, rewrites of history distill the same sets of biases, leaving out the same things. These omitted things become important when we need to correct our course as a people, to recognize that some of our most cherished assumptions are doing us harm. Then we turn to the lessons of the past to see where we went wrong, only to find homogenized accounts endlessly confirming that our way of doing things is best, declining to tell us what *else* happened—what other people thought, what alternatives were possible, when another course of action might have been better.

Here are some of the things that have been almost entirely distilled out of our history.

- The identity and origins of the Scotch-Irish, who in colonial times comprised one of the largest ethnic groups in America. They were instrumental in the creation of the American West and the American Republic. Why are they almost forgotten today?

- The identities and beliefs of the people who had been living on this continent for more than ten millennia when the first Europeans took up residence a mere four hundred years ago. They are portrayed in our culture either as projections of our primal fears ("heathen savages") or of our romantic notions ("noble savages"). Even the names we have assigned to them are bogus. Who were they?
- The intriguing anomaly that the Scotch-Irish and their fellow pioneers in the Shenandoah Valley, unlike white settlers in the other regions of the country, had little contact, and almost no conflict, with native inhabitants during two decades of settlement and growth.
- The explanation for the recurring explosions of savage war as the Scotch-Irish and others started to move west from Shenandoah. The traditional reasons do not withstand close inspection.

The surprising explanations of these mysteries were the eruptions that reshaped my narrative over the years. In its present, volcanic terrain, the book presents four sections. The first looks at the origins of the Scotch-Irish and their migration to America that carried John Lewis and his family to the Shenandoah Valley. The second inquires into a much earlier migration—by twelve thousand years or so—and the identity of the descendants of the First People. Part Three examines the great and apparently unbridgeable gulf between the two cultures, among other things in the way they valued and used the land. Here is one of the volcanic eruptions: a new evolution of land manipulation that was led and facilitated by the Scotch-Irish and that emerges from its own smoke and fire as a leading cause of war. Part Four tells the story of the first of those wars.

Another thing missing from our history is the great majority of present-day Americans. Our society suffers massively from cultural amnesia. We wander through the world not knowing where we have been, remembering so little that we try to manipulate vast human and natural systems as if they were simple machines, despairing when we fail, like children refusing our parents' help while trying to ride a bicycle for the first time. Contrary to the conventions of television, no situation we face today is new. The counsel of our ancestors is available to us on every subject, but we do not consult it, and the price we pay for that ignorance is excessive and repetitive.

As a way of making the argument, with Faulkner, that "the past is not dead . . . it isn't even past," I have appended to each section of the book a personal journal of my discovery of this story and the value of heritage. I have done this not because I regard my life as exemplary, but because I regard my youthful stupidity as emblematic of a larger, generational problem. Such progress as I have made toward connection with the great, sprawling, untidy, and erratic progress of my fellow humans, I believe, is a source of hope for our future.

The seventh man on the monument, the fellow in the hunting shirt whose name so few remember, is now a constant companion of my life, as I hope he will be of yours.

Mention must be made of the persistent controversy over the proper nomenclature for the Scotch-Irish. "Scotch is a drink," many Scot, Irish, and politically sensitive acquaintants have pointed out to me over the years, "the people are known as Scots." It is true, and that is how natives of Scotland should be designated. But that is not who we are talking about here. These people were no longer Scots when they lived in Ulster and never became Irish in the traditional sense. The identity they created arose in America and was labeled at the time—by William Penn's administrator James Logan, for example, and by the Irish writer Edmund Burke—as Scotch-Irish. So have they been known for nearly three hundred years, so will they be known here.

The Shenandoah Valley Today

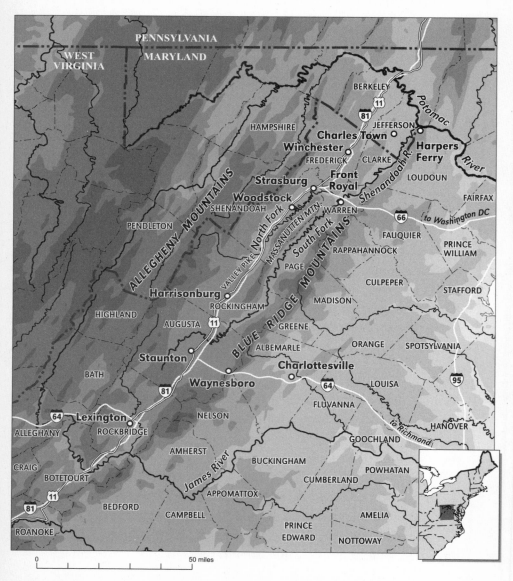

The Valley of Virginia widens from its narrow terminus at Roanoke, in the southwest, to a broad plain where the Shenandoah and Potomac rivers meet, at Harpers Ferry in the northeast. Although the streams south of Augusta County make their way into the James River, the Shenandoah drains the rest; because it flows northward, residents speak of going north as going "down" the valley.

Part One

———

The Scotch-Irish

Lord, please make me always right, for Thou
knowest I am hard to turn.

—*Scotch-Irish prayer*

Chapter 1

—◦—

East Wind Rising, 1729

The humour of going to America still continues, and the scarcity
of provisions certainly makes many quit us. The humour has
spread like a contagious distemper . . . it affects only Protestants,
and reigns chiefly in the north.

—*Archbishop Boulter, Primate of Ireland, 1728*

FROM ITS BEGINNING, this story is about the land.

The mob that came for John Lewis on a day in 1729, in
County Donegal in the Province of Ulster in what is today Northern Ireland, was after his land. We do not know the hour or the day
it happened, and indeed we cannot be sure of the season or the
year. Most of the story is long lost, its details shrunken in memory
even as its concept was enlarged to mythical dimensions, eventually
recalled in fragments by elderly grandchildren nearly a century after
it happened (when at last someone thought to write it down). They
chiseled a reference to it on John Lewis's gravestone, because what
happened that day made his life legendary and led to everything
else, but stone-carvers are necessarily cryptic, and they referred only
to a conflict with an "Irish Lord."

The man who led the mob was armed with a musket and most
likely self-medicated with rage and whiskey. He was not a lord of

the realm, as the tombstone half a world away would later imply, but one Sir Mungo Campbell, John Lewis's landlord. Campbell was most likely a baronet (a rank roughly equivalent to that of knight) who had inherited his father's land and minor title, but not his father's character.

John Lewis's father, Andrew Lewis, and Mungo's father, Hugh Campbell, had passed a generation in a settled and prosperous relationship. Lewis had a leasehold on a portion of Campbell's Donegal County land, and as the tenants were diligent and reliable, so the landlord was fair and responsive. Thus John Lewis had grown to manhood, there he had eventually brought his wife, Margaret Lynn, there he had seen his parents into the grave and five children into the world. There his family had enjoyed a remarkable island of stability and peace, in a country that all the while had been seething with ancient hatreds and sparking with sudden violence.

About 1725 things had started to unravel for the Lewises. Hugh Campbell died, leaving his land to his self-indulgent son just as a long drought settled in, withering the crops year after year. Meanwhile nothing reduced the taxes or relaxed the tithes that every resident, regardless of religion, owed to the established Church of England. To these burdens one was now added that was common elsewhere in Ireland but had not affected John Lewis while Hugh Campbell was alive. It had long been the habit of the English landlords, most of whom were living in England, to raise rents on their Irish properties whenever they needed money, regardless of the effects on their tenants. Apparently Mungo Campbell liked this idea and decided to impose the rack rents, as they were called, on John Lewis.

Just as Campbell was no lord of the realm, so Lewis was no downtrodden serf. He had a good lease—"for three lifetimes," as his grandchildren would recall it—had met his obligations, and knew his rights. He took the case to court, according to one version of the story, and won. Perhaps he thought that with the dispute thus settled, he could go back to his home and resume his life. But Mungo

Campbell was not to be dissuaded by a court. He had become overly impressed, apparently, with the ways of imperious English aristocrats. Forgetting that he was no lord and his tenant no vassal, the young Campbell decided to impose his will by force. He collected a band of supporters, either hired hands or raucous friends, and marched out to eject the Lewises from their home.

Forewarned, John Lewis gathered his family in the house, shuttered the windows, and barred the door. He had living with him at the time his brother, who was ill and bedridden, in addition to his wife, Margaret Lynn, and five children: Ann, an infant; Margaret, a toddler; William, five years old; Andrew, nine; and Thomas, the eldest at eleven. Mungo pounded on the door and demanded that the Lewises leave the premises. Hotly, John Lewis refused. The ruffians surrounded the house and tried to break down the door, but succeeded only in splintering it. Inside, disbelieving, John Lewis waited for his young landlord to come to his senses.

Instead, Mungo Campbell stuck through the cracked door a musket loaded with buck and ball, and fired. The ball struck John Lewis's brother where he lay in his sickbed, wounding him mortally. A pellet of buckshot tore through Margaret Lynn's hand. With his wife and brother wounded and bleeding, the one dying and the other no doubt shrieking with pain and fright, John Lewis was transformed. He wrenched open the door, charged outside, and with his shillelagh split open the skull of the young Mungo Campbell.

Deprived of leadership and of the prospect of reward, the other outlaws fled, leaving Lewis to comfort his wife and children, bury his brother, and contemplate his hollow victory. Knowing there could be no justice in Ireland for any tenant rising up against any landlord, he prepared to flee for his life.

⸻

A strong wind was blowing through Europe as the eighteenth century began. The pressure gradient ran away from the tyranny, religious oppression, frequent wars, and grinding poverty of the corrupt old monarchies, westward toward a fresh New World where, it was said, one could speak and worship as one chose, own land, improve one's lot in life, make a safe place for a family, and live to see it grow. Those who had something solid in Europe—land or money or family or maybe just a title—hung on to it and let the wind blow. Of the multitudes who could claim neither possessions nor hope, only a small minority would try to sail this wind to a new life, and most of those who tried, as was the case with John Lewis, were pushed by circumstances into an adventure they would as soon have missed. The wind they tried to ride was strong and cruel; those who lacked strength or character or cunning, whatever their dreams, could be dashed to destruction before it.

A paradigm shift—any vast new idea—begins in the hearts of individual people who act anew because of a powerful notion or circumstance. Often they are spurred to action by what they find unacceptable in their world; often they are led to change by religious fervor or by greed. Individuals who tack across the prevailing winds of culture can be dismissed as merely eccentric; if small groups join them, they will still be seen as aberrant malcontents; but when like-minded groups grow to critical mass (not necessarily an overwhelming majority—not even, necessarily, a majority—just enough) then culture itself is suddenly transformed.

This family's crisis was created by the forces that had shaped them and their world; their reaction to their crisis would help reshape those forces and that world. Andrew Lewis, nine years old when he saw his father kill, his uncle killed, and his family uprooted, would live to consider, embrace, and then powerfully enact into the history of the world a new paradigm of human entitlement and personal freedom embodied in a new republic that would bestride the world. Yet for all that new paradigm and that new republic would ennoble human history and enable human progress, it would embody as well significant evils. It would do so, as most cultures do, without discussion, dismissing the wrong it felt required to do with simplistic rationalizations followed by a profound forgetting. And yet, ignored, two of these offenses—a virulent form of racism and a new kind of greed—would continue to irritate the body politic to the point of abscess, even cancer.

To understand the end of a story we need to comprehend how it begins. Our story begins with that strong wind blowing toward the west, taking certain sailors with it.

By the time Andrew Lewis was born in County Donegal, the English had been trying to subdue the tribes of Ireland for five and a half centuries, King Henry II making the first attempt with an invasion in 1171. British overlords regarded the emerald isle, as they would later view the New World, as a country with some interesting economic prospects that was unfortunately infested with natives. English armies were able to correct this situation and maintain the crown's authority in Dublin, on the nearby east coast, but beyond the city and its immediate environs, beyond the area called the Pale, the authority—and the armies—had a way of dissolving.

During the first half of the sixteenth century, Henry VIII had been able to gain somewhat tenuous control of the whole country of Ireland, and in the latter decades of the century, Elizabeth's armies had crushed the organized resistance of most of the native chieftains. Yet when James I took the English throne in 1603 (to become famous for establishing a new version of the Bible, for espousing the divine right of kings, and for persecuting Catholics), Ireland was still in turmoil.

Francis Bacon, a principal advisor to King James and an advocate of England's manifest destiny to rule the British Isles and the world, had nothing but contempt for Ireland. He did not know which was worst: "the ambition and absoluteness of the chiefs," the "licentious idleness" of their soldiers, or the "barbarous laws, customs, their brehon laws, habits of apparel, their poets or heralds that enchant them in savage manners, and sundry other dregs of barbarism and rebellion." The crown was motivated not merely by a desire to export law and order, but by national security: England's enemies—the Catholic pope, the crowns of Spain and France—saw in any Irish insurrection an opportunity to gain a foothold on British soil for their priests and their generals.

As James took the throne, a bloody, eight-year insurrection by the clans of Ulster had just been brought to an end. The last stand of the Gaelic chieftains against the English juggernaut had been ground down by a scorched-earth policy that had left Ulster, the northernmost of Ireland's four provinces, largely depopulated. Yet the principal leaders of the revolt, Hugh O'Neill of County Tyrone and Rory O'Donnell of Tyrconnel (the ancient name for Donegal), had been allowed to retain their vast real estate holdings and their titles (they had been made earls by Queen Elizabeth in an attempt at pacification). Both were soon involved in new intrigues and, learning that they had been found out, fled the country in September of 1607, an event remembered in Irish history as the Flight of the Earls. The crown confiscated their estates and those of the chieftains who went into exile with them, an area of land extending over much of the province of Ulster. The earls were soon replaced as chief rebel in Ireland by one Sir Cahir O'Dogherty of Innishowen, who was in his turn hunted down and killed in 1608. King James, perplexed, wanted a final solution to the Irish problem. Francis Bacon and other advisors thought they had one.

They focused on Ulster, the source of most of the recent troubles. As the English historian Thomas Babington Macaulay would observe, the Irish "were distinguished by qualities which tend to make men interesting rather than prosperous. They were an ardent and an impetuous race, easily moved to tears or laughter, to fury or to love." Such men did not pull well under a yoke.

Sir Arthur Chichester, Lord Deputy of Ireland, proposed that establishing law and order in Ulster would require planting among the wild Irishmen "colonies of civil people of England or Scotland."

(By "civil," Chichester did not mean polite, but civilized, a word not yet in general use.) By "planting," he meant what had been undertaken in 1607 at Jamestown in Virginia: the forceful establishment, in an area populated by primitive tribes, of an English system of plantation agriculture, common law, established religion, and pitiless subjugation of the natives. In 1609 King James ordered the plantation of six of the nine counties of Ulster.

Four times before, in the 1560s and 1570s, Queen Elizabeth had given adventurers large tracts of Irish land on condition they settle them with civil English farmers. All three had failed in the face of fierce opposition from the natives, just as Sir Walter Raleigh (who had come to the queen's attention by putting down an Irish rebellion in 1580) had failed to establish Roanoke Island in the New World.

This time the Ulster plantation was better organized. Those taking up estates (offered in three sizes, of 1,000, 1,500, and 2,000 acres) were required to live on the land and improve it with buildings and fences. Additional lands were set aside for churches, schools, and villages; everything was properly surveyed and recorded. If a native pressed a prior claim to ownership, some treason was rooted out of recent history and another tract of land was confiscated. By 1610 half a million acres of land were made available to planters, who were sternly cautioned to avoid relationships with the natives. Hiring "mere Irish," as the Catholic residents were called, renting land to them, and, above all, marrying them were strictly forbidden.

On Francis Bacon's recommendation, "to allure by all means fit undertakers," the king created a new order of baronet. Gentlemen who agreed to take up Ulster land, and who paid £1,000 into a fund for the support of troops in Ireland, were permitted to assume a dignity roughly on a par with a knight although a baronet remained a commoner.

The offers of Irish land and titles did not raise unqualified enthusiasm in England. Established gentlemen there were "a great deal more tenderly bred," recorded the Reverend Andrew Stewart at the time of the plantation, "and entertained in better quarters than they could find here in Ireland." Those who did leave the comforts of home and the intrigues of court for the hard and remote circumstances of Ireland often found the "marshiness and fogginess of this Island unwholesome to English bodies." Many, according to Stewart, died "of a flux, called here the country disease, at their first entry." But the perspective was quite different from the hardscrabble farms of lowland Scotland, whose tenants were also British subjects and eligible for the offer of free land. From the beginning of the plantation, more Scots than Englishmen moved into Ulster, where they presented the king with a new population that was fully as bull-headed as the old.

It was a community set apart not only by the circumstances of its origins and by surrounding events, but by hard-won and vigorously defended religious and political ideas. To a remarkable degree, in a world just emerging from feudalism, these people (who left feudalism behind when they left Scotland) had a sense of personal worth. Unlike the Irish Catholics, they bent their knee to no pope, bishop, or priest. Their Presbyterian religion, founded in Scotland by John Knox in the mid-sixteenth century, gave an unprecedented amount of authority to the ordinary members of the congregation. They elected their elders, including the minister, who together governed the church as a session. Lay elders served with ministers on the presbytery, the regional body that administered groups of churches and supervised the ordination and discipline of the ministers.

The Presbyterian church had taken the Reformation further than the Lutherans or the Anglicans in rejecting not only the authority of the pope and the supremacy of the mass, but the doctrinal authority of priests and bishops and virtually all forms of liturgy (they would not even bend their knee to God, but prayed standing). To prepare themselves for finding the meaning in the word of God and the life of Christ without the necessary interdiction of clergy, Presbyterians placed great emphasis on universal education. Knowledge and free will notwithstanding, the individual was not free to act however he pleased; to maintain the strict morality of their lives in the absence of higher church authorities, the congregation took the authority to supervise in minute detail the affairs of its members.

This, to modern eyes, appears to be an odd kind of freedom. No one wandered about exercising free will at random or learning alone whatever seemed interesting. That kind of independence was unthinkable, and would have been considered dangerous—to the individual soul, to the community, and to the very order of society—had it been considered at all. This was a kind of corporate freedom, the right to march in lockstep with one's right-thinking co-religionists and neighbors, knowing that at the slightest misstep one would be herded back into the group. Yet no distant king or bishop told this herd what to do, and that was a new and precious freedom indeed.

"We met every week," recalled the Presbyterian Reverend John Livingston of his work in Ulster after 1630, "and such as fell into notorious scandal we desired to come before us." Those who appeared, confessed, and repented had their misdeeds recounted before the congregation; those who "would not be convinced to acknowledge their fault" were "debarred from the communion; which proved such a terror that we had very few of that sort." The zealousness of this oversight—from the admonishment of scolds to the persecution of witches—became characteristic of Puritanism.

Whatever the excesses and limitations of the sessions and presbyteries, the great underlying reality was that this religion was homemade; it was something for ordinary people to study, discuss, and act out, individually and in community. It was in fact a new birth of freedom, and the Scots Presbyterians of Ulster found it a bracing tonic indeed.

Unlike the English Anglicans, the Scots gave no place to their church in the affairs of state, but held separate their sacred and secular institutions. As British subjects, they were nevertheless required to pay heavy tithes to the established Church of England, an additional tax on their livelihoods that acted as a constant gall. But while tithes could be collected, respect could not be forcibly imbued; the monarchy might well be the highest evolution of statehood, it might well be the instrument that lifted men from feudal servitude and constant tribal war, but kings were subject to the cool appraisal of any Scots Presbyterian. And resistance to the crown was required, in the words of the great Christian reformer John Calvin himself, "if we are inhumanly harassed by a cruel prince; if we are rapaciously plundered by an avaricious or luxurious one; if we are neglected by an indolent one; or if we are persecuted on account of piety by an impious and sacrilegious one."

Thus reverence for the English king and his divine rights was no part of this community's heritage. War with Britain had been a tradition of many generations in the Borders, the counties of Lowland Scotland from which most of the Scots settlers in Ulster had come. King James, a Scotsman himself, was able to suppress overt rebelliousness with years of hangings, drownings, brandings, whippings, and banishments; but the hostility to the British crown simmered on.

Nor did the Lowlanders have any kind feelings for tribal clansmen, such as they had once feared in the Scots Highlands and such as they now found in Ireland. From the beginning of their sojourn in Ulster, the settlers' principal enemies were wolves and wood-kerns, the latter being Irish fighting men who traditionally had claimed their food and shelter from the community as a right due their profession. Although most such swordsmen had been deported, small bands of them remained who, with the wolves, preyed constantly on the planters' cattle and possessions. Thus from the beginning the Presbyterians were preoccupied with defending themselves from the maraudings of barbarian and beast.

The Scots—proud of their own emergence from what they considered to be barbarism into religion, morality, discipline, and learning—reviled the people who remained in a state that seemed to them lawless (because the laws were different from their own) and without culture (because the traditions were alien to their own). These prickly, moralistic Christians had no compunctions whatever about hanging as malefactors or burning as witches any miscreants who belonged to a culture less advanced than their own. Nor did they see anything wrong with visiting on those of a lower station precisely those persecutions for which they despised the British.

The same King James who ordered the Plantation of Ulster had seen, when he had been king of Scotland, that the democratic and independent ideas of the Presbyterians posed a threat to the authority of the monarchy. He preferred the outcome of the Reformation in England, where a prince could still exert influence over the church by way of the bishops. With this in mind, he deftly maneuvered his own countrymen into accepting the idea of life terms for the moderators of their presbyteries.

British impositions on the Scots continued under King Charles, who was not as diplomatic as James had been, and who set off a firestorm when he dictated in 1637 that the Presbyterians would henceforward use the Anglican liturgy and prayer book. True to Calvin's advice, the Presbyterians resisted this "impious and sacrilegious" prince, joining English Puritans in a Solemn League and Covenant (for which they became known as "Covenanters") to maintain their religious independence and resist what they regarded as an attempt to revive Catholicism. Charles marched into Scotland at the head of an army to impose his will. It was a big mistake; the flinty Scots faced him down and made him sign a humiliating treaty that retracted his earlier demands.

Charles's treasury had no money left with which to support a distant war, and when the parliament refused to raise any more he dissolved it, and in 1640 he challenged the Scots anew. By way of response they marched across their border, occupied much of northern England, and demanded to be paid for their trouble while a peace treaty was devised. The much harassed Charles was forced to convene a new parliament in order to raise money; but the parliament he summoned turned out to be more interested in curtailing his powers and establishing a constitutional monarchy. Within two years their conflict would become a great civil war.

While confronting Scotland, Charles never stopped worrying about all those Scots in Ireland. In 1639 he had required every Presbyterian in Ulster to take what became known as the Black Oath: to swear never to oppose the king's command or to make any contrary oaths or commitments. Agents of the crown expended a great deal of energy taking a census, sending commissioners to ceremoniously administer the oath, and keeping records of those sworn and not sworn.

Then the British administration set out to raise an army in Ireland. It intended to recruit only Protestants, but when King Charles let it be known that the army would be deployed to enforce his will in Scotland, his commanders decided it would not make much sense to rely on Ulster Scots. The only other fighting men to be found in sufficient numbers in Ireland were Irish Catholics, who were duly inducted. Then, after introducing them to and training them in organized military service, Charles abruptly changed his mind, disbanded the army, and sent these newly dangerous men back to their homes.

In October of 1641, the native Irish, led no doubt by these recently trained soldiers, rose against their Protestant overlords and began a great slaughter in Ulster. Fighting at first directed primarily against the English spread across the island and soon involved the Scots as well. Something like fifteen thousand Protestants were killed, many of them tortured to death. The fighting went on for eleven years, a period of war and privation during which the potato became the staple food of Ireland, primarily because a potato crop could not easily be confiscated or destroyed by marauding troops.

Meanwhile, in August of 1642, the struggle between Charles I and parliament turned into civil war. Scotland's Covenanters fought at first on the side of the parliament, in the vain hope that in victory the Presbyterian church might become the established church of England. After two years of reverses, the parliamentarians, or Roundheads (a term of contempt referring to the short haircuts of some lowly apprentices who joined an early antiroyalist mob), began to prevail, especially after their victory at the Battle of Naseby in

1645. While Roundhead generals such as Thomas, Lord Fairfax (who commanded the victorious troops at Naseby), and Oliver Cromwell steadily improved their military skills, King Charles was a chronic blunderer and in 1646 got his army overwhelmed and himself taken prisoner.

But Charles escaped, somehow made a treaty with the Scots Covenanters, and led them into England and another defeat by Oliver Cromwell at Preston in 1648. This time the Roundheads took no chances with Charles and beheaded him, only to see his son continue the war with the help of the Covenanters (who still hoped to establish their church in the place of the Anglican church) and their brethren in Ireland. By 1651 Oliver Cromwell had brutally extinguished resistance to the parliamentarians in England, Scotland, and Ireland and had driven Charles II into exile. For Ireland, Cromwell's triumph meant more confiscation of land—some six million acres handed over to Cromwell's troops, most of whom soon intermarried, converted, and became mere Irish.

After the death of Cromwell in 1658, a newly elected parliament invited Charles II to return from exile and remount the throne on condition that he ensure amnesty for his former enemies and toleration for all religions. The deal was consummated in 1660, but in less than a year Charles reestablished the Anglican church, restored the episcopacy, and declared illegal the Scots Covenants. For three decades the Covenanters of the Western Lowlands, unlike the majority of Scots Presbyterians, resisted fiercely, maintaining their religious freedom in the face of imprisonment, torture, and massacre, three times rising in organized rebellion that was each time harshly put down by a king who had discovered at last how to apply military power. These decades were to be remembered as the "killing times." Their harshness, contrasted with the comparative religious freedom of nearby Ulster, prompted the migration of thousands more Scots to Ireland.

It was into these times that John Lewis was born, in County Donegal in 1678.

When King Charles died in 1685, his brother James ascended the throne, thus introducing another schism into the hopelessly tangled animosities of the British Isles. James, a convert to Roman Catholicism, tried to establish religious freedom in the face of intractable resistance from parliament and the princes of the Church of England. When in 1688 James had a son who stood to succeed to the crown, the parliament deposed James and invited his son-in-law, the Dutch Protestant William of Orange, to take the English throne.

James sought to reclaim his crown by way of Ireland. He gathered there in 1689 an army consisting of Irish Catholics and troops provided by the Catholic Louis XIV of France. The Ulster Scots stood firm for William of Orange and Mary, holding out at Enniskillen, in western Ulster, and through a 105-day siege of Londonderry in the north until William arrived in 1690 and crushed James at the Battle of the Boyne. Another million and a half acres of Irish land were confiscated and made available for planting. But William of Orange brought religious toleration, political union, and economic prosperity to Scotland, and thus removed the causes of Scots migration to Ireland. A few years into the eighteenth century, the migration stopped.

As the seventeenth century waned, the population of Ireland was estimated at just over one million, 70 percent of whom were dispossessed Irish Catholics living in serflike conditions and smoldering with rage. About 200,000 English Anglican overlords or civil servants were scattered across the country, living in baronial splendor. The Presbyterian Scots, about 150,000 strong, made a place between, most of them in Ulster. (In that province, the population of 1641 was estimated to be 100,000 Scots and 20,000 English.) Among them lived other displaced people, including French Huguenots and English Puritans left over from Cromwell's armies, with whom the Scots not only lived but intermarried, something they only very rarely did with the Irish natives.

Mungo Campbell's father Hugh was of Scot descent, but John Lewis's father Andrew was not. There are two traditions in the John Lewis family, each based on the hazy recollections of his aged grandchildren: that the original Lewis in Ulster was a French Huguenot named Louis who had fled French repression; and that he was a Welsh Cromwellian soldier taking up land as a reward for his service. Whichever was the case, the Lewis family by the 1720s was fully assimilated in the Scots Presbyterian community that lived in Ulster and tried to avoid the constant plots, risings, alarms, repressions, riots, and contentions that constituted the story of Ireland at the turning of the eighteenth century.

Values were changing in Ulster. At the close of the previous century land had been cheap and people scarce, especially in the aftermath of the 1688 revolution. Driven from Scotland by the Covenanter troubles and drawn to Ireland by good land and long leases—typically of thirty-one years, or "a lifetime," in duration—Scots had flocked to Ulster anew and had built up their leaseholds. By the time these leases began to expire, about 1720, there were other offers to consider. Native Irishmen got together and offered two or three times the rent that the landlord was getting; not that they were necessarily going to be able to pay it in the future, but they could make the offer. And the landlord, beguiled by the idea of ready cash, might convince himself that the Irish natives were as productive and industrious as the Scots, and set a new price for his land.

It was all too much. Repeatedly, the government of Britain had wrecked the Irish economy, by prohibiting the export of cattle, sheep, and swine or their products; of woolen manufactures; of dyed linens—of virtually any product that became successful enough to compete in any way with any English interest. In 1704 the Test Act, directed against Roman Catholics, excluded Presbyterians, as well, from civil and military office, and imposed fines on any Presbyterian minister who dared to celebrate a marriage. Meanwhile the tithes to the Church of England continued to come due, and now came the droughts and the rack rents.

Not for the first time, and not for the last, the Scots refused to accept injustice. They would not make a foolish bid just to keep the land. In the face of the rack rents, in 1717, the first wave of Scots Presbyterians once again set their faces westward and sailed to a new land. Twelve years later Robert Gambie wrote from Londonderry that "there is gone and to go this summer from this port 25 sail of ships, who carry each from 125 to 140 passengers to America; there are many more going from Belfast, and the ports near Colrain, besides great numbers from Dublin, Newly and around the coast. Where this will end God only knows."

That was the year that John Lewis and his family joined them.

Chapter 2

———

Finding America, 1730–1732

It looks as if Ireland is to send all its inhabitants hither.
The common fear is that if they thus continue to come they
will make themselves proprietors of the province. It is strange
that they thus crowd where they are not wanted.

—*James Logan, Pennsylvania provincial secretary, 1729*

ABOUT THE YEAR 1730, John Lewis and his family plunged into one of the great diasporas of history. The Protestants of Ulster (many of them originally lowland Scots, but also French Huguenots, Welsh veterans of Cromwell's armies, and others), impelled alike by their history and their character, pushed by tyranny and drawn by a new and powerful notion—that ordinary people should have the hope of improving their condition—had been migrating to the New World, looking for a better chance, for more than a decade. By the thousands and the tens of thousands they fled the sad island where they had prospered for a few generations to face a new world of unimaginable size and terrors.

First they had to face the voyage across the Atlantic Ocean, a grueling affair that could take eight weeks or longer depending on the winds, that could lead to death by starvation if supplies ran out, by drowning if the vessel gave out, or at the hands of pirates if the luck ran out. Those who were very old, young, or weak could die from sheer stress. "We went on shipboard the 14th of September," wrote one Robert Witherspoon of a typical voyage in 1734, "and lay windbound in the lough at Belfast fourteen days." They had been at sea only two days when "my grandmother died, and was interred in the raging ocean, which was an afflictive sight to her offspring." Storms raged, the ship leaked, the pumps had to be manned "day and night; for many days our mariners seemed many times at their wits end. But it pleased God to bring us safe to land, which was about the first of December."

Another vessel became famous as "The Starved Ship" for its passage in 1740, during which the food on board ran out and the passengers resorted to systematic cannibalism, by lot, to sustain themselves until they encountered another ship. And there were pirates; on one occasion a band of them captured a party of Ulster émigrés, one of whom was a Mrs. Wilson who amused the pirate captain by going into labor and giving birth to a child. The pirate leader, charmed, gave her a silk dress and set the whole party free in the baby's honor. The newborn child was to have a grandson one day whose name would be Horace Greeley.

The details of the Lewises' crossing were not recorded, and the traditional family accounts differ on many of the specifics, but some things are clear. While John Lewis was far from frail, he was also far from young. About fifty-two years of age when he made the crossing, he had lived as long as a man of his time could expect to live, and could hardly have foreseen or relished the prospect of starting life over. (He set no records in this regard: in 1730 a man named John Young died in Worcester, Massachusetts, at the age of 107, having emigrated there from Ulster at the age of 95.) Margaret Lynn Lewis, fifteen years his junior, still in her childbearing thirties but fortunately not pregnant, had little to fear from the crossing except the weather and the tedium of caring for Ann, a toddler of two, and four-year-old Margaret. William, Andrew, and Thomas, aged six, ten, and twelve respectively in 1730, would have been on their own while on board ship. William told his daughter Agatha, late in his life, that their voyage took three months, "during which we suffered from awful storms and came near being lost, when finally we landed in the Delaware, with our stock of provisions exhausted and the entire crew almost famished with hunger."

Although the details are tangled and beyond certainty, it is probable that John Lewis crossed the Atlantic first, alone, in 1730, sailing to Virginia on board a ship captained by John Patton, a cousin of Margaret Lynn Lewis's mother. It would have been natural, in his family's distress, to appeal to his seafaring relative, as it would have been to go visit another, Dr. William Lynn, Margaret's brother, who was already established in Fredericksburg. Dr. Lynn and some friends had applied in 1727 for a patent for fifty thousand acres of land on the Cowpasture River, a tributary of the James River running through the Appalachians west of the Shenandoah Valley. The rest of the family probably crossed later, when John Lewis had settled on a place.

The Lewises, unlike the vast majority of their fellow émigrés from Ulster, were able to pay for their passage. Archbishop Hugh Boulter, primate of the Anglican Church of Ireland at the time, thought that about nine of ten passengers "either hire themselves to those of substance for passage, or contract with the masters of ships for four years' servitude when they come thither." On arrival in port in America, the ship's captain would conduct an auction of his contract passengers, which, with its crowd of buyers inspecting and speculating on the worthiness of workers, must have resembled a slave auction. But the term of the indenture was limited to four years, sometimes seven; conditions were regulated and supervised by the colonies to prevent cruelty; and rewards for those who fulfilled their contract included, in Pennsylvania for example, a lump-sum payment, a kit of tools, and fifty acres of land. There are cases on the record of people who could afford to pay for their passage who nevertheless became indentured in order to learn the ways of the country in a protected situation before starting out on their own.

For most Ulster émigrés, and probably for the Lewis family when they followed John to America, the first sight of America was of Cape May and the beaches of New Jersey. Their ships gained the protection of Delaware Bay and sailed upriver to Chester, New Castle, or Philadelphia, where the weary travelers trooped ashore. They shared their ships and the docks with a similar stream of German families from the Palatinate in southeastern Germany, whence for twenty years emigrants had been encouraged to head for enclaves on the Neuse River in North Carolina, the Hudson in New York, and the Shenandoah River in Virginia. Now, after weeks of confinement and helplessness, it was time to confront the new world and begin a new life.

British America consisted of a thin swath of settlement along the eastern seaboard from Maine to the Carolinas, its population numbering in 1714 about 375,000 whites of European origin and 58,000 blacks of African descent, almost all of them slaves. For the whites, the early dreams of easy living were long gone, and it was well known that what rewards America offered were gained only by long, hard labor. But dreams of freedom—the freedom to worship as one chose, to own one's home and land, to live as one saw fit— persisted, and were confirmed in different ways, and to different degrees, in the different colonies.

Maryland's offer of religious freedom and toleration had been taken up by a party of Ulster Scots as early as 1680. (They included the Polk family, later of North Carolina, whose descendants included James Polk, eleventh president of the United States, and Leonidas Polk, Episcopal bishop and Confederate general.) Shortly thereafter, Presbyterians arrived in the Carolinas, but wrote home that the area from Virginia south was dominated by slave-holding planters and the established Church of England. Of the two evils, the immigrants from Ulster were no doubt more repelled by the idea of living once again under the established church than that of living amid slaves, but those who inquired further into the matter would have learned that as a practical matter, both slavery and Anglicanism became more diluted as one traveled westward.

Between 1717 and 1720, fifty-four ships from Ulster had arrived in Boston bearing immigrants who moved to the western frontier of New England, pushing that frontier westward against Indian indignation. They wrote home that although the settled parts of New England were Calvinist, the people there were none too friendly to immigrants who tried to join them in their safe and settled townships. However, if newcomers were willing to go to the frontier of Maine, Massachusetts, or New Hampshire, they were welcome to thus provide a living buffer between the settled coast and the wild Indians. (In 1724, in the midst of Indian troubles, the people of Worcester chose an Ulsterman named James McClellan as town constable; 160 years later his descendant would command the armies of the United States at the outset of the Civil War.)

By the time the Lewis family set sail from Ulster, the favorite destination was Pennsylvania. William Penn had been laboring since 1681 to establish a place where freedom of conscience and religion were guaranteed, where virtually every man could vote, where justice was tempered with mercy and even the native tribes could expect fair treatment. Moreover, the land was of the best quality, the climate was good, and the people were friendly. In fact, the Proprietor's administration had extended a formal invitation to Ulster Presbyterians.

James Logan (a Scotch-Irish Quaker who served William Penn and the Proprietary as administrator) recalled that about 1720, "considerable numbers of good, sober people came in from Ireland, who wanted to be settled. At the same time, also, it happened that we were under some apprehensions from the northern Indians. I therefore thought it might be prudent to plant a settlement of such men as those who formerly had so bravely defended Londonderry and Inniskillen, as a frontier, in case of any disturbance." Thus the Ulstermen were being planted in western Pennsylvania in much the same way that their forefathers had been planted in Ulster, and for similar reasons.

"There is no part of British America in a more growing condition," wrote the Irish writer and politician Edmund Burke in 1761, describing Pennsylvania in the 1720s. "In some years more people have transported themselves into Pennsylvania than into all the other settlements together. In 1729, 6,208 persons came to settle here as passengers or servants, four-fifths of whom at least were from Ireland. These are chiefly Presbyterians from the northern part of Ireland, who in America are generally called Scotch-Irish."

Thus appears one of the first uses of the much-despised term "Scotch-Irish." These people were not Irish and, after generations of sharing contempt for the "mere" or "wild" Irish and their "papist" religion, did not relish being thus associated with them. Moreover, as any denizen of Scotland or Ireland will gruffly announce today on hearing the abominable appellation, Scotch is a drink; the people are Scots. Nevertheless, Scotch-Irish is what they became in America, where one does not choose one's nickname but must survive it. And there is a certain justice here; after all, these people insisted on referring to the natives of their new country as Indians.

By the time the Lewises arrived in 1730, the previously hospitable Quakers were not so interested in sharing prime land within easy reach of Philadelphia markets. The indentured servants had their place, of course, but those who came as settlers, who wanted places of their own, found that things were changing in Pennsylvania. Provincial Secretary Logan had decided by this time that his fellow Ulstermen were in fact neither "easily dealt with" nor "a leading example to others" as he had expected when he had invited them to emigrate. By 1729 he was sick of them: "a settlement of five families from the North of Ireland gives me more trouble than 50 of any other people." They were proving to be "troublesome settlers to the government and hard neighbors to the Indians." He decided, in fact, to issue no more land patents to the Scotch-Irish, but few had bothered to get them anyway. The newcomers simply headed west until they found unoccupied land and occupied it. When challenged as squatters by provincial authorities, the Scotch-Irish resisted, making the argument, as Logan reported to William Penn, "that it was against the laws of God and nature, that so much land should be idle, while so many Christians wanted it to labor on, and raise their bread."

Newcomers to America in 1730 soon realized that from Boston to Savannah the best coastal and tidewater lands of the British-American crescent were already occupied. Royal charters granted to individual proprietors such as William Penn, to development companies (the Massachusetts Bay Company), or to the colonists as a body (Connecticut) conveyed an interest in and power over the land in return for the assurance that people would be settled on it, for that was the value to the crown: a thriving, taxable, raw material–exporting colony. By 1730 that settlement had been accomplished as far west as the first range of mountains, at least to the extent that no one wanted a sudden infusion of alien people in communities of established ethnic and religious identity. Few knew or cared what might lie beyond the western mountains: "Our country has now been inhabited more than 130 years by the English," wrote Colonel William Byrd, who in 1728 surveyed the boundary between Virginia and North Carolina, "and we still know hardly anything of the Appalachian Mountains, that are nowhere above 250 miles from the sea."

Known or not, it was to this territory that the Scotch-Irish, determined never again to bend their knee to landlord or bishop, had to look for a home. Beyond the first mountains, the few people who had obtained royal charters by 1730 were so eager for the settlers they needed to perfect their grants (one of them, William Beverley, would resort to naming his cows and reporting them as heads of families in order to meet his quotas) that few questions were asked, restrictions applied, or laws enforced. The landholders wanted not only to fill their quotas but to create a human buffer between them and the increasingly resentful Indians who populated the western wilderness, many because they had been pushed there by white incursions into their former homelands. One did not have to make many promises or be of particularly high stature to qualify as tomahawk fodder.

So the Scotch-Irish headed west from Philadelphia, most of them on foot, some who could afford it leading pack animals, the well-to-do on horseback. By the time the Lewis family made the journey, former Ulstermen had founded a thriving frontier town at Lancaster, sixty miles west of Philadelphia; thirty-five miles farther west, John Harris operated a trading post and ferry across the Susquehanna River that had become the locus of another bustling Scotch-Irish settlement. This was the gateway through the continent's first range of western mountains (called in Pennsylvania the Catoctins, in Virginia the Blue Ridge, and in the Carolinas the Great Smokies) into the Cumberland Valley, into which Scotch-Irish Presbyterians and German Lutherans flowed in the search for land beyond the reach of officialdom. The two cultures—the one Celtic and Presbyterian, the other Germanic and Lutheran—had little to do with each other. They played a kind of hopscotch, settling alternate areas as they moved steadily to the south and west.

They were thus breaking a long-held principal of William Penn: that no white occupation of Indian land should take place before a fair settlement had been made. But the farther one got from Philadelphia, the less it mattered what William Penn believed or what the law was rumored to be. In European eyes, if a man owned land he occupied it, or had someone else occupy it for him, and this land was, where not staked out by an enterprising white family, spectacularly empty. Moreover, people from Ulster were familiar with dispossessed natives, the "mere" Irish or "mere" Indian, having no rights to the lands of their ancestors.

Yet these were civilized people, these settlers, and they knew that they could not descend into utter anarchy in the matter of land rights, or they would be helpless to defend themselves from the next wave of squatters, once they had made their choices and settled down. And so they worked out a generally recognized set of unwritten ordinances they called the "forest law," which took the place of royal charters as long as you were far enough removed from the king. Forest law described three basic rights under which land could be claimed. The "corn right" permitted a claim of one hundred acres of ground for every acre of cultivated corn; the "tomahawk right" reserved the ground whose boundaries were marked by blazed trees; and the "cabin right" applied to a hundred acres around any built structure.

These rights were extended by white Europeans to other white Europeans. Most, but not all, of them simply ignored any native claims to the land, an attitude that was encouraged by the fact that the native population for a long time made no such claim; their culture had no concept of, and thus no language for, "owning" land in the sense meant by white men. There were a few among the Europeans willing to assert the claim for them; William Penn, at least at first, was careful that each advance of his domain was in his view properly negotiated and settled. The Society of Friends, or Quakers, was strident in calling on the settlers to treat the natives fairly.

One of them, Thomas Chaukley, offered advice in 1738: "As nature had given them and their forefathers the possession of this continent of America (or this wilderness), they had a natural right thereto in justice and equity; and no people, according to the law of nature and justice and our own principle, which is according to the glorious gospel of our dear and holy Jesus Christ, ought to take away or settle on other men's lands or rights without consent, or purchasing the same by agreement of parties concerned." Chaukley's was a minority view, especially on the serrated edge of the advancing white frontier in western Pennsylvania.

That advance, the Lewis family not the first but certainly among the vanguard, now pressed to the southwest, along the wide valley between the mountain ranges, across the river variously known as the Cohongoruton, the River of Wild Geese, or the Wapotomaca, at its confluence with another broad river flowing along the valley from southwest to northeast, called the Shenandoah.

And here they encountered what seems to us now a great mystery. From this broad valley of sweet waters, springing grasses, and vast forests, with its gentle climate and abundant wildlife, something was missing. Unlike every other place where the white settlers had arrived on this continent for the past century or so, no delegation stepped forward to welcome or oppose them; no native tribe could call the Shenandoah Valley home.

Journal

⟞⟝

Coming to Shenandoah

When I had been a man for many years, and had children of my own, I was visiting my parents in some winter season and of course we commemorated the time together, which was rare because we lived two thousand miles apart, by visiting a shopping mall. We were passing the display window of a liquor store when my father gestured toward it with his chin and said, "That's what we are."

Since my father and I were pretty much limited to two subjects of conversation—what the weather was doing and how the car was running—I paid attention to this uncharacteristic remark, but as I looked at the window full of festive bottles and signs I could not make sense of it. "What are we, drunks?" I asked.

"No. That." And the chin zeroed in on a particular section of bottles, over which hung a sign that said Scotch, comma, Irish. Thus was I introduced to my heritage.

By that time, some of the stories to be encountered within these pages had already snagged me, drawing me into a dance of thirty years and more with their elusive meanings. And it was not just the stories that beguiled me and led me on; it was the place, which exerted its hold on me long before I heard any of the stories or knew that I was Scotch, comma, Irish. Or cared.

The wind I sailed away from home in 1958 was a west wind, blowing back and away from the western frontiers of my grandfathers, drawing young people to glittering anonymous cities and a life my ancestors would neither have imagined nor desired. This wind did not take the best of us, although we assumed we were such at the time, it took the chaff first. It filled the sails of people who had been raised without privation, stuffed with education, indulged to the point of spoilage, and who regarded the extended families (including parents who did not divorce) and tightly knit communities that had nurtured them as shackles on their free will, impediments to their fulfillment.

We were hedonists. We drank cheap whiskey and smoked unfiltered cigarettes while driving gas-guzzling behemoths at high speed (without seat belts) in search of unprotected sex. We wanted instant and constant gratification and found it difficult to sustain under disapproving gazes, hence our need to move, to replace family with the company of fellow hedonists, community with isolation in a sea of strangers who, not knowing or caring for us, would not bother to judge us. We knew we would have to do some kind of work to support all this, but we also knew it would not be the work of our fathers; no sweating in sun-stricken fields for us, we would poke at typewriters, shuffle papers, murmur into telephones, and be supplied with enough money to live like princes.

Literally. We rambled the world at will and took our pleasures where we might, as only the richest and most degenerate noblemen of previous centuries could have done. In 1958 I left the family and farm for university and work in broadcasting; in 1963, minimalist college degree in hand, I left the country for a broadcasting job in Bermuda—a two-year-long beach party among fellow nomads.

No one told us we were wrong, not even the families we had spurned. They read in the newspapers that Science was mastering the universe, planning to seed the clouds for rain on demand, to deploy the new "atom bombs" to unwind hurricanes, divert the

Gulf Stream to de-ice Russian ports or pop an instant new harbor for Alaska. We were on our way to supersonic travel, to the moon, to the stars; everything new and scientific was "progress" and good, everything old was discredited. Emphatically included among the things that were tainted by having existed previously were the values and structures of family, community, and heritage. This is what we young nomads acted out, and even our parents were not sure we were wrong. They read the headlines promising the advent of a new world without disease, obesity, halitosis, Communists, or mosquitoes; they read our infrequent letters with the exotic stamps, shook their heads, and said nothing.

We were a migration, larger than that of the Scotch-Irish in the eighteenth century, but we were not fleeing from tyranny, we were disconnecting from humanity. We went in search not of liberty but of money and fun. We did not seek the New World, we sought a New Economy, and the only revolution that interested us was the sexual one. Of course we had worries. The Russians might win the Cold War, or at least beat us to the moon. Someone might unleash a nuclear war and incinerate us all. But this was background stuff, plots for movies, excuses for doing what we wanted to do ("Come on, honey, we might all get blown up tomorrow").

Then the assassin's bullets struck down John Kennedy. And the war in Vietnam spun out of control. The 1950s were over. If one of the richest, most powerful, and most capable men on the planet could be erased with a flick of fate's finger, what hope was there for any of us? And if the best and the brightest among us—scientists, strategists, statesmen, warriors—could not defeat a bunch of jungle peasants, what hope was there for all of us? How were we expected to party on when any of us was—all of us were—subject to sudden death at the hands of savages?

Of course we were convinced that none of this had ever happened before. Television was our primary source of information, and like all things new and insistently forward-looking, it had no memory. It left us with the impression that America had never lost a leader to an assassin's bullet before (oh, sure, Lincoln, but my God, that was prehistory); that a civilized, technological country had never been humbled at the hands of small brown primitives before (even when George Armstrong Custer's very unit, the Seventh Cavalry, was surrounded and virtually wiped out in the first major action of the Vietnam War, we did not get the irony, or the lesson); and that an advanced society on the brink of controlling all of nature surely had never threatened to tear itself apart with race riots and antiwar demonstrations (well, yes, the Civil War, but that was just a succession of battles, and besides, those people were not evolved, like us).

The steady wind of hedonism became a succession of anarchistic tornadoes. The mantra ceased to be "Enjoy yourself" and became "Save yourself." A few young nomads ran away to some tranquil foreign country, renouncing their country in order to be safe, thus severing the last bonds but those of blood that bound them to their people. Many plunged ever deeper into the counterculture, trying to drown out the sounds of gunfire and rage with drugs, sex, and rock 'n' roll, or with organized and sometimes violent dissent. Others turned to face the beast, volunteering to serve their afflicted country mostly to get it over with.

A few went back home, and I might have been one of those, had not providence played a cruel trick on me.

Any second thoughts I might have had about abandoning the community that raised me were obviated when, in my absence, the community was obliterated as thoroughly as if it had been the object of a bitter war. The family farms I had known were melded into corporate, chemical operations tended by fewer and fewer people and more and larger machines. One by one the businesses of our town—the lumber yard, the barber shop, the hardware store, the auto repair shop, the farmers' co-op—withered and died for lack of customers. They closed the railroad station, then the post office. These thrifty farm folk did not leave the buildings to rot down, they jacked them up, put them on wheels, and towed them off to other uses; the school I had attended was converted to someone's chicken coop, they towed the church away to use somewhere else. Even the huge grain elevators that lined the railroad track to house the annual harvest were dismantled and taken away, and there was talk of actually tearing up the railroad track. The scenes of my childhood were struck like the set of a play that has closed for lack of attendance and will never be produced again, to become blank stretches of anonymous prairie.

In the midst of the country's turmoil and dislocation, I took as my mission the covering of the turmoil of Washington, D.C., as a broadcast journalist, and within a few weeks of taking up residence and my duties there I was drawn to do something that would change the rest of my life. On a day in June of 1965, I drove west from the city, got out of the car, and stood for the first time on the banks of the Shenandoah River. I do not know what impelled me to go. The river and its valley, Virginia itself, had been no part of my family's history, as far as I knew—but then, neither had any other place. I never knew three of my own grandparents, rarely saw the sole survivor (my paternal grandmother, who lived a thousand miles away), and I had never asked, nor had I ever been told, who their ancestors were and where they had come from. As far as I was concerned—and I was not concerned about it at all—I had no heritage, was connected to nothing that was old or unseen.

Yet here I was, responding to a summons that was as urgent as it was intangible. I do not know the nature of that summons. I wonder sometimes if there is such a thing as genetic memory, vague but powerful impressions of experience recorded along with all the codes of creation in our chromosomes and passed unvoiced, beyond the range of consciousness, to the last generations. I do not know about that, but there I was, and two things I do know: my first sight of the glittering river that day, the sound of its quiet watery eternal passing, the smell of its fecund banks, remain stark and clear in my mind, in the first rank of indelible memories; and, with the exception of brief physical absences, I never left that river again.

Deprived, like John Lewis, of the home of my birth, like him I traveled many thousands of miles as part of a historic migration and built my life and family and community anew on the banks of the Shenandoah, and of all the things I found there not the least was my connection with him.

Part Two

The First People

The Prehistoric Shenandoah

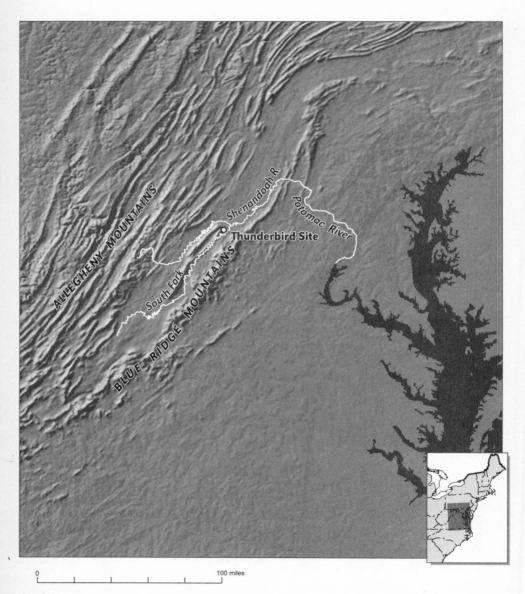

Seen without the structures of industrial society, the rippled mountains flanking the Valley of
Virginia bespeak their origin in continental collision, and the broad ribbon of the valley offers
a sheltered and inviting causeway for northeast-southwest travel. The oldest remains of human
habitation ever found on the continent were unearthed at the Thunderbird Site.

Chapter 3

———

Finding Jasper, 10,000 B.C.

For eleven millennia, that particular outcrop of jasper provided perhaps four hundred generations of people with the basis of their wealth, the mineral resource without which their life would have been untenable. Yet in all that time no one tried to assert exclusive ownership.

IMAGINE, TWELVE THOUSAND YEARS before Scotch-Irish eyes ever fell upon its waters, a band of brown people making its way along the river that will be known as the Shenandoah, heading upstream beside the broad and shallow stream that flows in sluggish gray braids among many islands, bogs, and sandbars. (In the millennia since, the river has cut itself a much narrower and more convoluted course.) The travelers, swathed in skins and fur, are on an urgent quest, moving south between the river and the mountain that will be called Massanutten. (Today the round-shouldered mountain is entirely covered with a forest that is mostly hardwoods; then, although it was already an ancient landform, it reared sharply above a tree line of dark pines that cloaked its flanks like green fur. From October to May its stark upper ridges glistened with snow and ice, fading memorials to the great glaciers that had come as close as present-day Pennsylvania before retreating toward their Arctic lairs.)

The people are nomads who have been traveling for generations through a world forever new yet always familiar, wandering for so long that home was everywhere and nowhere in particular. Memories of the plains of Mongolia had faded from their minds generations ago but lingered in their angular, copper-colored faces, in their glittering brown eyes, and in their songs and stories. They had come to this continent and eventually to this valley not to discover it or claim it, but simply because they were following the herds on whom their life depended. For a time, the great ice sheets that covered half the world had locked up in them so much of the planet's water that the oceans receded, baring a land bridge between Asia and America across which these hunters had trotted.

The people in the valley watch the cottonwoods and willows along the river margins for signs of prey or predator, alert to a chance to trap a deer or to stay clear of a saber-toothed cat or a brown bear. The danger, from even the largest carnivores, is negligible, for the simple reason that the animals are unfamiliar with humans and have not yet identified them as either prey or threat. Across the river, a marshy savanna stretches away to the east, a vast expanse of yellow grass dotted with widely spaced clumps of trees: spruce and fir where the ground is dry, oak and hickory in the many swamps. Another range of old mountains (today's Blue Ridge) rises a dozen miles away.

The men and older boys carry spears. Some have only a wooden haft, with no elongated stone point bound to its tip. Others carry weapons with only stubby remnants of a proper point. This is the subject of their urgent search; they have to find a source of the special rock that fractures predictably, whose surfaces can be worked to a tough sharpness. They have no idea where to look, so they have to look everywhere, and they have to find it soon. Survival requires that every one of them be fully equipped, to maintain the supply of meat, sinew, antlers, bones, and hides for the people's food, shelter, and clothing.

At last they hear an excited shout from one of the scouts who has gone to inspect a likely looking ridge on the other side of the river. He comes splashing through the shallow stream now, bearing a fist-sized rock that he shows to the leader and the band's foremost craftsmen, who trot to meet him at the water's edge. One of the craftsmen leans down, selects a rounded cobble from the riverbed, and with it sharply strikes the proffered rock. It splits cleanly, to the immense relief and pleasure of the group—and of the whole band, who have been watching them closely. The elders now look more sharply at the topography of the area. The ridge where the scouts made their find faces the north; it will be cold and windswept. The river runs closely beneath it, leaving little flat land. Across the river from it, however, not far from where they are now, the lush bottomlands are flat, expansive, and open to the southern sun. He indicates a slight rise not far away. This is where the people will stay.

The first people have come to the Shenandoah Valley, have discovered there a source of great wealth, and have decided to settle.

The extended family does its work quickly. The young men gather large saplings at the river's edge and bring them to the campsite where the men have dug a double line of shallow post-holes. Each young tree is placed, thick end first, in a hole and bent into its opposite number to form a low arch. The women and the girls unfurl the hide coverings from their bundles and spread them over the framework. The work is soon done and a fire is struck against the advancing dark and cold.

With the urgency and the worry lifted from their hearts, knowing now that tomorrow will see their weapons and tools replenished, the people make a feast of their carefully husbanded supplies, thank the gods, and celebrate into the night. After dances, songs, and prayers the old men tell stories, learned from their grandfathers, of the beginning of the world, of how the people came to be and got their name, and of the old, heroic days when the earth shook to the tread of giant mammoths, vast herds of horses, camels, caribou, and musk oxen. All gone now, with all the ancestors, fled from a changing world.

Of course the stories and the legends did not begin to grasp the enormity of what was happening around them. They had been focused on their immediate problem of how to continue to make use of the animals among which they lived, whose flesh and hides were essential to their survival. They were aware only marginally of the larger fact that the grand beasts of their ancestors' world—the mammoths, giant bison, great shaggy horses, and camels—were dead. Extinct. The world would not see their kind again, and the saber-tooth cats and mastodons would soon follow them into oblivion. (Caribou and musk oxen were missing from the valley, too, but they had simply moved northward, following the glaciers' grudging retreat to the polar haunts where the ice would wait for its time to come again, in another ten thousand years or so.) The brown people were struggling to sustain their lives in the midst of the greatest dying the planet had seen since the death of the dinosaurs 65 million years before or would see again until the twentieth century A.D.

The relationship of causes to effects has never been simple. There are degrees of linkage, of which logicians recognize two. An efficient cause is one that, by itself, brings about a result. Kick a pebble off a cliff, and the force you applied is the efficient cause of the pebble's descent. Lean against a twenty-ton rock that has been unbalanced by eons of erosion, and the force you applied, minuscule by comparison to the enormous mass of the boulder, may be sufficient, in combination with all the other factors, to topple a rock you could never have moved by yourself. It is in this latter sense that the people may have caused the great dying of the megafauna.

The advent of their ancestors to the North American continent was an event at least as distant in time from the first people of the Shenandoah as, for example, Joan of Arc and the Battle of Agincourt are from us. The nomads had stepped aboard a continent that, during the tens of millions of years since the last giant reptile had thudded dead to the ground, had reached an exquisite ecological balance. Lush, diverse plant growth sustained a remarkable bestiary of huge grazers: bison with six-foot horns, ground sloths weighing several tons, beavers the size of today's bears, huge hairy horses, and of course the shaggy, seven-ton mammoths. These populations were preyed upon by correspondingly large saber-toothed cats, dire wolves, lions, and bears.

It was a world of enormous productivity that had balanced all its equations of birth, life, death, and renewal without allowing for the thinking, practiced hunters who suddenly appeared among vast herds of animals that had no fear of them (as well as predators that had no taste for them). As the immigrants from Mongolia moved into and across the new land, their effects on the ecosystem may have spread outward from them like ripples that somehow gathered force with distance, becoming destructive tsunamis. Killing an animal now and then, erecting a temporary camp here and there, the people affected the populations of their prey in tiny but incremental ways. Moving a herd away from its customary grazing area here, deflecting a migratory route there, the people caused the densely nestled populations of animals to jostle each other with increasing force and effect. Similar dislocations affected the other predators, with amplified effect because a predator requires a much larger range for survival than does a grazer. The canids, big cats, and bears found their territories altered by both the unaccustomed movements of their prey and the unprecedented challenge of the humans for space of their own.

The outcome was swift and monumental. Within four hundred years, a mere eye blink in geological time, migrating humans had reached South America and the Shenandoah Valley. And by that time, in their wake, 100 million large animals, dozens of species—a biomass equal to all the cattle now alive on the continent—were dead. Their niches in the ecosystem remain empty to this day, like ghostly rooms in a partially abandoned mansion.

Had there been anyone to comprehend and relate these events (they are not well understood, or unanimously agreed upon, even today) to the family making its camp on the Shenandoah in that long-ago time, they would not have believed that such a thing had happened, let alone that they had helped to make it happen. They would have hefted their simple stone-tipped spears, thought about the scant harvest of animals required for their survival, surveyed the plains around them, still teeming with deer, elk, and moose, and they would have snorted their derision. That their actions could have helped derange the ecology of a continent, sending unbalanced systems reeling into each other and crashing to destruction like a house of cards, would have been as incomprehensible to them as, for example, the notion that twentieth-century humans helped blow a hole in the ozone layer with their air conditioners or began an unnatural and potentially cataclysmic warming of the planet by generating electricity and driving cars.

The life of these simple people, long represented in modern society as one of continuous fear of privation, fang, and claw, was more likely one of relative ease and plenty. Studies of surviving hunter-gatherer societies such as the !Kung of the Kalahari show that adults spend about ten hours a week in subsistence activities. There were at hand not only vast herds of meaty animals that had no fear of humans, but abundant and diverse plant growth offering greens, nuts, fruits, berries, grains, and tubers. After the retreat of the glacier line above the modern-day Canadian border, the rivers warmed and began to teem with fishes, mussels, turtles, and water birds. Roaming from place to place, changing their diets with the seasons, the people never came close to depleting their supplies of food. A harsh winter or a sudden drought could bring hunger, but privation was hardly the rule. For beings smart enough to preserve and store some food, to plan ambushes and design snares, to remember and predict the behavior of game animals, living was easy. The populations of the First People exploded even as those of the megafauna vanished silently and unnoted around them.

In the morning the men and boys head out to begin the work for which they had come to this place. They wade the icy, shallow strands of the broad river and approach a modest ridge on the other side, its jumbled vertical side facing northwest, into the harsh, early-winter wind. They clamber up the rubble at its base until they find what they have been seeking: an outcrop of yellow-brown jasper, a form of quartz, embedded in a layer of sedimentary limestone that accumulated on the floor of an unimaginably ancient sea.

The seabed may already have been a relict when, a quarter of a billion years ago, the planet's two existing protocontinents collided to form one enormous landmass. The force of the collision along a front thousands of miles long slowly drove the edge of one land-mass, borne by massive currents of molten rock on its tectonic-plate raft, up over the other. The earth's hide shuddered with earth-quakes, erupted with volcanoes, and wrinkled into mountains (the same process that today continues to raise the Himalayas and the Alps) until, 100 million years or so later, the subterranean tides changed, ripped apart the landforms they had created, and bore seven fragmentary continents away to their current, separate sta-tions. At the boundary of the ancient collision, unimaginable pres-sures acted on the sediments of ancient seas, the skeletons of bil-lions of microscopic marine organisms and solutions of young minerals recently disgorged from the earth's bowels to form, among other things, certain crystalline veins and nodules of silica, stained brown with iron and copper, known today as jasper, found scat-tered along what geologists have christened the Blue Ridge Over-thrust Fault.

The brown people are not intimidated by the massive boulders that confront them. The young men fan out, gathering tinder and kindling, so that the elders can strike a fire at the base of one of the huge stones. They all pile on branches, enjoying the welcome heat reflected from the rock. They haul up a couple of large animal-skin bladders full of icy water from a nearby stream and, when the stone is sufficiently heated, fling the frigid water on the rock. There is a hiss, a gout of steam, and an explosive crack as a slab of rock breaks loose and falls. They push it to one side to let it cool, and while some of them build the fire back up to repeat the process, others hammer at the warm slab with rounded hammer stones scrounged for the purpose from the riverbed. The senior craftsmen appraise the chunks thus cracked loose, discarding some and selecting those with the most workable grain for transport back across the river.

There, away from the chilling shade of the ridge, the craftsmen settle down to their patient work. Taking up one fist-sized core at a time, the workmen deftly shape it by chipping away with a cobblestone. The shape that emerges will dictate the final product—perhaps a scraper for the women to use when preparing hides, an ax for felling trees and breaking bones, a knife for butchering. Most important, however, are those cores that yield an elongated triangle suitable for finishing as a spear point. Occasionally, just as the treasured shape appears in the stone, there is a grunt of frustration as one blow too many fractures the emerging point.

When a point has been roughly shaped, the craftsman sets aside his cobblestone and begins the finishing work with a piece of deer antler, pushing one small flake at a time off the stone with a twisting outward thrust against its edge. After many minutes of this delicate knapping, he holds up a finished point. The first to be done is immediately bound to the head of the man's spear, to replace the one worn down to a nub by frequent resharpening. Soon the family's tool kit has been replenished, and there is a sack of blanks to provide replacements in the coming year.

This seasonal routine was to continue from about 9500 B.C. until around A.D. 1650. For eleven millennia, that particular outcrop of jasper provided perhaps four hundred generations of people with the basis of their wealth, the mineral resource without which their life would have been untenable. Yet in all that time no one tried to assert exclusive ownership. The culture of the Paleo-Indian, like the ecology of the megafauna before it, achieved an exquisite balance with the natural resources that nourished it. Fundamental to that balance was the concept that land and minerals, like air, water, and game, were for all to use as they needed. It is not that the First People cared for their environment in any active, premeditated way. They simply did not have the means to exploit it or to resist the operation of biological laws that achieve harmony among populations and their resources. And the idea that any individual could claim for private advantage anything the people needed for their survival simply did not exist.

In the traces of the structures used by the First People along the Shenandoah, in the scraps of their handiwork in stone, and especially in the source of their wealth, the jasper outcrop that still juts over the river they traveled twelve thousand years ago, there are important lessons for the human race.

Chapter 4

—⁖—

Leaving Shenandoah,
1400–1732

We have burned all our songs, all our dances, all our
superstitions and everything that the Devil has taught our
forefathers.

—*Montaignais convert to Christianity*

IN 1734, TWO YEARS AFTER John Lewis arrived in the Shenandoah
Valley, Benjamin Allen staked his claim on the broad bottomlands
between the North Fork of the river and Massanutten Mountain,
south of present-day Mount Jackson. The historian of the valley
Samuel Kercheval relates the "tradition," as he labeled many of the
stories he recorded, that Allen was often visited by an elderly native
who identified himself as the last of the Senedo people. The old
man related that his entire tribe had been wiped out in a massacre
that had occurred when he was a boy, which Kercheval calculated
would have been in the mid-seventeenth century. All the Senedoes
had been killed, the old man said, except for him and one other.

The "tradition" that a people called the Senedoes once lived
along the river that now bears their name has been discredited.

Kercheval set it down a century after Benjamin Allen's time, and the editor of the fourth edition of the work, published another century later, dismissed the account because a 1725 treaty between the English and the Iroquois, purporting to list all the tribes living in the area, did not mention Senedoes. But as we will see, the editor (who also ridiculed Kercheval's belief that the natives of America originated in Mongolia and crossed to the continent via the Kamchatka Peninsula) relied on a slender reed in believing that English treaty writers knew whom they were dealing with. There is reason to listen to the old man's poignant tale with fresh ears.

But his is not the mystery that brings us up short when we consider the record of the advent of white settlers in the Shenandoah. As we slowly realize in considering the chronology, the fascinating question is not how the white newcomers dealt with the native inhabitants, but why they did not have to. The natives they encountered (with the possible exception of the elderly Senedo) were travelers, on their way from a distant place to another distant place. For nearly twenty years after the arrival of the settlers, contact between the two races in the Shenandoah Valley was infrequent and for the most part benign. In fact, there were no native inhabitants in one of the world's most beautiful and productive places. How could this be?

John Lewis and his family were not intruding on some idyllic Paradise where happy aborigines lived in peaceful abundance. The gates of Eden had slammed shut behind the inhabitants of the Shenandoah three hundred years before the white man appeared, but until 1400 or so, the Shenandoah Valley had been occupied by widely dispersed families living in peace and plenty. Plenty, in this context, meant they almost always had enough to eat. Even then they did a little farming, scratching out small plots of corn, beans, and squash. But their subsistence depended on hunting, fishing, and foraging in a bountiful land. They moved readily and often, to be near the fishing in its season, the hunting in its time, the berries and nuts when they were ready. They lived in round huts, fifteen to twenty feet in diameter, whose walls were sharpened posts driven into the ground, little changed from the shelters of the First People. There is no sign in the archeological record that they had any need for defensive palisades. Their community graveyards contained the remains of the very young (under two years of age) and elders over sixty; most who survived infancy apparently could expect a long life.

This and other evidence suggests a picture of hunter-gatherer life that stands in stark contrast to the assumptions of modern people that hunter-gatherers lived in constant fear of predators and enemies, endlessly frenzied about finding their next meal, hanging on the edge of extinction. To the contrary, recent studies indicate that the hunter-gatherer enjoyed plenty of leisure time and had no concept of either work or worry. In a balanced ecology, food was at hand, had always been at hand, and there was no reason to worry about the source of the next meal. If there was some contraction of the food supply, for example during a drought, the human population adjusted, but not necessarily in an agony of famine (indeed, there are those who argue convincingly that there was no such thing as famine before the invention of agriculture). Instead, birth rates declined because females who did not achieve a certain ratio of body fat to muscle did not conceive; the elderly perished a few months before they otherwise might have; a few more infants died at, or shortly after, birth. Predation occurred, of course, as it does in every natural system, affecting the weak and thus constantly pruning the tree of life. (Modern people find it inconceivable that predation upon humans could be tolerated without continuous fear, yet Americans today accept the slaughter of about fifty thousand of their number every year in automobile accidents without outcry, without even a moment of personal reflection while slipping behind the wheel and into mortal danger. Moreover, this predation does nothing to improve the gene pool.)

The death of a child or a grandmother may be biologically neutral, even an evolutionary advantage, but it is always a human sorrow, and humans do what they can to avoid it. In some cultures, and the natives of America were no exception, it began to seem obvious that the best way to secure the future was to cultivate plants, managing natural abundance in order to produce reassuring surpluses. The existence of the surpluses removed the natural controls on population, and as the numbers of people consequently increased, each village required larger fields and more extensive ranges for hunting and wood-gathering—and, of course, larger surpluses, which among other things had to be defended from confiscation. These trends were accelerated by the onset, after 1350, of the Little Ice Age, a four-centuries-long shift to cool, dry weather that substantially reduced vegetative growth. Farming became less productive and hunting required even larger territories. Even then, for a time the vastness of the continent easily absorbed the increasing sprawl of human activity, but inevitably boundaries collided.

After 1400 the negative effects of agricultural advancement became obvious in the Shenandoah. Villages became not only larger but fortified against attack. The population of the valley contracted eastward, flinching from the threat posed by ever more numerous and aggressive people to the west. Large villages quickly exhausted the surrounding resources and had to be moved often. This was no longer the simple matter of a seasonal move by nomadic hunter-gatherers; it was an industrial operation, involving the construction of new fortifications and the establishment of large new fields. Eden had been lost.

Yet by about 1500, the jostling for place achieved a new equilibrium, one less kind than had been the case in Eden (cemeteries of this time contain more frequent evidence of death by violence than had been the case for millennia) but stable enough for another century. Then came cataclysm.

Disaster came in two forms, both related to the arrival of the Europeans on the eastern shores, but it was not the Europeans themselves who wreaked the destruction: it was their diseases and their trade goods. The newcomers did not know, at first, that their diseases ran before them like an invisible forest fire, consuming perhaps half the human population of the continent before the agents of the destruction ever advanced into the interior. And while the Europeans knowingly initiated trade with the natives, they were oblivious to its effects on their trading partners. The tribes quickly became dependent on things for which the whites were the only source: firearms, powder, ammunition, steel knives, iron pots, cloth. Such things seemed to make life more convenient and survival more assured. Like the benefits of agriculture, they were embraced as a new standard of wealth with little thought for their true, long-term costs: loss of independence, disruption of long-held beliefs, the unleashing of the dogs of war.

One of the largest, longest, and most disruptive wars the continent has ever seen was waged for seventy years beginning about 1630, not between natives and whites but among the tribes. Called the Beaver Wars, these conflicts were fought for domination of the beaver trade. The pattern of apparent prosperity followed closely by unmitigated disaster was established toward the end of the sixteenth century by French explorers of the St. Lawrence River Valley and the residents they found there, the Montagnais. What happened to the Montagnais was relatively well documented because the French were not as disdainful of the natives they encountered as were the English and because of the pervasive presence of literate Jesuit missionaries wherever the French operated. What is known about the Montagnais sheds light on what happened to every other tribe that was caught up in the Beaver Wars and on the resulting native geography that confronted the first settlers of the Shenandoah.

━━

French cod fishermen had been visiting the shores of the Gulf of St. Lawrence for decades, finding the Montagnais friendly and eager to trade for metal tools and trinkets. All the natives had to offer in exchange were the furry hides of various small animals, for which the French had little regard. But they accepted the pelts to be polite and to maintain friendly relations, and as the years passed they began to pass the novelties around in Europe. Eventually, hat makers in Paris discovered they could make a high-quality felt from beaver fur and began to offer their special customers a few very expensive hats made from this new material. Wealthy Parisians began to sport them, the less wealthy began to emulate their sartorial leaders, and soon a fad was raging. In 1583 a French merchant named Etienne Bellenger sold a cargo of furs for ten times the value of the goods he had traded for them. A consortium of merchants sent five ships up the St. Lawrence in 1584, ten ships the following year.

The Montagnais joked about the newcomers they were out-smarting, people who, as one jubilant trader put it, "have no sense; they gave us twenty knives like this for one beaver skin." But both sides were soon taking this trade very seriously. The occasional visits of French fishermen trading for their own amusement became a steady flood of fur traders who came to stay. Never mind gold, or a route to Cathay, they were on the track of a new source of fabulous wealth; the fur rush was on. They learned how to travel inland with birchbark canoes on the rivers and lakes in summer, with snow-shoes and toboggans over the thick snows of winter. They got used to eating corn, moose, beaver, and dog. They tried smoking tobacco and before long, as a disgusted Jesuit reported, became "so bewitched with it that, to inhale its fumes, they would sell their shirts." Another observer noted that once Frenchmen were accustomed to tobacco, "they can no more be without it than without meat or drink."

Such changes in the behavior of the fur traders were minor, however, compared with the transformation of Montagnais life that occurred within a few decades, first disrupting and then replacing the ways, learned over the millennia, with which the Montagnais had come into balance with the demands and opportunities of their austere, subarctic environment. Montagnais families traditionally had traveled familiar routes within relatively small areas, following an annual routine of hunting and gathering. They had moved across the land as guests at a great buffet, sampling fish in the summer, eels and bear in the fall, porcupine and beaver in early winter, caribou and moose in late winter, geese and partridge in the spring, eating their fill and moving on. Because they did not rely heavily on any single area or species for their food supply, they were never a threat to any single kind of animal, nor were they threatened when some animal went into a decline, as, for example, the snowshoe hare did periodically.

Trade with the French changed everything, immediately. Hours of working fragile edges onto flint knives, scrapers, hatchets, and arrow points were obviated by the availability of manufactured metal knives, hatchets, arrowheads, and, especially, guns. The owner of a flint-and-steel could carry fire anywhere without the bother of transporting embers. A woman who had an iron kettle no longer had to bother with making bark or earthenware vessels and heating rocks with which to warm their contents. It was much easier to decorate clothing and accessories with ready-made glass beads than to gather, polish, and mount seashells and porcupine quills.

With the time their new implements saved them, the Montagnais became specialists. Instead of drawing on the whole range of animal life in their environment, taking from each species a little of what they needed for survival, they began a relentless pursuit of beaver. Instead of their former accommodation to a whole web of relationships with the natural world, the focus of Montagnais life became finding and killing beaver, not for an occasional supper but to supply all the needs of the tribe. In short order, the supply of prime beaver in the familiar home ground was depleted. To satisfy the insatiable demand for more pelts, the Montagnais were forced to do something they had not done before: travel great distances in search of new beaver-hunting grounds. Not only did this pattern of destruction and migration drastically alter their traditional, stable relationship with the natural world, it brought them into contact first with other Montagnais families, then with other tribes with different ways and languages. At best these competitive contacts changed the cultures of the people forced to forge new relationships; at worst they led to warfare.

The laborsaving innovations were thought of by Europeans as improvements in the Montagnais standard of living. But once the exacting skills of subsistence were lost, they could not be revived when trade was interrupted—when, for example, a supply ship failed to make the Atlantic crossing on time. In such an event, people died of starvation. Meanwhile, prolonged contact with the French brought diseases and parasites—influenza, smallpox, measles, and rats—with which the Montagnais had no experience and against which they had no defenses. "They are astonished and complain often," reported the Jesuit Father Pierre Biard, "that since the French are among them many of them die and their population is decreasing."

While the French may not have intended to restructure the Montagnais' material life, they deliberately set out to reorient the Indians' spiritual life. After about 1540 the kings of France, in order to secure for their colonial ambitions the blessing and support of the powerful Vatican, professed religious motives for all their expeditions to the new world. Their real objective was not land nor money nor power, they declared at every opportunity, but merely to go among the savages and, as King Francis I put it, save "an infinity of souls for God."

Thus as the fur trade developed, the increasing number of traders was paralleled by an influx of missionaries, most of them Jesuits, who found it was much more difficult to change spiritual beliefs than it had been to transform work habits. Father Paul Le Jeune, who for a quarter of a century after 1632 was the Father Superior of all Jesuit missionaries in New France, lamented the difficulty of appealing to a people who seemed to need nothing: they were "harmonious among themselves," he wrote, "rendering no homage to any one whomsoever, except when they like." Moreover, "as they are contented with a mere living, not one of them gives himself to the Devil to acquire wealth." No one gave orders, either in the household or in the tribe, no one enunciated or enforced rules of behavior, even among the children. Everyone participated fully in the life and the decisions of the community.

This would never do, Father Le Jeune lamented: "Alas! If someone could stop the wanderings of the savages, and give authority to one of them to rule the others, we would see them converted and civilized in a short time." The Jesuits were implacable in urging the Montagnais to give and obey orders—husbands to wives, parents to children, leaders to followers—as they were in insisting that the Montagnais forsake their casual relationship with their familiar spirit world and accept a remote and authoritarian God along with His reproachful priests. At first, the Montagnais received the remonstrances of the Jesuits with unflappable courtesy and affable tolerance. "They said that when I prayed to God they greatly approved of it, as well as of what I told them," recalled Father Le Jeune; "and hence, that I must also approve of their customs, and I must believe in their ways of doing things." But the Montagnais customs were crumbling under the onslaught of trade goods, liquor, disease, and dramatically changed ways of doing things. As one Montagnais convert to Christianity proclaimed proudly, "We have burned all our songs, all our dances, all our superstitions, and everything that the Devil has taught our forefathers."

By the time the French traders had succeeded in addicting the Montagnais to trade goods and the Jesuits had convinced many of them to begin giving and taking orders, the beaver were gone from their country and from the country next to theirs. The traders deserted the Montagnais, moving farther inland to deal with the Hurons, who had plenty of beaver. The Montagnais now had nothing to trade, but they were utterly dependent on trade goods. The old ways were gone, the new ways had betrayed them, and the proud people were reduced forever to a humiliating reliance on the charity of strangers.

For nearly half a century the juggernaut fur trade rolled on, pitting white nationalities and red tribes against one another, but the nature of the contest changed when it reached the country occupied by the Iroquois League. The pattern of exploitation—in this case by Dutch traders based in the Hudson River Valley—was the same, as was the conversion of the native culture. But the League was a different kind of organization, and its reaction to the new circumstances would determine the patterns of native settlements in the eastern third of the continent, including the Shenandoah Valley. It is not likely that John Lewis ever knew what the Iroquois League was. There is no evidence that his sons understood it, though they would spend their lives in wars whose outcomes would depend on the alliances of the Iroquois.

They called themselves the People of the Longhouse, but are known to our history by the contemptuous term Rattlesnake People. The word Iroquois does not occur in the Iroquoian languages, but in the Athabascan, the tongues of their enemies, who called them Iroqu, or Rattlesnakes, to which name the French appended "ois."

Here is how this nomenclature worked: white newcomers would ask a tribe with whom they had become familiar to identify the next tribe upriver or overland. "Oh, them!" would come the response. "They're man-eaters (Mohawks)!" Or "little snakes (Sioux)!" Or "rattlesnakes (Iroquois)!" The white explorers would dutifully memorize, repeat, and write down this term as the official name of the people who labor under it to this day. Each of these tribal groups, of course, had a name for itself, which invariably translates as some version of, simply, "The People." Thus the Iroquois were *Ongwe Honwe;* the Sioux, *Lakota;* the Delawares (given the name of a British lord they never saw) called themselves *Lenni Lenape.* But since the advent of the whites, who immediately labeled them "Indians," the tribes have been denied that most fundamental of human rights—the right to be known by a name of one's own choosing.

The five major tribes living within, and just west of, the present-day states of New York and Pennsylvania progressed, just as did the inhabitants of the Shenandoah, from peaceful abundance prior to 1400 to managed abundance thereafter, with the consequent increases in population and thus in the size and importance of fields and villages. Thereafter, war became a part of life, and among the five tribes—the Mohawks in what is now eastern New York and to the west the Oneidas, the Onandagas, the Cayugas, and the Senecas—fighting became constant and bloody. At some point there arose among the five tribes an advocate of peace named Deganawida who preached relentlessly against what had become a destructive orgy of killing. He eventually won the support of an influential Mohawk war chief named Hiawatha (with whom Longfellow's later, epic poem had nothing to do), and together they crafted a remarkable confederacy.

To comprehend it, we whose culture is based on certain basic assumptions about human behavior must suspend those assumptions and consider a world in which they do not exist. To consider just one example: to white Europeans, few words are more powerfully iconic than "father." From "Our Father in Heaven," to "Father" Le Jeune, to "Great White Father," the term calls up an image of power and benevolence that requires no explanation, except to people in whose culture there is no such concept. Ask a European who he is and he will name his country, probably his religion, and his family, embodied and named by his father. But to most native populations in the New World, the first and most important identifier (after whatever name was used to signify "The People") was the name of the clan.

Clan membership defined one's role and possibilities in life; youngsters were taught to behave as a member of their clan should behave, to rely on clan elders for help and advice, to regard only certain other clans as appropriate sources of a marriage partner. The clans extended across tribal lines; members of the Wolf clan of the

Senecas, for example, would be welcome in the longhouses of the Wolf clan of the Mohawks (and forbidden to marry their daughters) although they might well need interpreters in order to speak to each other. And clan membership, this core of identity on which everything in life depended, was inherited, in most of the tribes, from the mother.

It is difficult for anyone for whom the assumptions of patrilineal tradition are as normal as the sunrise to conceive of the degree to which everyday life and thinking would be different in a matrilineal society. When a man married a woman, he moved in with her clan, and any children of the marriage were born into her clan. The biological father had little to do with bringing up his children; his responsibilities for education, guidance, and leadership were directed toward his sisters' children, who, unlike his own offspring, were members of his clan. His children were schooled in all the important attitudes and practices of life by fellow clan members, which is to say the mother, along with her brothers and sisters. Thus when any boy reached manhood, and reflected on the source of his knowledge of hunting, of weapons, of woodcraft, it was not his father to whom he directed his gratitude but his uncles, and in these tribes the most meaningful term of respect one could offer was the honorific "uncle." Those on equal footing showed respect by using the more neutral "brother." When a person died, possessions and any hereditary titles did not pass to his children, but returned to his clan, to be assigned by the matriarch to brothers, sisters, or cousins (yes, cousins; the children of my mother's sister are in the same clan as am I).

In a patrilineal society, the father embodies not only knowledge but power. The power to direct others, as a father directs children and a king his subjects, is assumed to be a fundamental and necessary ingredient of society. People inculcated in such ways can imagine only with great difficulty a world in which no one had the duty, or even the right, to give orders to another. In the tribes, even young children were seldom rebuked or forbidden to do something.

It was assumed that as the family lived the right way, the child would soon comprehend and adapt to it. Husbands had no right to instruct their wives, and there were no counterparts to mayors, constables, judges, or kings. There was not even a counterpart to what white people to this day assume was an Indian chief.

As in any human society, there was frequently a need to make community decisions, and it was not always possible to gather the entire community to deliberate. So it was the job of councils to make these decisions, but when they had made them, they had no power to impose them. The sachems who gathered, each holding an office conferred by the matriarch of his clan, had the responsibility of representing their community's thinking, not of controlling it. If they made a decision the community did not like, the community simply ignored it. Even a declaration of war could easily be derailed by the matriarchs, who, if they disagreed with it, would refuse to prepare the food supplies required by the warriors. War chiefs were given, by consent of their warriors, the power necessary to make tactical decisions in battle, but their offices were temporary and quickly removed should they prove unequal to their task.

Deliberations within a council, communications from one council to another, and the history of the people were all oral. There were no written or otherwise recorded constitutions, laws, resolutions, or histories. Certain people had responsibility to remember and communicate essential information. To help them remember, they used wampum belts made from shells stitched on hide in symbolic designs that represented a summary of the case to be presented. These were used as utilitarian aide-mémoire, and were never afforded the significance that Europeans attached to written records. The only thing that mattered was the case made by the speaker.

When the sachems in council received a proposal, such as, for example, Deganawida's idea of a peaceful union of five tribes, it would not occur to them to make a decision on the spot. They would first have to take the information to the people, wait while the families considered it, talked about it, and eventually, at a time that could not be predicted, much less dictated, reached consensus. This amorphous process was the bane of every foreign negotiator who tried to impose an outcome on it, but Deganawida mastered it and won approval for a confederacy that was to bestride the affairs of much of the continent for centuries to come.

An important symbol of the Iroquois League was the fire around which the great council met, and that fire was maintained and the great councils convened by the Onandaga. To these councils came fifty sachems representing the five tribes, approximately according to their population. But decision making involved much more than a simple vote. Any question was first taken up by two separate groups—the Younger Brothers (the Cayugas and Oneidas) and the Older Brothers (the Mohawk and Senecas)—who then took their conclusions to the Firekeepers, the Onandaga. Any differences were referred back to the councils as many times as was required to obtain a unanimous result.

The vision that Deganawida had described to the many councils, and that the resulting League held up as its main idea, was of the Tree of Peace, a great white pine whose roots extended to the extremities of the world and whose crown was watched over by a fierce eagle alert for threats to the Great Peace. As one Iroquois described the dream, for those in the shade of the tree and under the gaze of the eagle, "the land shall be beautiful, the river shall have no more waves, one may go everywhere without fear." The vision was not of a passive peace, but one imposed and maintained by armed power. Other peoples would be invited to sit beneath the Peace Tree and to "clasp their arms around it'" (as when, in 1722, the Tuscaroras became the sixth member of the League).

But peace was not an option for those who were invited into an alliance with the League and refused. In this case the League representative extending the invitation was to make patient arguments in the council of the invitees until rebuffed for the third time. Then, he was to ceremoniously drop a handful of white shells on the ground and club his opposite number to death in front of the council, commencing a war that was to be fought until the Great Peace of the Iroquois could be imposed by conquest.

In this manner the Iroquois League had pacified its members and many of its neighbors by the time the first white men made contact. The League's focus on peace, its artful combination of a central authority with local autonomy, its mixing of proportional representation with checks and balances based on other considerations, made it the most successful and powerful political organization the continent had yet seen (and would be considered carefully by Benjamin Franklin and others when they began crafting their own league of thirteen nations).

Thus, when the fur trade came to the Iroquois, it affected more than an extended family. And when the League decided that it intended to monopolize the trade, the effects on their competition were calamitous. The power they had accumulated to protect the Great Peace proved murderously effective in imposing the Great Fur Monopoly.

By about 1630, the Iroquois had exhausted their supply of beaver and in the familiar pattern now found that in order to maintain their new prosperity in trade with the Dutch in the Hudson River Valley, they had to range to the northwest, toward the beaver-rich country near the Great Lakes. There they encountered the powerful Huron tribe doing the same thing while trading with the French. Here the Iroquois broke the pattern. Instead of jostling ineffectively with their competitors until they were passed by and marginalized, the Iroquois drew on their long experience in subjugating neighboring tribes, applying to the task their formidable political focus and their ferocity. They declared and prosecuted a war that would last for seventy years and would reshape the population of nearly half the continent.

In the ensuing twenty years they conquered the Hurons, destroyed the French fur trade, ejected the Jesuit missionaries, took firm control of the Ottawa River (the primary French trade route to the interior), and reduced the French presence in the country to an enclave in Montreal. With the Hurons subjugated and the French suing for peace, in 1650 the Iroquois laid siege to virtually every tribe they encountered, from the Lenape (later called Delawares, of present-day Pennsylvania) to the Catawbas of South Carolina, from the Susquehannocks and Nanticokes of Virginia to the Shawnees far to the west in the Ohio Country. All these tribes and more the Iroquois defeated and incorporated into the Covenant Chain, making them a kind of second-class member of the Iroquois League without representation in the Great Council.

By 1680 the Iroquois bestrode most of the native populations east of the Mississippi River and dominated utterly the native dealings with the European settlers on the eastern seaboard. No force in the country, native or European, could have withstood the League at this point, but the Iroquois were not fighting for their way of life, they were fighting for trade, and trade required European traders. They decided to play the Europeans against each other to get the best deals, while preventing any European power from achieving dominance over the others, which would pit a European monopoly against their monopoly with unfavorable effect on prices.

When King William's War broke out between the English and the French in 1687, the French were allied with many traditional Iroquois enemies and remnants of tribes defeated by the League, and England had proved to be a more stable and profitable trading partner. So the Iroquois fought on the side of the English. This time the French proved a far more formidable enemy than they had been previously and took the war fiercely into the Iroquois homeland, in the process spreading smallpox among them. The English and French concluded their war in 1697, the victorious English in the peace treaty grandly recognizing Iroquois assistance by taking them "under protection," a gesture that had little significance at the time but was to take on enormous import.

While the French and English temporarily suspended their hostilities, the French and Iroquois continued theirs for another four years. In fact, their war was entirely separate, fought for dominance of the beaver trade and continued partly because the Algonquin allies of the French saw a chance to destroy the League, which was now in trouble. When it became apparent that no one was going to win an absolute victory, the French and Iroquois declared peace in 1701. That year the French and British resumed their war, this one called Queen Anne's, while the League remained neutral.

As the French and English continued to spar over their spheres of influence, the Iroquois held sway from the St. Lawrence River in the north to the valley of the Catawbas in the Carolinas, from the Shenandoah in the east to the Mississippi. It was the Iroquois who had determined the geography of the tribes that John Lewis and his fellow settlers of the Shenandoah would encounter. The settlers, unaware that the natives had a geography, left little in the record about them. To learn what they saw, we must reconstruct it at a distance of nearly three centuries.

The stories of the various points of contact between colonists and natives in eastern America are fairly uniform, varying mostly in the length of time the two sides took to progress from amazement to curiosity to hostility and violence. Given the intensity of many decades of such strife in Tidewater Virginia, in Pennsylvania, and in the Carolinas, it is mystifying to scour the accounts of the first white settlers to stake their claim in the Shenandoah Valley and find no tribal delegations—welcoming, greeting, or warning off— no tribal villages, no tribal residents. What they did see they could not identify at first, having neither knowledge nor curiosity about tribal identities, but all accounts indicate the occasional presence of parties of Senecas and "Delawares" from the north, traveling to the country of the Catawbas and Shawnees in the south, and vice versa. One of the hoary traditions often repeated is that the Shawnees were in the habit of setting fire to the dead prairie grasses each fall to refresh the grass and prevent the growth of trees in the grazing land of the elk and buffalo. When the settlers expressed concern for their homes and fences, the Shawnees, it is said, amicably abandoned their practice.

Having resisted white encroachment elsewhere, and having fought a seventy-year, highly territorial war with each other, why did the tribes of the Shenandoah care so little about the intruders?

In fact, there was no tribe that called the Shenandoah home. In the wake of the Beaver Wars, the Iroquois League laid claim to the valley, but they lived far to the north and cared little about the Shenandoah because it was too far south to be prime beaver country (not enough cold weather to stimulate thick fur), and its river, flowing up from the south, was not a route to prime beaver country. The League declared the Shenandoah a *cantuckee,* a hunting ground for all, that no tribe could claim as its territory. While League warriors had reason to travel frequently through the Shenandoah, as we will see, they were not there to defend it.

The natives encountered by white settlers in the Shenandoah were for the most part wanderers, displaced people grieving for the familiarity of a homeland far away, now receding into memory, rankling at the brutality of their ejection by the Iroquois, dreaming of an eventual return.

The Shawnees who were most often seen by the arriving Europeans were a fragment of the tribe ejected from the Ohio Valley early in the Beaver Wars. As they had not yet engaged in the beaver trade when the Iroquois appeared in their country, they had possessed no firearms with which to withstand the fierce assault. Those who had scattered to South Carolina and the Cumberland Basin (now Tennessee; others went to southern Illinois and eastern Pennsylvania) often traveled, hunted, and camped in the Shenandoah, but they were intent on regaining their former territory south of

Lake Erie, which is where Great Lakes tribes had given them the Algonquin name *Shawun,* or People of the South.

Of Algonquin derivation themselves, the Shawnees accepted the name. Like their neighboring tribes, they organized themselves along clan and tribal lines. Unlike the Iroquois, but like all the other tribal groups, they had no mechanism for organizing their separate factions, and each of the five dispersed groups of Shawnees was fiercely autonomous. Unlike most of the other tribes (and like the Europeans), they observed patrilineal lines of family and clan organization and of heredity.

Other travelers through the Shenandoah as the eighteenth century began were Catawbas from the river valley that bears their name near the border of North and South Carolina. Oddly, they spoke a variant of Siouan, a family of languages usually associated with territories much farther to the west. It is probable that they, like the Shawnees, were victims of the Beaver Wars and were driven from the Ohio Valley about 1650. Like the Shawnees, they had been assigned a relatively benign name meaning "river people," although they called themselves *Iyeye,* "The People." A half century after being driven south by the Senecas of the Iroquois League, the Catawbas and Senecas maintained a bitter, long-distance war with each other involving frequent, long-distance raiding parties that traveled through, and often chased each other through, the Shenandoah. In addition, the Catawbas clashed frequently with their neighbors the Shawnees and Cherokees. For all this combat the Catawbas needed guns, powder, and ammunition, and to get them they forged a close alliance with the British colonists of the Carolinas.

The frequent forays of the Senecas through the Shenandoah often included warriors from another tribe subjugated to the Iroquois League in the Beaver Wars—the Delawares. Of course they called themselves The People, *Lenape,* or more formally *Lenni Lenape,* "The Original People." But the first Englishman to sail into the large bay north of the Chesapeake named it for the first governor of Virginia, Sir Thomas West, Lord de la Warr, and eventually the people who lived on its shores became Delawares. Outside the Iroquois League, the *Lenape* were afforded great respect as the "grandfathers," the people from whom sprang all other Algonquin tribes.

In an 1836 book the French-American naturalist Constantine Rafinesque (whose thinking on the origin of plant species foreshadowed Darwin's) recorded the traditional history of the *Lenape* on which rested their reputation as the "grandfathers" and their title of Original People. This saga recalled the exodus of their forebears from Siberia across the land bridge and across the continent to the Atlantic. Rafinesque recorded that this oral history was supported not by wampum belts, as used by the Iroquois, but by a set of wooden sticks carved with pictographs called the *Walam Olum*. The sacred sticks subsequently disappeared, and western scholars who trust only words written on paper have written down their grave doubt that any oral tradition could persist for ten thousand years.

This marks another chasm between the two cultures that affected everything that happened between them for centuries. When people steeped in an oral tradition entered into negotiations, however complex or important, they focused exclusively on what was said in council. People with special abilities for recalling and re-creating discussions were the record keepers (and historians) for the tribe. Any physical record of the proceedings, whether wampum belt or carved stick, had no value other than its ability to stimulate the memory of a speaker.

European negotiators, on the other hand, would say almost anything during verbal negotiations because to them nothing mattered but the written document that resulted. Thus it frequently happened that the two sides would leave a council fire, one side satisfied with what it had heard said, possibly casually or deceptively, the other side happy with the written document it carried away, signed dismissively by the speakers. Later it would emerge that the two sides understood their agreement differently, usually with grave results.

Before, and outside of, the Iroquois League, other tribes often turned to the *Lenape* to act as arbiters of disputes. The grandfathers did nothing to extend or organize this influence, but remained clannish, autonomous in their various villages and extended families, amorphously communal in their oral decision making. Representatives of the French, Dutch, English, colonial, and eventually the United States governments were endlessly frustrated in their attempts to find one person to speak for the Delawares. Such a person never existed.

The various bands of Delawares did authorize one sachem, whose name was Tammamend, to represent them in negotiations in 1682 with one William Markham. Markham represented William Penn, who had received a grant of land from Charles II on which to found a colony that would be open to, and tolerant of, all religious faiths. Penn, oddly, did not assume that the king's grant extinguished the rights of the native inhabitants and was determined to treat them fairly. On his behalf, Markham struck a deal to "buy" the area that would become southeastern Pennsylvania. (In subsequent American lore, this event would somehow be transposed into an account of "Tammany" selling Manhattan for $26.) The Iroquois were furious with the Delawares for negotiating anything without permission from the Great Council, and spent the next several decades expressing their displeasure and reinforcing the Covenant Chain that bound the Delawares. Thus Delaware warriors were often impressed to accompany Seneca bands heading south to pound the Catawbas.

Meanwhile, the flow of settlers into Pennsylvania turned from amicable to implacable, and the Delawares, too, were pressed relentlessly westward until, by the time John Lewis arrived, they occupied only a fraction of their former homeland, in Pennsylvania's Wyoming Valley. They, too, began to move westward, to the Ohio Country.

Thus nearly every tribe encountered by the settlers of the Shenandoah was in the valley for some temporary purpose, intent on gaining another place: the Forks of the Ohio. This was the place where the Allegheny River, running southwest from the vicinity of Lake Erie in French Canada, met the Monongahela River flowing northwest from Virginia to become the Ohio River. From their confluence (at the place now known as Pittsburgh) the Ohio curved northwest, then recurved to the southwest, eventually joining the Mississippi River. The rivers were the roads—for fur traders transporting the wealth of the backcountry, for war parties seeking or fleeing their enemies, for hunters and explorers and fugitives—and in the great northwestern territories, all roads met at the Forks of the Ohio.

As long as John Lewis and the other settlers of the Shenandoah merely occupied their farms, they lived in relative peace with the native tribes who passed through the valley. It was when they, too, turned covetous eyes on the Ohio Country that trouble became inevitable.

Journal

⟿

The Thunderbird Site

By 1970 I was the proud "owner" of a hundred feet or so of the bank of the North Fork of the Shenandoah River, on the western flank of Massanutten Mountain in Shenandoah County near Woodstock. I had turned my back on the big money and huge hypocrisy of large-market television news in Washington for the lesser rewards but more honest work of journalism in a small place—and, of course, life in the Shenandoah Valley.

You cannot stay for long in this valley without becoming aware of the palpable presence of the past. People who have lived a long time here tend to talk as much about (and, you think sometimes, *with*) their long-dead ancestors as about their next-door neighbors; as much about the details of a Civil War battle that took place down the road as about the latest news from Richmond; as much about the visits of George Washington and Stonewall Jackson as about those of George Bush or Magic Johnson. These are the subjects not only of formal ceremony and education, but also of casual conversation and passionate kitchen-table argument. It is not possible to live among such people without becoming aware of the patina of past lives and happenings that colors the mountain ridges and the hollows, the ancient byways and elderly houses, clinging like the mists of a crisp fall morning.

By the time Dr. Bill Gardner reached out to me for help one day, asking me to give some publicity to his cause, I was accustomed to the reverence for the past that imbued the valley, and by osmosis I had begun to absorb the stories. I was by then familiar with the notion that life in the valley had not only a spatial horizon—the comforting mountain ridges to east and west—but a temporal one, offering vistas stretching back two hundred years. Now Bill Gardner was about to take me on a journey of ten thousand years and confront me with an epiphany about the people of the earth and what it means to own land. That is not what he said, of course. He said he was the director of something called the Thunderbird Museum, that it was in serious trouble, and that some public exposure would help.

A rangy man with a deceptively casual manner, Dr. Bill Gardner had a fierce curiosity about the past and a short fuse, ignited when people or events conspired to waste his time. When we talked about the story of the Thunderbird Site, years afterward, he was rueful about its unsatisfactory end. "I was not the person to do this," he said when it was all over, "I'm too irritable, I didn't know enough about fundraising and politics." Yet it was to him that the discovery of a lifetime came, and no one checked his qualifications first.

Had he not been curious, and had he not been able to distinguish between an apparent and a real waste of time, he could easily have missed the whole thing, so quietly did it offer itself. In 1969 he was a professor of anthropology at Catholic University in Washington, D.C., working on a comprehensive map of prehistoric sites in the basin of the Potomac River. He was trying to cover a vast area of western Virginia and eastern West Virginia, and appealed for help through the Society for American Archaeology. The Northern Shenandoah Valley chapter of the Archaeological Society of Virginia responded that they had some good stuff to show him if he would make a speech to their membership. He agreed, but encountered a last-minute schedule conflict and sent a graduate student, Stephen Gluckman, in his place.

Gardner was not especially fond of amateur archaeologists: "I've seen too many sites just looted and trampled." But Gluckman returned to Washington to report that the Shenandoah Valley group had an impressive number of stone points, all made from the same material, all collected from the same small area. Curiosity kicked in. Bill Gardner scheduled a trip to the Shenandoah Valley.

To reach his destination, Gardner drove to Front Royal, where the North and South Forks of the Shenandoah River conjoin, sixty miles west of Washington, D.C. He turned south on U.S. Route 340, passed the northern entrance to the Shenandoah National Park and Skyline Drive, and proceeded another six miles or so to the hamlet of Limeton. There he met Lanier Rodgers, who was to play a principal role in the drama to come.

Rodgers took Gardner to and across the South Fork of the Shenandoah north of Limeton (see map on page 42), onto a broad floodplain on the inside of a horseshoe bend of the river. Old rivers—and the Shenandoah is one of the oldest on the planet—meander in ever-lengthening and tightening oxbows in obedience to basic physical principles. In any bend of a river, water on the outside of the curve has to flow faster than the water on the inside. (For confirmation of this principle, check with anyone who has been last in line for a game of crack-the-whip.) Thus a river is constantly wearing away the material on the outside of the bend, the swift current scouring it away, while on the inside of the curve the slow water and eddies allow silt to settle out and build up. Thus, over centuries, every bend becomes more pronounced, its outer edge extended and inner edge filled in, until it looks as the North Fork looks today, with most of its length flowing at right angles to its overall course.

Rodge, as everyone involved would soon know him, showed Gardner where the amateurs had found the spear points that had impressed Steve Gluckman. They were Clovis points, a name assigned to them for the site at which they were first identified, near Clovis, New Mexico. They had been crafted about ten thousand years ago by Paleo-Indians, which is to say a precursor people to the Native Americans encountered by the first white immigrants to America. They had been worked from jasper, a reddish brown form of flint, and they had turned up by the scores in a couple of hot spots along this riparian plain—in particular, a half-acre or so along the south-facing quadrant of the horseshoe.

Gardner had seen hot spots before, but this one was special, primarily because the amateur archaeologists who had worked it thus far had been careful not to disturb the site. This is vital because only undisturbed layers of soil allow firm conclusions about the order and age of depositions. The first foot or so of ground, known as the plow zone, is assumed to have been dug and stirred over the ages, but below that archaeologists hope for undisturbed layers that can be read much as tree rings are read: this year there was a flood, that year there was a drought, and this was put here before that. Moreover, the site's location on the inside of the oxbow meant that it had been protected from the worst erosion by floods and had experienced regular sedimentation over the millennia. Gardner declared this to be a primary site and set in motion the machinery of a major excavation. By the summer of 1971, with a grant to finance preliminary work, he was ready to begin.

The location was on a two-thousand-acre property, backed up against the flank of Massanutten Mountain to the west, facing the river and the Blue Ridge to the east, that was being operated as a resort called Thunderbird Ranch. Thus according to usual practice, the site took on the nearest place-name and was henceforward known as the Thunderbird Site.

The practice of archaeology was more advanced in the American West than in the East for the simple reason that eastern soils are acidic and yield few traces of ancient wood, bone, and organic remains, including structures. In the drier, alkaline, and less populated West, well-preserved prehistoric sites are more common. Gardner had learned his trade in the West, and brought that experience to Thunderbird with two practices not before used in the East.

First he set up a controlled surface collection, in which the site being worked was first delineated in grids—defined by crosshatched twine stretched between set stakes—with every find meticulously mapped on a corresponding grid map for each incremental level of excavation. The second innovation for the area was the addition to the excavating team of a soil scientist, John Foss, whose job was to perform chemical analyses of the soils through which the dig was proceeding. He was looking for a background history of the river in the area: where it had flowed in prior ages, when it had flooded, when it had been shrunken by drought. In addition, he analyzed the soil layers to determine their age and to seek out any chemical deposits such as phosphorous and calcium that would indicate the presence of residues from the human digestive process. (The discipline is known as pedology—the study of soil samples called peds—and Gardner remembers that his funding requests to attend pedological conventions "raised a lot of questions at Catholic University.")

Within a few weeks, both approaches to the site paid off. The initial stages of the excavation confirmed that this hot spot was huge, deep, and prolific. They had discovered the first buried Paleo-Indian site on the North American continent. And there was much more to it than that.

The excavators soon came upon a series of dark circles in the soil. What they immediately suspected was quickly confirmed by soils scientist Foss: these were the remains of posts that had been set in the ground by human hands and that had rotted in place. No trace of the wood remained, just the discoloration left behind by its reconversion to soil. These were the first post molds ever to be associated with a Paleo-Indian site. And there was still more.

As the excavators painstakingly plotted the location of the post molds on their grid maps, what first appeared to be a random jumble took on a broad pattern. It was the clear outline of an oval shelter about thirty-five feet in length that had been built, replaced, and restored countless times over hundreds of years. Gardner's team had unearthed the oldest remains of human habitation ever discovered in the Western Hemisphere.

It is the dream of such a discovery—one that changes everything, requires the rewriting of textbooks, opens a clear new window on the human condition—that sustains any scientist through years of painstaking research, observation, and thought. Such a revelation, one assumes, will electrify the academic world, make headlines in the general press, earn its authors enduring fame and lasting fortune. For a short time, it looked as though Thunderbird was going to do all that. The National Science Foundation approved a generous grant to support three years of research on the site beginning in 1972. "We assembled a cast of thousands," Gardner recalled, although it was actually dozens of graduate students and researchers who flocked to the site to participate in the summer excavations.

But the politics of academia are as bitter, as Byzantine, and as dominated by money as any election campaign. And in political terms, Thunderbird had two big problems: it contradicted conventional anthropological wisdom, thus offending the conventional wise men; and it confirmed long-held anthropological theory, thus repelling the disbursers of grant money.

Until Thunderbird, it had been assumed that the people who came before the Indians were nomadic savages incapable of such complex tasks as building a community shelter (which, of course, implied community, a fairly advanced social organization). In part, the nomad hypothesis was an extension of the habitual arrogance of white Europeans who never acknowledged the humanity, let alone the accomplishments, of Native Americans and could hardly be expected to credit earlier peoples with anything but lesser abilities. But it was also a logical error against which every rookie cop and prosecutor is often cautioned with the reminder that *the absence of evidence proves nothing.* Before Thunderbird, the artifacts of the Paleo-Indians had been found only in scattered, shallow deposits indicating a temporary occupation of the ground. But at Thunderbird, the deposits went down three feet in neatly layered successions of river silt that proved continual, deliberate, repeated occupation of the site for *three thousand* years. These were not nomads, but the apostles of the nomad hypothesis did not want to hear it. "The old guard just denied what we had found," says Gardner, "they insisted the stuff had just washed in there."

On the other hand, the time line established by the Thunderbird research unfortunately confirmed the prevailing theory about the first human residents of the continent. The accepted scenario was that during the most recent Ice Age that crested about twenty thousand years ago (with glaciers reaching as far south as Pennsylvania), so much of the world's water was trapped in ice that the level of the oceans dropped, exposing a land bridge across the Bering Strait between present-day Siberia and Alaska. Mongolian nomads wandered across this temporary connection, it is thought, to become the first Americans. The Thunderbird Site, with its first artifacts dating to about eleven thousand years ago, offered circumstantial evidence in support of the land-bridge theory, at least offered nothing to contradict it. This, as it turned out, was unfortunate, because as Gardner explained it, it is easier to raise money for a project that holds out the hope for some spectacular evidence that would upend all the theories and demonstrate a dramatically earlier date of human settlement than allowed for by the land-bridge hypothesis.

(Thus, for example, in early 2000, the annual meeting of the Society for American Archaeology gave respectful attention to a series of papers claiming the discovery of human occupation dating to more than sixteen thousand years ago at Cactus Hill, a sand quarry east of Petersburg, Virginia. Traces left there, said the discoverers, not only predated Thunderbird by five thousand years but more closely resembled artifacts found in northern Spain than Clovis points. When I offered him a newspaper story about these claims headlined "Explosive Prehistoric Find," Gardner glanced at it and tossed it back with a snort: "Bad archaeology.")

Despite the scoffing of the old guard and the indifference of the headline writers, Thunderbird gathered considerable momentum during the summer of 1972, and it was not academic politics that brought it to its knees. In late June, Hurricane Agnes came ashore on the Florida Panhandle and began a leisurely northward progress. Its winds were not notable—it was almost immediately downgraded to a tropical depression—but it was huge. It measured about a thousand miles in diameter, and that was before it merged with a vast low-pressure system approaching from the northwest. The resulting behemoth dumped up to fifteen inches of rain on the Shenandoah watershed and produced a Noachian flood, of a size the statisticians say can be expected once in five hundred years, that inundated the Thunderbird Site and obliterated the careful excavation with an overlay of several inches of muck and debris. Stubbornly, Gardner and his grad students began the lengthy cleanup, toiling for weeks, trying to get back to where they had been.

They were still engaged in this frustrating process when even worse news arrived: the entire property had been sold to a real-estate developer, one John T. Flynn, who apparently had big plans for selling "five-acre farmettes." Such schemes were becoming increasingly common in the valley in the 1970s. The growing, aging and affluent population in the nearby Washington metropolitan area (soon to be connected to Front Royal by a new interstate highway) was increasingly responsive to the notion of owning a "second home" in the bucolic Shenandoah. As one disgusted elderly farmer put it to me one day after bidding unsuccessfully on a run-down, hardscrabble farm that sold at auction for an astronomical price, "Show these Washington people a tree, they think they're in heaven."

Gardner and his team hunkered down and kept digging. As he put it, "I decided we would just keep excavating until somebody kicked us off. We kept working, and one day this young kid came hopping through the corn field to the site, and stuck out his hand, and said 'Hi, I'm John Flynn.' We looked each other in the eye, and in that moment it began: each of us thinking, 'What can you do for me?'"

Flynn, as it turned out, was not the prototypical land developer determined to cram as many houses as possible onto his land. "He was at the cutting edge of concern for the environment," Gardner marveled, "and he actually saw the archaeology as an asset to his development—a marketing asset." Instead of being shunted aside, Gardner and his researchers were invited to participate in the planning of the proposed Thunderbird Farms. Gardner was worried about more than the original Thunderbird Site; scattered across the two thousand acres were clues to twelve thousand years of human history, including not only traces of the First People but village sites and burial mounds left by later tribes.

Flynn not only set aside from his development plans the one hundred acres containing the key archaeological finds of the Thunderbird Site (by now Gardner and his teams had found evidence of other, smaller Paleo-Indian camps in the area) but professed to be willing to keep builders away from other key areas as well, to include nature trails and historic interpretation in his site plan, and to consult the archaeologists to make sure that planned roads and buildings would not harm valuable artifacts. Moreover, he wanted the Thunderbird Site discoveries to be the first thing people encountered when they visited Thunderbird

Farms; he made available a house he owned across the river from his property, on the Route 340 side of the river, for a combination museum and visitors' center.

Working feverishly, Gardner tried to capitalize on his good fortune. He and his wife, Joan Walker, set up the museum "more as an interpretive center than a museum," he said, "an archaeological laboratory." He formed a nonprofit foundation, the Thunderbird Research Corporation, and struggled to put it on a stable financial footing. A key to these plans was attracting tourist traffic to the museum in order to make it profitable. It would be one of the earliest examples of heritage tourism in the Shenandoah Valley.

It was tough going. The Virginia Department of Transportation would not allow the museum to erect large signs at its turnoff from Route 340. Officials of Warren County and the Town of Front Royal were, in Gardner's view, sullenly uncooperative, resentful that the developer and the scientist were planning to benefit from resources of which they had until then been oblivious. It was about then that Gardner called on me for help.

If you are active in political campaigns, you might once or twice in a lifetime be a part of an enterprise with the energy, the focus, the save-the-world zeal combined with the seize-the-day humor evinced by the Thunderbird people. Everything was crude, jury-rigged, bargain-basement, and holy. The run-down rambler that housed the museum was crammed with displays of artifacts from the dig, sketches showing how the Paleo-Indians quarried and worked the jasper, built and maintained their shelters, and hunted mastodons in the river-bottom swamps. What these displays lacked in professional finish was supplied in more than full measure by the missionary fervor with which Gardner, his wife, his fellow scientists and students, and even some local workers and visitors who had been converted to the cause explained the meaning and the promise of this discovery.

After examining the contents of the museum and being cheerfully harangued, one clambered aboard an army-surplus, World War II–era amphibious landing craft called a DKW or "Duck." There followed a ride worthy of any amusement park, in which worry competed with hilarity as the huge combination of tank and boat roared down the riverbank, flopped into the water (floating helplessly downstream for endless minutes while Rodge, at the controls, tried to jam the worn transfer case from "wheel" into "prop"), churned across the river, and lurched up the other bank and over to the excavation.

Here the mood was less revival meeting and more churchly. Graduate students moved reverently around and into the staked and strung grid, some of them on their knees removing soil a few particles at a time, with the concentration and delicacy of surgeons, carefully exposing and mapping anything they found embedded in the ground before removing it. Anyone who visited Thunderbird in these heady days came away convinced that scientific history was being made here, that this was important and would have enormous implications for the Shenandoah Valley.

The discovery of the oldest known human habitation in the hemisphere seemed especially exciting in the context of the emerging debate about the future economy of the Shenandoah Valley. There was growing concern about the number of land developers who, like John Flynn, were buying up large acreages of "waste" land—too steep, rocky, forested, and/or remote to be of use as farm fields, orchards, or traditional home sites. The developers saw enormous profits to be made from dividing these acreages into five-acre tracts, bulldozing in a few white-knuckle roads, throwing up a few A-frame cottages, and selling them to rich Washingtonians as weekend getaways or retirement homes.

Those who worried about this trend, who predicted it would destroy the very assets it was selling, were challenged to propose another source of wealth for the landowners. It was as if by discouraging someone from committing a holdup, you became responsible for finding another source of loot. Some took up the challenge out of political necessity and proposed an alternate source of loot: tourism. The business of giving leisure travelers something to look at or do, pampering them meanwhile, was emerging as a leading industry of the region, the country, and indeed the world. It was not only profitable, but had the further advantage that the customers, after shedding their disposable income, went home and relied on another jurisdiction to provide them with water, treat their sewage, educate their children, and so on.

In the Thunderbird Site, it seemed to me, the valley had been presented with a winning ticket in the tourist lottery, a compelling reason for people to visit the valley, spend money, then leave. I did more than give Bill Gardner the publicity he had been seeking; I joined the board of directors of his nonprofit organization and began to advocate the preservation of the Thunderbird Site.

But things were falling apart. John Flynn was not meeting his development's sales targets, or controlling its expenses, or both, and his creditors were threatening foreclosure. Gardner wanted to launch a public campaign to raise money to buy the archaeological sites, in order to snatch them from the coming collapse, but Flynn did not want him to do anything that would signal the gravity of the financial problem, and Gardner felt obligated to wait.

They both ran out of time in the fall of 1976. Flynn's financial structure collapsed, and the land was sold at auction in the fall. The part with the Thunderbird Site on it was bought by Haynes Anderson Trustees, a Front Royal firm whose principals, Bradley K. Haynes and Charles Anderson, were becoming players in the new Monopoly—buy land by the gross, sell it by the piece—that was consuming Shenandoah Valley real estate. Like most players, Haynes Anderson had to sell some of their lots to keep the rest of their land, and the twenty most salable lots they had were the riverfront ones whose river-bottom area comprised the Thunderbird Site. They were all sold by spring.

In the end, all that was saved was a covenant written into the deeds of the critical lots, forbidding excavation or disturbance of the archaeological sites and, eventually, four central lots repurchased with money raised by the Archaeological Society of Virginia and set aside for future study. Try to get at them now, try to see the site from either side of the river, try to remind yourself of the giddy time of a great discovery and its vast potential, and you will confront forests of "No Trespassing," "Keep Out," "Lot Owners Only," and "Beware the Dog" signs.

But other things remain. There is the knowledge of the First People revealed by the Thunderbird Site artifacts and the memory of a long-ago, zestful crusade whose only quest was for knowledge. And there is the memory of a visit to an outcrop of rock and a startling epiphany about owning land. It is not now possible to approach that store of jasper that was the principal source of wealth for the First People for eleven thousand years. The surrounding five-acre retirement lots are much too valuable.

Part Three

The Land

Chapter 5

——

Building Shenandoah,
1732–1739

A Scotch-Irishman is one who keeps the Commandments and every other thing he can get his hands on.

—*American proverb*

THE SHENANDOAH VALLEY LANDSCAPE must have seemed familiar to young Andrew Lewis and his family on their journey from Philadelphia to rejoin his father in Virginia. As their mounts plodded southwest along the Shenandoah Valley's Indian Trace (the path of least resistance along the length of the valley, defined over the millennia by continuous animal and human travel, later known as the Valley Pike), the ancient, tree-clad mountain ranges of the Blue Ridge rose to the east, those of the Alleghenies to their west, and the fertile river-bottom lands sprawled away between. (See the map on page 42.) Indeed, this land was more than familiar, for a reason he could not have known.

A quarter of a billion years before, the planet's two proto-continents had collided, the edge of one, borne on its tectonic-plate raft by massive underlying currents of molten rock, riding up over the other with ponderous geological force. Along the zone of collision, thousands of miles long, the earth's hide shuddered with earthquakes, erupted with volcanoes, and wrinkled into mountains (the same process that today continues to raise the Himalayas and the Alps) until, a hundred million years or so later, the subterranean tides changed, ripped apart the landforms they had smashed together, and bore seven fragmentary continents away to their current, separate stations. Two of these continental rafts carried remnants of the old mountains. Thus the ranges of Wales, Ireland, and Scotland are not merely similar to those of eastern North America—they are the same mountains.

In this familiar landscape, the exiles from Ulster were free to an extent previously unknown in their civilization to any but kings, free to write on what they considered to be a blank slate—the vast, fertile country before them—what they believed about economic and social order. Their freedom would be constrained at first only by their personal histories and limitations, and of course the capabilities of the land. Before long, however, they would find themselves confronting other sets of ideas about the land and the society to be built upon it, some of which they would resist and some, adopt. As they did so they would shape a region, spark wars and revolution, and help create a new country.

The first reconciliation that would be necessary would be with the rulers of their new country—Virginia—and the second would be with its natives. In both cases, the first, foremost, and most lasting issue would be: who owned this land?

The first Europeans to make their home in Virginia were not especially interested in the land. The wealth they sought in the New World would be derived, they assumed, from gold or other precious metals and in trade with the Orient when they had discovered the way to sail there. Land was something to stand on, to build on, to raise a few vegetables on, little more; ownership of it was handled in an offhand manner. Ownership, in any case, was for kings, not ordinary people: the crowned heads of Europe assumed they owned whatever land had been discovered, conquered, or in any way occupied by people carrying their flag. They conveyed to others certain rights to parcels of this land in various ways, to various degrees, and for all kinds of reasons. As a result, from the very beginning in Virginia, land rights were mired in confusion and conflict.

White settlement in Virginia—the name applied at the time to all the land in the New World not already claimed by France or Spain—had begun with the Virginia Company of London, one of two companies given nearly identical charters by King James in 1606. The company headquartered in Plymouth was authorized to settle northern Virginia, the London company to colonize the south, and they were to stay one hundred miles away from each other. The initial expeditions of the Plymouth Company, like those of Sir Walter Raleigh and Sir Humphrey Gilbert before them, had failed. But in May of 1607, three ships of the London company bearing one hundred gentlemen adventurers sailed into the great estuary to be known as the Chesapeake Bay, made their way into the mouth of the first river they came to, and established a town, naming it and the river in honor of their king.

From its beginning, the story of Jamestown was not a pretty one. The gentlemen adventurers had begun to fight like cats in heat before their vessels were out of sight of England and had disembarked with John Smith, the only one of their number with the temperament and experience to deal with the challenges ahead, shackled in chains for some offense (for which he was quickly forgiven when the king's sealed orders, opened on landing, named Smith to the governing council). The bickering intensified as the adventurers were beset by hostile natives, malaria, and hunger. They did not like each other very much, appointing and then deposing a succession of council presidents, but they truly despised their corporate masters in London, who sent them, at the intervals of about six months imposed by the width of the Atlantic, a succession of ships bearing inadequate supplies, more incompetent colonists, and intemperate demands for gold, commodities, anything that would make them rich. The colonists had no time to think about wealth, they were trying to survive, and were not succeeding. Of the five hundred or so who began the winter of 1609, only sixty-five survived.

The little colony struggled mightily, with the Indians it was displacing, with hunger and disease, with the strenuous labor required to build their fortified town, with the ravages of fire that twice destroyed it, and with the uncertainties of their supply line across the sea to England. As years passed, they barely hung on to survival, let alone finding the source of revenue that would justify all their travail. During this time all the land they occupied and used was held in common by the company. Continual dissatisfaction with the ruling council, on the part of colonists and company managers alike, moved the company in 1609 to install a governor with executive authority, the council functioning as an advisory body. Thereafter, dissatisfaction with the governor became continual.

In 1612 some of the colonists began to grow a curious and little-known plant called tobacco, whose use by the natives had fascinated Europeans from the first contact. The whites were oblivious to the religious and ceremonial context in which the natives used tobacco; not for personal satisfaction (there were at the time no chain-smoking Indians), but in ceremonies, to signify transformation to, and communication with, the spirit world. What intrigued the white men was the physical practice of igniting some dried leaf and inhaling it. (It was as if, observing the sprinkling of holy water in a Catholic ceremony, non-Christians had begun soaking themselves with water periodically and waiting for effect.) Explorers demonstrated smoking in the courts of Europe, where early adapters took it up as an affectation that quickly became a habit.

The practice was offensive to King James, who condemned it in an article he published anonymously, titled "Counterblast to Tobacco," in which he asked, "What honor or policy can move us to imitate the barbarous and beastly manners of the wild, godless, and slavish Indian especially in so vile and stinking a custom?" The king went on to observe that doctors regarded smoking as unhealthy and that as far as he was concerned it was "a custom loathsome to the eye, hateful to the nose, harmful to the brain, dangerous to the lungs and in the black stinking fume thereof, nearest resembling the horrible Stygian smoke of the pit that is bottomless."

Nevertheless, the fad grew, and supplying it became a lucrative business for the West Indies, where the locals had developed a strain, *Nicotiana tabacum,* that was less bitter than that grown by Native Americans. In 1611 Governor John Rolfe of Jamestown somehow got his hands on some *tabacum* seeds, despite the fact that the Indies imposed the death penalty on anyone who allowed any of the precious strain to fall into foreign hands. The very next year Virginia shipped its first *tabacum* leaf to England. The virgin bottomlands along the James River easily produced 1,600 pounds of leaf per acre, and demand in Europe was virtually unlimited. Suddenly the Virginia Company was prosperous, Jamestown was a boomtown, and a flow of import duties into the coffers of the cash-strapped King James induced a sudden tolerance for the "vile and stinking" custom.

The colonists overhauled their affairs completely in 1619. They reorganized themselves with increased powers for the local council (predecessor to the current Virginia State Senate, whose lineage thus gives it claim to being the oldest deliberative body on the continent, although the Great Council of the Iroquois League predates it by perhaps four hundred years) to control the governor, with a "General Assembly" of people representing the population, not appointed by the king or his agents (the first representative assembly in America, again except for the Iroquois League and countless other tribal organizations), and with a declaration of independence: no order of the king, the colonists proclaimed, "shall bind till ratified by the General Assembly."

Two other developments made 1619 a momentous year. Ironically, the land the colonists had ignored while looking for gold or silver or a passage to the Orient had turned out to be the source of wealth they and their company craved. Now the people abandoned the concept of communal property and took personal ownership of their land. Also that year, they took possession of the first African slaves to be imported to Virginia.

The idea of his orders being subject to review did not please King James. He had not rewritten the Bible and propounded the theory of the divine right of kings to be thus insulted by colonials. For this and other reasons, he sent a Royal Commission to take names and record evidence, whereupon he revoked the charter of the Virginia Company of London and converted Virginia to a crown colony. However, the right of a paid-up member of the company to own his land remained established. Land, because it could grow tobacco, had become the source and the signifier of serious wealth in Virginia.

The colonists spread their vast estates, now privately owned, throughout Tidewater Virginia, brought in increasing numbers of slaves to tend the tobacco plants, and used their swelling wealth to build baronial houses and fund lordly ways. The language changed; heretofore, the word plantation had meant a royal colony planted in a foreign place, as in the plantation of Ulster and Plymouth Rock; now plantation came to mean the acreage on which tobacco was planted, acreage overseen and owned not by the king, but by the planter. Dangerous as these tendencies were to the authority of the king, they were tolerated because they were producing a great deal of revenue for the crown and because of the distractions of a series of religious, dynastic, and civil wars that continuously embroiled the throne—occupied after 1625 by Charles I, son of James and like his father a believer in the divine right of kings, the absolute authority of the Church of England, and the worthlessness of elected parliaments.

For nearly a century the planters flourished, spreading their estates along the tidewater James, York, and Rappahannock Rivers. Their only serious problem with land, aside from the normal vagaries of life in agriculture, was the distressing way it played out, refusing after a few years to push up any more tobacco plants. At first this problem was easily avoided by simply opening fresh fields, leaving the "oldfields," as they were euphemistically called, to revert to brush. But early in the eighteenth century, those trying to expand, relocate, or establish plantations north of the Rappahannock, along the Potomac River, for example, discovered to their disgruntlement that there was in Virginia another proprietor with vast holdings not subject to the colony's government.

In the 1640s and 1650s, while engaged in his losing and eventually fatal struggle with Oliver Cromwell's Roundheads in the English revolution, King Charles I had received loyal service from one Thomas, Lord Culpeper, which service was rewarded by Charles II (while exiled and in poverty in France with Cromwell ruling England) with a casual gift of Virginia land. Of little meaning at the time, it took on significance with the restoration of the English monarchy under Charles II in 1660, although for decades the recipients of the gift and their heirs showed little interest in it. However, in the early 1700s the legacy passed into the hands of Thomas, Lord Fairfax, a young and profligate baron whose mother was a Culpeper. That the gift of land should pass to him was ironic, in that it was his ancestor and namesake who had won the Battle of Naseby for the Roundheads in 1645. By the time the grandson inherited in 1719, his English estates were so exhausted and debt-ridden that he began to think seriously about his New World possessions. At that point the casual nature of the gift began to cast a long shadow over the affairs of Virginia.

The king's gift had conveyed rights to all the land lying "within the heads" of the Rappahannock and Potomac Rivers. No one knew exactly where those rivers flowed or what precisely the king had meant by "heads." Did he refer to the heads of navigation, at the falls of the rivers, thus confining the grant to the Tidewater, or did he mean the head springs, somewhere far to the west? That issue was addressed by an amended charter, issued in 1688, that specified the "first heads or springs" of the two rivers as the boundary markers. But that resolved nothing, because no one knew where the rivers originated. Now the colonial government claimed the rivers sprang from the Blue Ridge, limiting Fairfax's land to the so-called Northern Neck east of the mountains and north of the Rappahannock, while Fairfax claimed the rivers originated in the Alleghenies, making the northern Shenandoah Valley his as well.

Meanwhile the government of Virginia, now with its capital in Williamsburg and its focus on expanding the substantial wealth it had achieved with the tobacco economy, had done its best to ignore the Fairfax grant as a throwback to feudalism and had disposed of substantial acreage within it. What had worked so well in the Tidewater, it was assumed, would work as well throughout Virginia, whose boundaries were assumed to be, as Thomas Lee would express it in 1749, "The Atlantic on the east, North Carolina on the south, the Potomac on the north and, on the west, the Great South Sea, including California."

While the governor, council, and burgesses of Virginia did not directly challenge the long-standing principle that they acted as agents of the crown, the notion that had first appeared in Jamestown in 1619—that once one had obtained official permission to occupy the land and had met the terms of the patent including payment of the so-called quitrents, ownership passed to the patentholder—had become entrenched in Virginia. Thus when agents for Lord Fairfax appeared to collect quitrents, even though the rents were substantially the same as those required by Virginia, both the colonial government and the property "owners" were offended by the idea of reverting from owning their land to holding it by the grace of their sovereign. In addition to the principle involved, there was of course the money and power.

The legal and political wrangle over the boundaries and legitimacy of the Fairfax grant would cloud the titles of Virginia landowners everywhere north of the Rappahannock River and would affect the patterns of settlement of the Shenandoah Valley especially. It would become, in fact, the longest-lived lawsuit in American history, one that would not finally be resolved until after the Revolution, by a United States court. This battle was joined almost immediately after the arrival in Virginia of a new governor (technically, lieutenant-governor: the appointment typically went to an English aristocrat who did not deign to visit his realm, assigning the work of administration to an underling), an amiable Scotsman named William Gooch.

Governor Gooch promoted the westward expansion of his colony despite the Fairfax problem. Like William Penn before him, he wanted a buffer of settlers on the western frontier between the savages who populated the western mountains and the increasingly populous Piedmont. He tried to encourage the formation of new land companies to do the job, but when no takers appeared (the value of remote western land was not yet apparent), he began to work through individual entrepreneurs, offering them land patents that required for their validation the settling of people on the land—usually one family per thousand acres—within a specified period of time.

Governor Gooch opened the bidding for the Shenandoah Valley in 1728, granting to Larkin and Thomas Chew the rights to twenty-six thousand acres near the forks of the Shenandoah. And during the next three years he doled out nearly a quarter of a million acres, including, in 1730, forty thousand acres to John and Isaac van Meter, who promptly sold most of their grant to an enterprising German named Hans Jost Heydt, whose name comes down in records and history books as the phonetically approximated Joist Hite. A similar grant went to a Scotch-Irish Quaker named Alexander Ross.

To each of these grants by the colony, Lord Fairfax's agent in Virginia, Robert "King" Carter, attached a caveat claiming on behalf of his proprietor ownership of the land being transferred. And in 1730 Carter began to issue Shenandoah land grants in Fairfax's name. But where Gooch's grants envisioned, indeed required, prompt and dense settlement, Carter's grants were to his own sons, grandsons, and in-laws, and he did not care if anyone lived on the land or not. Because his actions shaped the history of the lower valley, his motives are interesting.

More than anything else, Carter was bent on enriching himself, and it was this focus and his success in realizing it that earned him the appellation "King." (On Carter's death, the perennially cash-strapped Lord Fairfax would be astonished to read in the *Gentleman's Magazine* of London that his longtime agent's estate included £10,000 *in cash*.) Carter's strategy for accumulating wealth was based on the assumption that the future of Virginia would be exactly like the past in the Tidewater; that the tobacco-plantation economy would spread ever westward. There was by this time some urgency to this strategy, because more and more Tidewater land was exhausted; tobacco is a hungry crop, and with little knowledge or practice of soil restitution, established planters were having great difficulty maintaining their production. Thus Carter was not interested in having his claims cluttered with settlers. He was happy to wait for the planters and their slaves to come west.

This dream of extending the fabulously successful tobacco (and, later, cotton) plantation economy across the continent would persist for a century and a half and would be a prominent factor in the affairs of colonial America and later the United States, precipitating the American Civil War in 1861. It is one of the great ironies of American history that the dream was doomed from the start, as many people of the time understood. The climate and the soils beyond the southern coastal areas simply would not support sufficient yields from the plants, and no other crop could support the economics of slaveholding. Tobacco and cotton were labor-intensive crops, each plant requiring constant hand work from planting through hilling, weeding, debugging, and pruning to harvest. In the Tidewater, yields were more than enough to support the large number of slaves required to perform this constant labor; farther west they were not. Other crops, such as hemp, corn, and wheat, did not require as much attention, and field hands in large numbers were not needed.

The way people used the land, and related to each other, west of the Blue Ridge Mountains after 1730 differed radically from how they did things east of the mountains. In the eastern plantation country, each estate was huge and largely self-sufficient with respect to food, goods, and services—except for the manufactures imported from England. West of the mountains, the settlers from the north established small farms that could be tilled by a family, around small towns on which they depended for such things as their milling, smithing, dry goods, and staples. In the West there was no leisure class, there were very few slaves, and life was more egalitarian; in the East there were few towns, few roads, and much more attention was paid to one's family connections than one's abilities. The difference would shortly become entrenched in the language, with easterners becoming known as Tuckahoes, perhaps after the William Randolph estate of that name on a small tributary of the tidewater James, and westerners as Cohees, a corruption of the Scotch-Irish-Presbyterian way of saying somebody said something: "quoth he."

Thus did the American West begin at the crest of the Blue Ridge Mountains.

When they finally halted their pack train and declared their long journey over, the Lewis family had passed the broad lower Shenandoah Valley, where Alexander Ross, the Quaker from Ireland, was settling Scotch-Irish emigrants on his holdings five miles north of present-day Winchester, and Joist Hite was gathering a community of German Lutherans around his home ten miles to the south. Germans, Scotch-Irish, and English would stake out alternate areas of the valley for many years to come, like seeking like.

The Lewises had followed the Indian Trace along the strong bright convoluted stream of the North Fork of the Shenandoah, had journeyed forty miles in the shadow of Massanutten Mountain to the east, then continued twenty-five miles or so beyond its hulk into the broad, fertile plains of gently rolling land braided by countless streams that gradually collected themselves to become the North Fork. Along one of these streams, known today as Lewis Creek, on a slope facing south and overlooking a strong spring, John Lewis had marked his trees and now christened his new home Bellefonte in honor of the spring, and began to build.

First, the log house. The amount of labor involved in building the structure that Lewis first erected, and that became typical of the valley houses of the time, is staggering to contemplate. It began with grubbing out and dragging to the site the limestone rocks to be laid for the foundation. Then came locating and felling by ax the enormous oaks or chestnuts, with main trunks at least twenty feet in length and three feet in diameter. Once down, each log had to be trimmed of branches, hewn to its usable length, then squared along its length with broadaxes and adzes. Straining teams of horses dragged the timber to the building site, where it was notched, trimmed, and put in place. Placing the log was difficult enough on the first courses, increasingly so as the structure grew toward its final height; John Lewis's house walls eventually topped out at twelve courses, something over fourteen feet. One method of setting the higher courses was to lay massive timbers at an angle against the existing wall with the log to be placed lying at the bottom of the slope. Ropes tied to the existing top course ran down to and under the log on the ground, then looped back up to and over the structure to the other side, where horses were hitched to the ropes and hauled the log up the angle until it could be wrestled into place.

It took even longer to hew out and fit the smaller joists to support the second floor and the rafters for the roof. Puncheons—logs flattened on one side with the broadax and adze—were eventually fashioned for the first-story floor (although many settled for a dirt floor while other, more urgent work went forward). The floor of the second story and the underlayment of the roof required planks; workers set a massive, squared log on a timber stand about seven feet high, or across a pit dug that deep. Two men, one standing atop the log and another below, would use a five-foot whipsaw with handles on each end to saw boards from the log. Working to exhaustion through a long day, they could produce perhaps one hundred linear feet of planks. Then there were the cedars to find, fell, hew into two-foot lengths, and split into shakes for the roof. Fastenings were made using joinery wherever possible—if they had any nails, they were precious and few. It became common, when people for one reason or another decided to leave a house and move on, to burn the house down so that they could sift through the ashes and retrieve the nails.

Thomas and Andrew, now aged fourteen and twelve, would have been full partners with their father in the arduous work. Eight-year-old William probably spent most of his time at secondary duties: tacking, hitching and driving the horses, carrying water and food to the workers, fetching tools and supplies, and cleaning up at the end of the day.

However many families were building in the area at the same time as the Lewises (the best guess appears to be three), they would not have stayed away from each other; the work was too heavy, prolonged, and dangerous for a man and a few sons to undertake by themselves. As became customary, when it was time to raise a barn or a house the entire community pitched in. John Lewis's house was probably the first up and was henceforward available to the whole community as a temporary shelter, a lodge for travelers, a meeting-house, and, in times of trouble as a fort. In fact, not long after completing his residence, he would go on to build next to it a sturdy, slightly smaller structure with the first story made of stone, the second of timber, in a manner reminiscent of Ireland. In the troubles that were to come, this building would become known as Fort Lewis.

While the heavy work of construction went forward at a feverish pace, people in large numbers had to be fed, a project that in itself consumed countless woman-hours of labor, led by Margaret Lynn with some assistance from six-year-old Margaret, who at the least would have helped tend to Ann, who by now was four years old. Fires had to be kindled with flint and steel (a process so time consuming it was generally avoided by carefully banking the fires at night to keep embers alive) and maintained with cords of firewood; scores of gallons of water had to be carried each day to the iron pots, which typically weighed forty pounds empty and held about fifteen gallons; deer carcasses, in the first years no doubt the exclusive source of meat, had to be butchered. There would have been no fresh vegetables the first year (although even in the frenetic pace of building, someone had to prepare a place to grow them next year), and the main supplement to the meat was probably various treatments of aged cornmeal, along with berries, wild fruits, and nuts found in the nearby woods. In addition, clothes had to be mended, cleaned, and repaired, and thought and effort had to be given to the passing of the seasons toward winter, when stores of food and fuel would be needed for survival.

The details of the massive labor, privations, and worries of the first few years can only be deduced; no one had time to keep a journal or write letters. Scribes are luxuries that society can support only after someone has taken care of the necessities. Likewise, time for socializing, for the knitting together of a community, for building the structures of government, is not available while survival is at issue. Assurance of survival, in a new land, requires knowledge accumulated over years: of when winter finally eases its grip on the land and it is safe to plant corn (according to one valley tradition, when the oak leaves are the size of a squirrel's ear); of how dry a summer can be, how violent the floods of spring and fall; when the first killing frost can be expected; how much food and firewood are required to last through a winter.

Thus, for about four years after the work at Bellefonte began in 1732, there is silence, until at length the laborers looked up and realized that they were going to make it. Then, with homes secure, fields established, and larders filled, socializing began. (And other things as well: on March 11, 1736, the Lewises celebrated the arrival of Charles, the first of John and Margaret's children to be born in Virginia, and, as it turned out, the last of their children.) Soon, many afternoons at three, an hour after the main meal of the day had been served and the tasks essential to the day had been done, the women gathered at one another's homes for quilting parties. Now at weddings and wakes, hunts and horse races and dances, people gathered and talked about what they had in common, what they saw in the future.

Many who witnessed these early gatherings, especially traveling Quakers and Lutherans, were startled by the amount of drinking and the raucous nature of the socializing. Presumably they lacked experience of Ireland. Of the few recollections of John Lewis dredged up from aged memories, most are draped with memorial-service reverence, but one preserved by his descendant John Gilmer is of a more pungent character. At some social gathering, Lewis had set aside his shillelagh, the heavy, ornately carved walking stick/club that was his constant companion in America as it had been in Ireland. A man identified in the account as a visiting Tuckahoe (the tone implying that as an easterner he could not be expected to know better) picked up the shillelagh to examine it, to be told by Lewis that in Ireland, he who touched another's shillelagh must "fight or treat." Apparently the Tuckahoe took umbrage at being teased, and there followed a one-stroke "fight" that John Lewis politely lost.

Bellefonte, whether because it was the first residence, or because it was the most centrally located, or because it contained the most forceful personality, became the principal gathering place of the upper Shenandoah and the first stop for any visitor to the area. After it was established, no doubt according to the accepted traditions of tomahawk, corn, and cabin rights, the patriarch apparently gave some thought to the legalities of his situation and sought to perfect a deed to his property. The manner in which this was done was unusual, if anything could be said to be unusual in a place where ways of doing things were being invented as one went along.

Virginia's policy for thirty years, now being enthusiastically promoted by Governor Gooch, was to fill the western lands with human tomahawk fodder. Legislation passed back in 1701 for "strengthening the frontiers and discovering the approaches of an enemy" offered land in return for just one thing: the presence of one "warlike Christian man," heavily armed, for every five hundred acres granted. In practice, few warlike men applied for and received the land; instead, middlemen applied for patents, which were in effect rights to act as a real estate agent for the colony, transferring deeds to the eventual owner. Thus far, Virginia's conveyances had been to people such as the Chews, van Meters, Hites, and Millers who were living in the lower valley, or intended to, and who promised to bring in more people like them. Lord Fairfax's grants, thus far, had been either to planters providing for their own or their families' future residences or to people discovered squatting on the land already. But the first major grant of land in the upper Shenandoah went to a group of Williamsburg insiders who had no intention of moving to the Shenandoah. Their motivation was quite different from that which had been seen previously.

The applicants for 118,000 acres at the headwaters of the Shenandoah were scions of the First Families of Virginia, all of them substantial planters and men of affairs. Sir John Randolph was nearing the end of a distinguished life, having served the general assembly as clerk, speaker, and treasurer and the governor as his attorney general. His brother Richard Randolph was a planter in Henrico County, which he represented as burgess, and he would succeed Sir John as colonial treasurer. John Robinson, son of a longtime president of the governor's council, was a planter in King and Queen County who had just been elected to the House of Burgesses and was at the beginning of a thirty-year career in politics. The fourth grantee, William Beverley, was Robinson's uncle, owner of an estate on the Rappahannock River in Essex County. His father, Robert, had been a Knight of the Golden Horseshoe— the elite group of Virginia gentlemen who, with then-governor Alexander Spotswood, in 1716 had been the first of their kind to lay eyes on the Shenandoah Valley from atop the Blue Ridge Mountains. William served for thirty years as the clerk for Essex County, during which time he also served for six years as the burgess from Orange County (there being no residency requirement for the General Assembly, one could represent any county in which one owned land).

Not only did these gentlemen have no intention of moving to the Shenandoah, but three of them had no intention of staying in the deal. Like many of his fellow planters, William Beverley simultaneously enjoyed great prestige and suffered enormous debt. He had no doubt enlisted cosigners to help him make the required demonstration of financial capability to accomplish the required settlement. A few days after Governor Gooch signed the patent, in September of 1736, the Randolphs and Robinson signed over their interest in the land to Beverley (although Robinson, for one, was far from through with business deals in the Shenandoah and the West). The question arises: how did Beverley, with all his duties as a planter, merchant, and burgess in the Tidewater, propose to administer 118,000 acres beyond the mountains without moving there? The answer is not of the record, but emerges from events: he had a friend in the valley.

Beverley's friend and agent claimed the largest single tract of Beverley Manor land—2071 acres—and not only got it for the bargain price of £14 (about one-third of Beverley's standard price of £1 per forty acres) but had that small debt forgiven, as Beverley wrote, "for the extraordinary trouble of his house and charges in entertaining those who come to settle on Beverley Manor." He was, of course, John Lewis.

A man named Benjamin Borden (often spelled Burden), an Englishman who had lived in New Jersey and had served as an agent for Lord Fairfax, had the same friend. One of the persistent legends of the valley is that while visiting and hunting with John Lewis in 1736, Borden caught and tamed a buffalo calf, took it back to Williamsburg, and presented it to Governor Gooch. The governor, according to the oft-repeated story, was sufficiently amused to issue a patent to Borden for 500,000 acres, five times the size of Beverley Manor, adjoining it to the south. The traditional story obviously leaves out a great deal. Although the Virginia gentry often did their best to emulate the wretched excesses of the European courts, it is safe to assume that it took more to get this land deal done than a makeshift petting zoo.

Beverley, Borden, and Lewis had another friend who was indispensable to their plan. He was James Patton, the ship's master who may well have brought his relative John Lewis to America in the first place. Patton, the youngest son of an Ulster (County Donegal) shipbuilder, had spent most of his life at sea, first in the British Royal Navy and then as captain of one of his father's ships, ferrying emigrants from Ulster and returning with cargoes of tobacco and furs. By the 1730s it was said that he had made twenty-five crossings of the Atlantic Ocean. In 1738 he made one more, his last, on behalf of his friends and partners in Shenandoah Valley land.

Here is a change to note: where Patton had been hauling loads of desperate and frightened emigrants from Ulster, bound they knew not where, now he was recruiting them, offering to take them to the promised land and making the promises himself. He told John Preston, a ship's carpenter married to Patton's sister, that if Preston would serve as shipwright on the voyage, Patton would get him four thousand acres of land. (In the event, Preston got about four hundred acres.) To an Ulster craftsman of the day, the idea of owning that much land must have seemed as unlikely a dream as being made a lord of the realm and being asked to attend the king at court. Preston signed on, as did a total of sixty-five passengers, most of them bound for Beverley Manor or the Borden grant. The passengers included Patton's own wife and two daughters, for he had decided to leave the sea and claim his own acreage in the Shenandoah. And they may have included one Alexander McNutt who was to become famous as a tireless and successful promoter of the emigration of Ulstermen to America.

With the arrival of these families in what was now being called the "Irish Tract," with the Pattons and Prestons and Breckenridges joining the families of John Kerr, Gilbert Christian, John Campbell, and others, the structures of community became at the same time possible and necessary. There was a steadily increasing number of deeds to be recorded, for example, each of which required a laborious fifty-mile trip over the Blue Ridge Mountains to the seat of Orange County, which had jurisdiction over all of western Virginia. With more settlers, inevitably, came more disputes, more unfortunate people requiring care, and more scofflaws in need of restraint. In 1738 the colonial government created two new counties in the Shenandoah: Frederick (named for the Prince of Wales) in the north and Augusta (for Frederick's child bride, the mother of King George III) in the south. For several years, however, the colony did little more to organize Augusta, and what it did was stimulated not by the need to provide services, but by the perceived need for defense.

A good many well-armed Christian men had been spreading their farms through the upper valley for at least six years before the first serious trouble occurred between them and the "enemy" that had been the object of the 1701 land-for-defense legislation. Since the natives traveling the Indian Trace were usually war parties, thus viewed with suspicion and fear by the settlers, it is remarkable that two decades passed with only occasional incidents.

There were problems, of course. When members of war parties hunting for meat found cattle or hogs running loose in the woods, they killed and ate them as they took deer or any other wildlife, causing upset to the animals' "owners." Sometimes rough treatment of captives taken by the war parties somewhere far to the north or south, including torture and sacrifice, upset European witnesses greatly, and there would be talk of intervention. Yet it was not until 1738 that natives killed their first victim in the Bellefonte community, in circumstances not recorded. The result, of course, was a great deal more suspicion and fear, and a petition to the governor to do something. The response was immediate. Governor Gooch sent thirty muskets, sixteen pistols, and a supply of powder and lead balls—and appointed John Lewis the captain of militia for the area.

But the years passed with little need for defense, no enemy approach requiring a warning to the capital. As we have seen, the only natives in the valley were displaced people traveling through, pursuing old enmities and keeping old dreams alive. Year after year the German Lutherans poured into the lower valley, the Scotch-Irish into the upper, and still there was no trouble with the natives. Fences snaked around verdant pastures where cattle fattened and procreated; corn cribs groaned to contain the harvest; mills appeared, and towns, and lines of wagons screaming over the rude mountain trails (there was little grease, and the wooden axles made a fearful noise), carrying hemp and grain east, bringing salt and powder and manufactures back. The valley prospered and was at peace, and for many of its inhabitants, it was more than sufficient. Family prosperity and security were enough for the German Lutherans, the Quakers, and the Mennonites of the lower valley.

But for a few, John Lewis prominent among them, comfort was not enough. They wanted serious wealth, and like the first people to recognize the worth of a pelt of beaver or a hogshead of tobacco, they saw an entirely new way to get it.

Chapter 6

◦────◦

The Land Grabbers,
1739–1753

Beware a white man looking at the sky; he is thinking how to
fence it off and sell it.

—*Shawnee proverb*

BEFORE HE HAD PERFECTED the deed to his home place on Lewis
Creek, John Lewis, along with James Patton, had put in a request
for a patent for thirty thousand acres along the Calf Pasture River,
west of Beverley Manor and next to William Lynn's grant. The Governor's Council granted their request in 1739, provided they settled
thirty families there within two years. Two years later, another
thirty thousand acres "lying to the southwest and northwest of the
Calf Pasture" was similarly conveyed to a company of visionaries that
included one of the original partners in Beverley Manor, Speaker
John Robinson, along with his son Henry, Governor Gooch's son
William, and John Lewis's sons Thomas and Andrew.

These land deals had nothing to do with establishing homesteads, assuring the security of the families, not even providing land
for the children; the children were not yet of marrying age and were

still fully occupied with the original homestead. Everyone was busy, and little was done about these outlying lands for many years while more essential work was done. Yet the claims were there, and they represented something new. This was not hunger for a place of one's own, but lust for massive acreages of raw land that could be parceled into lots and, without further work, sold at tremendous profits. The model for this new attitude was William Beverley, who was becoming wealthy beyond dreams from his Tuckahoe plantation by treating everything as commodities; he was "conveniently situated," he advertised, "for the sale of Negroes, rum, sugar and molasses." Beverley had executed the plan that William Lynn of Fredericksburg probably had in mind for his Calf Pasture patent but had not yet brought to fruition. And Beverley had done it because of the forceful contributions of John Lewis and James Patton.

However tempting the prospects of the land business, it would have to wait until the Lewis family was firmly established. There was a mill to build on Lewis Creek. A famine in Ulster sent a new wave of emigrants up the valley to the Irish Tract, and the work of welcoming them, directing them, and getting them settled in was continual. Thomas and Andrew Lewis learned the surveyor's trade (at about the same time that, over in the country of the Tuckahoes, a young man named George Washington was teaching himself the same trade for similar reasons). The first Presbyterian pastor arrived to serve the community, preaching the first sermon in John Lewis's home.

About 1739 Patton built a home of locust logs rivaling John Lewis's in size and comfort, on a creek much like Lewis Creek ten miles to the south, near what is now called South River (it is the south branch of the north fork of the Shenandoah). Patton called his fourteen-hundred-acre spread Springhill, a name that described its principal asset much as did John Lewis's Bellefonte. He built a mill, as John Lewis had done, and turned his home into a center of business-related hospitality, welcoming newcomers and selling off tracts in the southern portion of the Beverley Patent, as John Lewis had done in the north of the Irish Tract. Obviously, these two alpha males were bound for conflict.

As Patton approached fifty years of age, he pursued his opportunities with remarkable vigor. He repeatedly traveled to Lancaster, Pennsylvania, to tout the advantages of life in the Shenandoah to arriving Scotch-Irish prospects. Having grown accustomed to human bondage while transporting indentured servants across the Atlantic, he set himself up as one of the very few slave traders in the history of the Shenandoah Valley. In 1741 Patton was appointed a commissioner of Orange County for the district yet to be organized as Augusta County. In 1742 Governor Gooch issued a commission naming the fifty-year-old Patton lieutenant colonel of militia for Augusta, superseding the captaincy of John Lewis, who was now sixty-four years of age and had been at the exhausting work of remaking his life for a decade.

"A difference happened between Col. John Lewis and Col. James Patton," wrote the harried Reverend John Craig (the first Presbyterian pastor in the area) of his two most influential congregants, "which continued while they lived, which of them should be highest in commission and power, which was hurtful to the settlement but especially to me." For more than a dozen years, the good reverend lamented, "I could neither bring them to friendship with each other nor obtain both their friendships at once." The reverend may not have had special gifts as a peacemaker; when the elders at Tinkling Spring Church voted on some matter contrary to his wishes, he vowed never to drink from the Tinkling Spring again in his life, and kept the vow (while preaching sermons there that began at ten in the morning and continued to sunset, with a one-hour break for lunch). During another disagreement, one of his congregants was moved to describe Craig as a "poor blind carnal hypocritical damned wretch."

Thereafter, Augusta County society became bipolar; there was the John Lewis camp and the James Patton camp, each contesting endlessly with the other. But enemies or not, Lewis and Patton were harnessed together in the formal organization of the government of Augusta County in 1745. If the younger Patton was preferred in military matters, John Lewis was still the elder statesman and as such became the chief magistrate of the twenty-one justices of the peace commissioned by Governor Gooch. Having governed informally for more than a dozen years, John Lewis wielded the gavel of state for the first time on December 9, in a rudimentary courthouse that William Beverley had thoughtfully erected on his "mill-place," in what would become the city of Staunton. The magistrates swore in James Patton as high sheriff and Thomas Lewis as the county surveyor, and licensed five attorneys to practice before them. As their first order of practical business, they ordered the building of the tools of discipline as stipulated in Virginia law: not just a jailhouse, but stocks (which confined a seated malefactor by the ankles), a pillory (which clamped the head and hands of a standing prisoner), whipping post, and ducking stool (used to punish women, typically on conviction of being a "scold," by immersion in cold water). Any court that did not have these implements in service within six months of its organization faced a fine of five thousand pounds of tobacco.

The magistrates were not the only governors of the county. Many important functions—the setting of property lines, the clearing and upkeep of roads, the care of the poor—were reserved by law to the vestrymen of the Church of England. This was the established church, and every resident was required to contribute to the support of its ministers, farms (called "glebes"), and parsonages. In each parish the first vestrymen were elected and thereafter appointed their successors. The problem in the new Augusta County was, of course, that virtually the entire population was Presbyterian, confirmed dissenters from the established church. But in the remote west, these things did not seem important; Scotch-Irish leaders happily took office in a church to which they did not belong and when named to civic positions swore the required oath—to be "conformable to the doctrine and discipline of the Church of England"—

without meaning a word of it. The authorities in Williamsburg never got around to checking the credentials of their officials in the west.

The children of John Lewis were establishing their own personalities. Andrew, twenty-five years old in 1745, was absent from the councils of Augusta County government, but not from the councils of the land companies with which his father was involved. Both Andrew and Thomas (now twenty-seven) had learned the surveyor's trade, but Thomas, being nearsighted, was less inclined to go adventuring alone. Andrew had become the primary hunter and pathfinder of the family, and from his boyhood had ranged the far country in search of either meat or land. William, twenty-one, was staying close to home and would not participate in county government; at the age of eleven he had embraced his Presbyterian religion with a zeal that made it impossible for him to indulge in the hypocrisy of swearing fealty to the Church of England. Although most colonial women married young, daughter Margaret at nineteen was still at home, and would wait another thirteen years before taking marriage vows. In 1745 Ann was seventeen and Charles nine years of age.

In the years immediately following the organization of the county government, the people of Augusta were drawn into larger spheres of influence in two ways, with Thomas Lewis in the forefront of both. John Lewis, relentlessly expansionist in his views, used his position as chief magistrate to promote a favorite project; the building of a road to carry commerce between Augusta and the east. It was hardly a foregone conclusion; to his considerable irritation, there were those who argued against his dream on the grounds that such a road would change everything by making it easy for strangers to come in and compete for land, hunt out the deer, and generally impair what today is called the quality of life. But Lewis prevailed, as he was wont to do, and Thomas Lewis was designated the surveyor of a route through the Blue Ridge via Rockfish Gap to Goochland, on the James River about twenty-five miles above present-day Richmond.

In 1746 the colony and Lord Fairfax agreed to remove a long-standing impediment to settlement in the Shenandoah by ending their long dispute over the location of the western boundary of the Fairfax grant. The disputants had agreed, finally, that the grant extended from the headwaters of the Rappahannock to the head-waters of the Potomac; that the Rappahannock rose from the head spring of the Conway River in present-day Orange County on the eastern slope of the Blue Ridge; and that the Potomac issued from the head spring of its north branch in what is now the western pan-handle of Maryland. The question that remained, however, was where exactly the boundary fell in the seventy-six miles between the two springs. A final, official survey was required.

The party that assembled in September to perform this task was large, about forty people in all. It included commissioners for Lord Fairfax and for the crown to oversee the work, surveyors for each side, along with servants and workers. William Fairfax, a cousin to the baron who had replaced King Carter as his principal agent, acted as commissioner for Fairfax, of course, along with William Beverley. Thomas Lewis acted as one of their surveyors. The commissioners for the colony included Joshua Fry, a retired professor of mathematics from Albemarle (who would be heard from in the valley again), and their surveyors included Peter Jefferson of Albemarle, whose son Thomas was then four years old.

Anyone who has traveled in roadless woods knows that as long as one is free to take the path of least resistance, the worst difficulty one is likely to encounter is the occasional long detour, or bewilderment from too many short detours. But the Fairfax surveying party had to strike a straight line across three mountain ranges, cutting through or climbing over whatever they encountered for nearly eight harrowing weeks. Thomas Lewis's journal of the expedition, which survives, should be read not as a general description of travel in the wilderness at the time, but of the difficulties of traveling in a straight line: "The swamp is prodigiously full of rocks and cavities, those covered over with a very luxuriant kind of moss of a considerable depth. The fallen trees, of which there was great numbers and naturally large, were vastly improven in bulk with their coats of moss . . . the laurel and ivy as thick as they can well grow, whose branches growing of an extraordinary length are so well woven together that without cutting away it would be impossible to force through them." Swamps were unusual, but rocky precipices squarely in their way were common. On Saturday, October 20, Lewis wrote: "The mountains made such a dismal appearance that John Thomas, one of our men, took sick on the same and so returned home." Not everyone could be an intrepid pioneer.

The valley was beginning to flourish. With the counties of Augusta and Frederick organized, homesteads were filling in the maps; mills dotted the streams; towns were growing; shops and stores and smithies were thriving. Exports of cattle, turkeys, hemp, and hides began to flow to Alexandria and Fredericksburg on river barges, ox-carts, wagons, and foot. (Cattle drives probably originated here, as did turkey drives, the turkeys being "shod" for their long journey by being herded first through a pond of tar, then through a pit of sand, the sandy "shoes" helping to keep their feet from breaking down.)

For the overwhelming majority of Shenandoah Valley residents, it was sufficient to perfect their farms, practice their trades, and watch their families and communities grow and prosper at an organic rate, as plants grow and fill out in season. But for over a decade now, John Lewis and James Patton and their relatives and partners had been incubating their lust to get on to the next big thing, the thing they believed would replace tobacco, as tobacco had replaced beaver pelts, as the source of fabled wealth in America. It was to be land speculation. They had been practicing it on a small scale, they had seen the way demand could easily be stimulated, and had been looking at the unlimited supply of acreage to the west. They had been waiting to break loose.

There had been some activity west of the mountains in the 1740s. A Pennsylvanian named George Croghan, along with his partner William Trent, had established a fur-trading post in 1741 near a location destined to become the fulcrum of American history for the next three decades: the place where the Monongahela and Allegheny Rivers combined to form the mighty Ohio River (the site of modern Pittsburgh). A combative Marylander named Thomas Cresap, a carpenter, surveyor, farmer, and trader, had set up at the confluence of the South Branch and main stem of the Potomac River. John, Andrew, and Thomas Lewis had been exploring land along the Greenbrier River (christened by John Lewis, it was said, in some exasperation after he became entangled in a thick stand of the vine) between the Allegheny ridges of what is now southeastern West Virginia.

One reason for the slow pace of westward expansion was the fact that in the Ohio River country beyond the Alleghenies there were resident Shawnees with strong attachments to their home-land—along with displaced populations of, for example, Delawares from Pennsylvania. In addition, groups of Iroquois hunters, mainly Senecas and Cayugas, had begun to move into the Ohio Country during the 1720s and had established permanent villages there, well outside the Iroquois homeland. (Displaced Delawares, with their bitter memories, called all Iroquois *minquas,* or treacherous people. British traders began calling the western Iroquois by a corrupted form of the Delaware name: Mingos.) By 1740 there were almost a thousand Mingos living in what is now western Pennsylvania and eastern Ohio. Although originally and technically Iroquois, they had begun to think and act like a separate tribe.

The white interlopers were at first oblivious to the intense emotions their incursions aroused in the tribes who regarded the Ohio Country as their last redoubt. But by the summer of 1744, so many disputes had arisen that a treaty council was convened at Lancaster, Pennsylvania, at which representatives of the Iroquois League, Virginia, Pennsylvania, and Maryland wrangled for three weeks to try to settle the issues between them. When it was over, all sides proclaimed victory to their constituents: the Iroquois exulted that they had finally won the white man's promise not to extend his settlements west of the Warrior's Road (the north-south trail used by the Iroquois to raid the Catawbas of North Carolina, and vice versa). The white signatories, on the other hand, took home a signed deed to 500,000 acres of Ohio Country land, described in writing as "all lands that are, or shall be, by His Majesty's appointment in the colony of Virginia." Afterward, the colonists remembered no promise to restrain settlement, and the Iroquois did not recall selling any land.

How could two sides recall the same agreement so differently? The whites would dismiss it as the ignorance of savages, while the tribes would see it as just another example of the white man's ethics. In fact, however, this misunderstanding again illustrates the enormous, unexamined gulf between the two ways of life that, because it was unexamined, led to immeasurable suffering and death.

As we have seen, the cultures of the tribes lived in spoken words, while in the European mind, conversation was merely a prelude to the creation of a written document, and only written records were meaningful. Thus when the Iroquois remembered the conference at Lancaster, they remembered what their sachem Canasatego had said:

> Brother Assaraquoa: The World at the first was made on the other side of the great water different from what is on this side, as may be known from the different color of our skin and of our flesh, and that which you call justice may not be so amongst us. You have your laws and customs and so have we. The Great King might send you over to conquer the Indians, but it looks to us that God did not approve of it, if he had, he would not have placed the sea where it is, as the Limits between us and you.
>
> Brother Assaraquoa: Though great things are well remembered among us, yet we don't remember that we were ever conquered by the Great King, or that we have been employed by that Great King to conquer others; if it was so it is beyond our memory.

Brother Assaraquoa: We will now speak to the point between us. You say you will agree with us to the Road. We desire that may be the Road which was last made (the Wagon Road). It is always a custom among brethren strangers to use each other kindly. You have some very ill-natured People living up there, so that we desire the persons in power may know that we are to have reasonable victuals when we are in want. You know very well when the White People came first here they were poor; but now they have got our lands and are by them become rich, and we are now poor. What little we had for the land goes soon away, but the land lasts forever.

This is, of course, a fragmentary record (set down by a white man) of one speech among many in a conference that extended over many days. Yet there are clues here to the great misunderstanding. "You say you will agree with us to the road" is perhaps the most important sentence. It implies that the white colonists agreed with the Iroquois "about the road," meaning they agreed to two major points: that the Iroquois would have free access to the Warriors' Road that ran from New England through the Shenandoah to the Carolinas and to the "victuals" to be found along it; and that the whites would regard the road as the western boundary of their settlements. A few, limited exceptions to this were talked about, but the Iroquois remembered that at Lancaster they had won the white man's promise to stop his invasion at the eastern edge of the western mountains.

At the very end of the conference, as a courtesy, the Iroquois signified their agreement in a written document. They probably did not know, and if they knew would likely not have cared, that the words written down differed greatly from the words that had been spoken. The treaty—at least as the leaders of Virginia later interpreted it—sold the Ohio Country to the whites.

Slowly, massively, the political machinery of land speculation was assembled, primarily in Virginia, where it coalesced into two camps, one dominated by Tuckahoes, the other by Cohees. Speaker

John Robinson, although a Tuckahoe, through his associations with William Beverley and hence John Lewis was at the head of the Cohee group, which by 1749 had completed patents for nearly a million acres: 200,000 acres west of the Beverley Patent for the Greenbrier Company, whose twelve principals included Robinson, John Lewis, his sons William and Charles, with Andrew as chief surveyor; and a staggering 800,000 acres south and west of the Greenbrier Patent, in what was to become Kentucky, for the Loyal Company—including Robinson, John Lewis, Peter Jefferson, Joshua Fry, and Dr. Thomas Walker of Albemarle County and five members of the Merriwether family of the Piedmont. The Loyal Company patent did not even bother to stipulate requirements for settling families (or even "warlike Christians") on the land, as all other patents did, in furtherance of what was supposed to be colonial policy (perhaps because Governor Gooch resigned his office and left the colony, leaving the government temporarily in the hands of the council). This lapse led a young Tuckahoe surveyor named George Mercer to complain bitterly that, after adding up all the various patents held by individuals and companies with Cohee leanings, "no less than 1,350,000 acres of land were granted by the governor and council to borrowed names and private land-mongers who were incapable of making effectual settlements."

But George Mercer was just jealous. He was to spend the next several decades in the employ of a competing, Tuckahoe-dominated company led by Thomas Lee, president of the council, who in 1749 engineered through London a royal grant of 200,000 acres west of the Allegheny Mountains and south of the Ohio River. This organization of a dozen planters and merchants, including Lawrence Washington (George's half-brother), was called the Ohio Company. Although it did not have the largest grant, it had as members the colony's most notable people, including the man who was about to become the governor of Virginia, Robert Dinwiddie.

More was being conceived in the Irish Tract during these days than land schemes. Andrew somehow worked into his schedule of western surveying trips several visits to the home near Augusta Stone Church of Elizabeth Givens. She was one of nine Givens children living with their mother, their father, one of the original Augusta settlers, having died. About 1745 Andrew and Elizabeth were married; no record survives, either because they did not bother to cross the mountains for a wedding in an alien Anglican church, required for legitimacy under British law, and simply married as Presbyterians, at home; or because they did execute the formality but disdained to preserve the record of it. Thomas Lewis, although busy laying out the new town of Staunton, found time to court one Jane Strother of Stafford County, whose girlhood home on the Rappahannock River, sold by the Strothers to Augustine Washington in 1738, had become George Washington's boyhood home. Wife hunting east of the mountains was becoming customary in the valley; Jane's sister had married the clerk of the Augusta County court, James Madison, and in 1749 Thomas married Jane. A few years later a prominent Augusta lawyer, Gabriel Jones, would marry another Strother sister. Thomas set up a new farm twenty-five miles north of his father's, on the broad South Fork of the Shenandoah, under the southernmost brow of Massanutten Mountain, where he and Jane would raise thirteen children.

Governor Dinwiddie arrived in the colony in 1751, welcomed heartily by the land speculators, who assumed that because he was one of them he would smooth their way. High on their list of things needing change was the tithing and other requirements imposed by the Church of England on the German Lutherans and Scotch-Irish Presbyterians who were the best prospects for resettlement on western lands. Lawrence Washington wanted German settlers for the Ohio Company, but the "Pennsylvania Dutch" he consulted in the lower valley told him that "they might have from Germany any number of settlers, could they but obtain their favorite exemption"—that is, if they did not have to pay tithes to the Church of England, to suffer the attentions of Anglican clergymen who did not even speak their language, and to be excluded from all public offices by their faith. Since Dinwiddie was a Scot and had been educated by Presbyterians, the land speculators were sure he would be sympathetic to easing the grip of the established church.

One of his first actions, however, was not at all to their liking and touched off a controversy heavy with portent. Dinwiddie discovered that, in the grip of their land fever, Virginia officials had assigned ownership of well over a million acres of land to themselves or their companies without completing the official transfers. They had recorded warrants of the surveys of these lands, but not the governor's patent, or seal of approval. The recording of the patent triggered the imposition of the annual quitrents, and the speculators often delayed the filing until they had settlers in place to make the payments. Dinwiddie not only insisted on prompt recording of patents, but he and the governor's council imposed a fee for each patent, on the assumption that since this was the colony's land, its manipulation ought to generate some funds for the colony's administration. The fee was pegged to the value of a Spanish gold coin called a *pistole* (there was simply not enough British currency available in the colony to carry the weight of commerce), worth about a pound sterling, the average price of a cow.

Dinwiddie regarded this as a minor administrative adjustment, a "silly fee" as he called it, "which I give small notice to." He was astonished, he wrote, by the "factious disputes and violent heats" that resulted. Some of the heat came from Cohee speculators (the Ohio Company was not yet ready to transfer any land), but most of the reaction came from individual property owners. Dinwiddie had done what his royal masters would continue to do for a quarter century: he had unwittingly prodded a throbbing American nerve. In certain American circles, among what Dinwiddie called "a most impudent, troublesome party," the idea was taking hold that there was an individual right to own land that at some point extinguished the king's right to dispose of it; that was one of the liberties of a country, not a colony, that was separate from and essentially different from its parent country. When the House of Burgesses next met, in

June of 1752, it protested the imposition of the fee in incendiary terms. William Stith, chaplain of the House and president of the College of William and Mary, spoke for the majority in calling the fee "subversive of the rights and liberties of my country." Stith proposed a toast that was soon being chanted in the streets, to Dinwiddie's consternation: "Liberty, property, and no *pistole*."

The *pistole* was as controversial in the Shenandoah as elsewhere. One James Calhoun contracted with James Patton for two parcels of land, and for the surveying and recording of them, but before the transaction could be completed the *pistole* fee was imposed, and Patton billed the fee to Calhoun, who refused to pay it. Whether he hated the fee or Patton more is hard to say; Calhoun had been telling it about that Colonel Patton had deeded over his land to his children in order to defraud his creditors, and Patton sued him for slander. Patton also sued Calhoun for the two *pistoles*. The issue came to trial at the fall session of the county court in 1752, but the jury hung and was ordered to return to the spring session in 1753. They did so, but when the case was called one of them leaped out a back window of the courthouse and escaped. Recalled to the fall session in 1753, not one of the jurors showed up. Pragmatically, the court discharged the jury, continued the case, and wearily implored the parties to submit to arbitration, which they did, and the matter was finally resolved in the fall of 1754 by the payment of one *pistole* by each party. It was that year, also, that the matter of the *pistole* fee itself, having been appealed to London by the General Assembly, was resolved in Dinwiddie's favor.

Meanwhile, Dinwiddie had become embroiled in a lot more trouble. Even as the *pistole* controversy was blowing up in his face, he was taking an avid interest and an active role in the affairs of the Ohio Company, whose aggressive start brought it (and Virginia, whose policies, through Dinwiddie, had become so entwined with those of the company as to be indistinguishable) into renewed conflict with the tribes of the Ohio Country. Dinwiddie's attempts to deal with this dangerous situation were logical, forthright—and disastrous.

The first step toward realizing the Ohio Company's extravagant ambitions was to clear a road to ease the passage through the western mountains of the thousands of settlers they expected. They established a staging area at a place called Wills Creek, where the North Branch of the Potomac wheeled from its northeasterly course to run southeast toward the Chesapeake Bay (see map on page 148). The spot was on the eastern edge of the Allegheny Front—the great divide between the rivers that made their way to the Atlantic Ocean and those that sought the Mississippi and the Gulf of Mexico—and was within sight of a gap, a notch carved like a gun sight into that forbidding barrier to westward travel. (Later named Fort Cumberland in honor of the captain-general of the British army, it is known today as Cumberland, Maryland.)

Wills Creek was then, and Cumberland remains today, one of the westernmost outposts of Maryland, whose aspirations for westward expansion were squeezed powerfully between those of Pennsylvania and Virginia, with today's map showing the resulting west-reaching tentacle of the state compressed to a long point by its more aggressive neighbors. (Thomas Lewis bears some responsibility for that map feature; as the representative of Virginia on the commission to set the Virginia-Maryland-Pennsylvania boundaries in the area, he was determined to truncate Maryland's westward tentacle, but missed the crucial meeting.) However narrow, Maryland's westward reach is a monument to Thomas Cresap, one of the most passionate of the colony's expansionists. Cresap previously had been advocating Maryland's claim to the fortieth degree of latitude as its northern border in a way that made him seem, as one who knew him wrote, "born unto trouble." Trouble had come to him in November of 1736, when a Pennsylvania sheriff with a twenty-three-man posse laid siege to Cresap's home on the Susquehanna River (and the fortieth degree of latitude) and, when Cresap resisted, burned the house down around him and took him in chains to Philadelphia.

His subsequent two-year imprisonment was the impetus for serious border warfare that led eventually to the running of the Mason and Dixon Line to settle the matter.

Cresap thereafter set his stake a little farther west than Maryland was thought to extend, near Wills Creek. There he encountered people of a like mind when it came to westward expansion, not Marylanders but certain gentlemen of Virginia, associated in the Ohio Company. In 1751, before Governor Dinwiddie's arrival, Cresap had built the first leg of the Ohio Company's road, from Wills Creek thirty-five miles northwest to the forks of the Youghiogheny River. The following year Christopher Gist had joined Cresap to extend the road another fifty miles, to the confluence of the Youghiogheny with the Monongahela, which in turn joined the Allegheny just ten miles farther to the northwest to form the Ohio River.

The Ohio Company was, of course, hardly alone in pushing westward. John Lewis's Greenbrier Company and the Loyal Company of which he was a part were located well to the south of the Ohio Company's starting point, and were not yet in direct competition, although all their aspirations overlapped to some degree in their westward dreams, which all eventually reached the Ohio River. But the mania was spreading; John Blair, a member of the governor's council, formed a company, wangled a grant, and hired Andrew Lewis as surveyor.

The competition among various Virginia companies was overlain by the continuing contest between Virginia and Pennsylvania, whose representatives had a different focus for their efforts but were no less aggressive. Pennsylvania's experienced wilderness hands, such as Conrad Weiser and George Croghan, were interested not in land speculation but in the more traditional trade in furs and hides. They wanted trading posts where the Ohio Company wanted towns, and intended to deal with the very tribes the Ohio Company wanted to run off. The Pennsylvanians found it easy to fan the embers of native distrust by pointing out at every opportunity that the advance of

Virginia surveyors and road builders could not be good news for the tribes.

Warnings and threats to the agents of the Ohio Company became so frequent and specific that the managers of the company and the colony (much the same persons) realized that something would have to be done to deal with the delusion these natives were under about having some right to the land. After all, the Iroquois League had sold the Ohio Country eight years before, in Lancaster, Pennsylvania, and there was a signed treaty to prove it. Governor Dinwiddie sent to the Iroquois on the Ohio River an imperious summons to come to Winchester and confer with their "Great White Father."

As we have seen, the use of the father image to try to convey the supreme authority of the king fell flat in a matrilineal society. Knowing this, and looking again at the few accurate transcripts extant of what the sachems said in council, we see that the forms of address they used were precisely nuanced. When speaking with equals (as Canasatego believed he was doing when he addressed the commissioners at Lancaster), one addressed them as "brother." In order to convey great respect, one addressed the listener as "uncle." The term "father" is never encountered unless introduced, and insisted upon, by the whites, because for the native cultures it had little meaning. Knowing this, one sees in the response conveyed to Governor Dinwiddie from the western Iroquois what the Virginians never knew was there—poisonous sarcasm: "Our brothers of Pennsylvania have kindled a council fire here, and we expect you will send our Father's speeches to us here, for we long to hear what our great Father the King of Great Britain has to say to us his poor children."

Even though they did not grasp the irony of the final clause, the Virginians knew they had been given bad news. Their Pennsylvania competitors, led by George Croghan, were at work among the residents of the Ohio Country, and the tribes obviously believed their bargaining position was strong enough to demand that the

Virginians come to them. The Virginians realized they had no option but to comply.

The conference was scheduled for June in Logstown, the principal settlement of the western Iroquois, or Mingos, located on the Ohio River about twenty miles downstream from the Forks, which the Ohio Company regarded as the focal point of their development. The commissioners who would conduct the conference for the Virginians were selected early in 1752, and it was in this regard that Governor Dinwiddie made the second great mistake of his administration.

It may be that Dinwiddie, who had been in the colony only since the previous November (although he had been aware of the colony's politics for a decade and had been a member of the Ohio Company for a year), simply did not yet have a grasp of the political geography. In any case, he allowed the House of Burgesses to name three of their members as commissioners to Logstown. Of course they named Cohee speculators: Loyal Company principals Joshua Fry, the mapmaker from Albemarle; Lunsford Lomax, a member of the House of Burgesses from Caroline; and the Scotch-Irishman John Patton of Augusta. Christopher Gist, Thomas Cresap, and William Trent of the Ohio Company were reduced to attending the conference without official standing. George Croghan, meanwhile, announced himself on scant authority (he was bearing a perfunctory message of goodwill from Governor Hamilton) as a commissioner from Pennsylvania, and managed to get himself treated as such throughout. Whether company men or not, the Virginia commissioners understood that their mission at Logstown was to gain the approval of the tribes for white settlement of the Ohio Country.

The Logstown conference did not start well, and soon got worse. The Shawnees were angry about some broken promise of help for their allies to the north, the Twigtees, about which the Virginians knew nothing and could do nothing except make some vague promises that, barely, placated the Shawnees. Then there was a problem with the Delawares. Every time the Virginians met with them, they found themselves negotiating with a different person— sometimes Tamaqui, on another occasion his brother Shingas, at still other times a sachem named Oppamylucah. That this was the way the tribes conducted their business, that they never invested the power of the people in a single representative, but arrived at communal decisions that were perfectly well expressed by whichever member of the community was at hand, never occurred to the Europeans, for whom power was a possession, a thing not to be given up once possessed, and a thing that could be used against the people as easily as for them. To regularize relations, the Virginians insisted on appointing Shingas "king" of the Delawares—the word "king" having even less significance for the *Lenni Lenape* than the word "father." Equable as ever, however, the Delawares allowed the Virginians to conduct a preposterous coronation ceremony for the man they wanted to call king, adorning the anointed leader in a fine British coat and such other decorations as came to hand. The Delawares, ever polite, did not consider spoiling the Long Knives' fun by letting them in on the fact that Shingas, being unable to make it, was represented at the coronation by Tamaqui, whom the Virginians unknowingly made a king.

However exasperating and time consuming, these matters were tangential to the business of the Logstown conference, which was supposed to be negotiation with the Iroquois League. Initially, the Virginians were horrified to learn that, although they had been welcomed to the conference "on behalf of the Six United Nations," the sachems of Logstown had never even notified the Great Council of the League, at Onondaga, that the conference was being held. Their despair was eased by the news that an emissary of the council was expected to arrive, three days after the conference had begun. When he did, things got no better for the Virginians.

The emissary was Tanacharison, one of the frontier's most influential individuals, and one of the most difficult to find in any history of the period. A sachem of the Senecas, he had been assigned by the Great Council as an emissary to the western Mingos (another sachem, named Scaroyady, had been sent to the Shawnees) in 1748. The whites persisted in thinking he was an overseer, but tribal customs admitted no such role; he was there to facilitate and comprehend the consensus of the Mingo sachems, to keep the Great Council informed, and to help the council reach consensus on how to react. All this consensus building drove the whites mad with frustration—too many meetings with inconclusive results. In their view, as an overseer Tanacharison was either seriously limited or seriously incompetent, but instead of trying to comprehend the difference of his approach, they gave him the contemptuous sobriquet of "Half-King" and continued to try to impose on him and the people he represented their iron precepts of power.

Even James Patton, the recording secretary for the conference, was impressed by Tanacharison, who swept into Logstown with a flotilla of canoes flying the English colors. "He seems to be a person of great dignity in his behavior," wrote Patton, who later—no doubt in light of succeeding events—went back and carefully crossed out the words of admiration.

First, Tanacharison disappeared from view into a series of private meetings with the Mingo, Shawnee, and Delaware representatives that lasted for five days. When he was sure he understood the situation, he convened the increasingly frantic commissioners and delivered a performance that would be a credit to any diplomat of any era. He was unaware, he said with smooth self-deprecation, that the Great Council at Onandaga had sold the Ohio Country to the Virginians; the council's failure to let him know what they had done had caused much unnecessary confusion, but the council would no doubt confirm their action as soon as he made contact. Until then, unfortunately, there was nothing he could do.

Faced with disaster, the commissioners tried one more gambit. They had been so sure of success that they had, as Patton recorded, "drawn an instrument of writing confirming the deed at Lancaster and containing a promise that the Indians would not molest our settlements of the southeast side of the Ohio." As a last resort, they sent one of the few members of their party who spoke the language of the tribes—a free lance named Andrew Montour—alone into a meeting with the sachems, the precious paper in hand. There is no record of how he did it, but he emerged with the required signatures on the paper.

Thus, once again the great gulf of misunderstanding yawned between the races. The tribes left the Logstown conference believing they had stalled the whites until consultations with the Onandaga Council could take place. The Virginians left with a piece of paper that said the Ohio Country was theirs. The Ohio Company ordered Christopher Gist to get the first party of settlers ready to move out, and he soon had fifty people assembled at Wills Creek. The company laid its plans for a string of trading posts to extend from the Forks of the Ohio two hundred miles downstream, with each to be a center of commerce and settlement.

One of the largest land-development schemes ever devised— certainly one of the largest undertaken without the participation of a king—was about to be realized, with revenues that any king would covet about to flow to the men who conceived it. Only formalities remained. The Virginia governor and council had to patent the first 200,000 acres, so that legal title could be conveyed to the settlers; and, if one were going to be fastidious about it, one should await confirmation of the Logstown deal by the Onandaga Council.

But the men of the Ohio Company were not the only ones who scented great wealth in the West, nor were they the only ones represented on the Governor's Council, nor was their company the only one claiming the land in question. The latter point was made dramatically when, just after Christopher Gist had gathered his prospective settlers at his plantation near Wills Creek, a surveying crew led by Andrew Lewis struck a line between Gist's home and the settlers' camp, across the Ohio Company Road, claiming the land for Councilman John Blair's company. The western air was still sulfurous from that confrontation when another council member, Richard

Corbin, filed a counterclaim to a large chunk of the land designated by the Ohio Company as its own. Perhaps these competing interests on the council contributed to a development that stunned the investors in the Ohio Company: the governor and council took no action on their urgent request for an initial patent.

Yet all these setbacks and delays began to recede toward insignificance in the face of a new and aggressive competitor now arriving in the Ohio Country—the soldiers of imperial France.

Journal

———

Leisure Point

I first came to live in the Shenandoah Valley because of a land speculator.

Five years had passed since my first, beguiling sight of the river. I had established myself as a broadcast journalist in one of the top ten "markets," as the venues for television-news performers are described, and had found it to be hollow, dishonest work, having little to do with journalism and everything to do with marketing. My angst was cured by a personal letter from the President of the United States requiring my presence, on a bleak and freezing December morning, at a bus stop in Alexandria, Virginia, where I was to surrender my sorry ass to the United States Army for two years. It was the height of the Vietnam conflict, and my country needed me; first to learn how to shoot, bayonet, club, and explode people and then, for the remainder of my enlistment, to run a public relations office at Fort Gordon, Georgia.

While in the army I continued to meet young people drifting across the face of the land, not connected to any particular place, thing, person, or idea—blowing in the wind, waiting for something to feel good. Occasionally, some outlandish passion would take hold, for a romance or a political party or an eastern religion

———

or a designer drug that, for a time, provided some actual feelings. But each diversion required a price that increased over time, and passion decreased as the cost increased. Only the drugs were addictive. Home and family meant little to these nomads. Home was a place you visited to get another year's worth of complaints about those provincial, unsophisticated people. Relatives were people to whom you could write for money when the bar bills became troublesome. The only standards of measurement the nomads used to assess behavior and make decisions were money and physical attractiveness.

I met no patriots in the army. I met a handful of jingoists, parroting lines from John Wayne movies, but no genuine, Patrick Henry patriots demanding, "give me a free Vietnam or give me death." It simply was not that kind of conflict. People were in the army because they were too poor or dumb to avoid the draft, because they had avoided it for so long they had run out of legal recourse and were not quite ready to flee to Canada, because they were tired of worrying about it and wanted to get it over with, or—and this is by far the majority—simply because this was what was happening to them now, and what the hell.

Every once in a while, I did meet people who believed in something: a Jesuit priest with whom I spent hours drinking red wine and arguing about the canons of Catholicism; a college chaplain, an Episcopalian as I recall, who specialized in fresh-air religion (expressed by slogans such as "God says, take what you want—and pay for it."); and any number of political firebrands on fire to prove that what they believed could save the country and make them president, all of whom soon burned out and dragged their blackened husks back to ordinary lives. I envied the truly committed, the passionate believers, and I wanted to be one of them. But I was not.

Back from the war, I continued to cast about for authenticity in post–John Kennedy, post-Vietnam America. The bullet-riddled, pot-reeking 1960s were coming to an end, the world was staring apprehensively ahead at the 1970s as my generation, with similar misgivings, considered turning thirty. As the rages and enthusiasms of youth burned out, the imprints of childhood and the imperatives of biology quietly reasserted themselves. One winter day a friend of mine, his shoulder-length hair brushing his worn, peace-symbol T-shirt, listening to his wife (she of the waist-length hair, wearing the tie-dyed blouse) at work in another room, having told some favorite stories of protest marches, group houses, and Volkswagen vans, jounced his baby on his knee, gazed out the picture window of his split-level suburban house at his station wagon parked outside, and marveled: "I never thought I would turn out this way."

Another great generational migration was under way. We who had become nomads, who had severed our ties to family, land, and past, now began to ache for connection. We married, and looked to our spouses to provide, alone, the nurturing that was once the shared duty of parents, aunts, uncles, grandparents, cousins, and neighbors—a small city of caregivers. We got in touch with the land by putting a down payment on a split-level on an eighth of an acre in the suburbs, and no indentured servant of the eighteenth century paid a heavier price or spent a longer time in thrall for his piece of land: a twenty-year mortgage, whose servicing required twenty to forty person-years of work, which in turn imposed additional person-years of sitting in traffic jams. As for the past, we didn't care about the past, we cared about the weekends, time when we could mow our lawns, which had no other purpose.

And when we had the spouse we lusted for, the child we craved, the house and car we had envied, we still ached for something, some contact with the bedrock of life, some sense of stillness at the center of things. When the spouses, children, houses, and cars no longer satisfied, we changed them. We committed additional person-years to therapy, to be told to get in touch with our feelings, our inner child, our self-esteem—and to make sure we wrapped it up at fifty minutes past the hour and paid the bill on time.

Into my drifting angst came frequent dreams of the Shenandoah, and, one day, Jim Thorsen. I am using his real name to protect the innocent.

If the height of art is the concealment of art, then Jim was at the top of his game as a promoter. His smile never alarmed, it warmed. His enthusiasm was not forced, it was infectious. Only after you had known him for a while did you realize that the smile stayed warm and the enthusiasm bubbly without regard for the circumstances of the day: if he were being led out to face a firing squad, he would be trying merrily to make a deal with the commander for the cigarette concession. But I did not know that about him when he invited me to "his" office building in Alexandria to discuss my preparing some advertising materials for a development he "owned" (I was to learn many gradations of meaning of the word "own") in the Shenandoah Valley. He did not need his persuasive powers to induce me to accept pay for traveling to and spending time in the Shenandoah.

Without delay, I drove out to the property, which Jim had dubbed "Leisure Point" for marketing purposes, to take pictures and form advertising concepts. But photographs and descriptive words could never capture what I saw there—it was one of the earth's truly sublime places. It was a four-hundred-acre peninsula bounded on three sides by one of the famous Seven Bends of the Shenandoah—a stretch through Shenandoah County west of Massanutten Mountain where the North Fork of the ancient river has gouged out a course so serpentine that most of its length runs perpendicular to its overall, downhill direction. The peninsula's base ran up the flank of the Massanutten and adjoined hundreds of thousands of acres of National Forest. The flow of the river along its mile-long sides and half-mile-wide nose was slowed and deepened by Burnshire's Dam at the downstream edge of the property. When I first saw the river there, in spring, the bright new leaves of the giant willows and sycamores lining its banks shaded and cooled the languid green waters, making a humid, fragrant tunnel down which you could float to destinations not shown on any map.

The land itself, the broad open plain of fertile river-bottom silt, offered everything that farmers most value: a reliable and abundant supply of water, flat fertile ground with few rock out-crops, and a gentle climate with a long growing season. Since nothing more could be asked of a farm property, it would seem to follow that farming there would be nothing but prosperous. Of course, real farming is never like that, no matter what your advantages. The first law of agriculture: Do everything right, and you might get a crop; do anything wrong, and you will not.

Through the 1960s, Earl Williams and his son Dennis had farmed this jewel of a property, with what was later described to me as indifferent success. When I met them, Earl had retired from a distinguished career as a trooper with the Virginia State Police, and Dennis had taken a job with the commonwealth calibrating weighing and measuring devices at gas stations and stores. I know nothing firsthand of their farming practices, but the fate of their land was something I saw again and again in the valley thereafter, so let me speak in general terms about what was beginning to happen to Shenandoah Valley land in the late 1960s.

Where I grew up, there was only one way to farm: you put seed grain in the ground in the spring, harvested it in the fall, trucked it to the elevator in town, and took what they gave you— we hoped for two dollars a bushel when I was a kid, and they don't get much more than that today. When I moved to the Shenandoah Valley, there was only one way to farm: you got some cattle, put them on pasture in the spring while you grew some corn and hay, fed the corn to the cattle in the fall to fatten them, then trucked them to market and took what they gave you. What they gave you was rarely enough. I once analyzed the rate of return on invest-ment that my parents were realizing on their grain farm, and it came to 3 percent; they could have doubled their income by converting their assets to cash, putting it in a passbook savings account, and doing nothing.

Like most people in the valley by that time, Earl Williams and his family did not rely on farming for a living. (Likewise my father, in the 1960s, had taken a job as the manager of the local co-op store.) Earl and Dennis worked off the farm, and so did Earl's wife, Estelle, a photographer. Earl and Dennis poked some corn in the ground every year and fed it to the cows every fall, but like just about everybody else they needed their day jobs to support their farming habit. Nothing much distinguishes the American commodity farmer from a compulsive gambler in a Vegas casino, who plays again and again against a house that has stacked all the odds in its favor, but allows a win just often enough to make sure the player can't quit. In all my life I never met a compulsive gambler or a commodity farmer who was truly enthusiastic or optimistic about the economics of what he was doing, although they all deeply love the ambiance of their respective pursuits.

So when a Jim Thorsen comes along and offers more money than you ever expected to see in your life for this land that has been a trial to you for a decade or a lifetime, you think about playing golf in Florida, about no longer worrying every time you see a thunderhead in August or a cow hanging its head low in April, about never again spending a Memorial Day sweating yourself down to a puddle of suet hoisting hay bales into the barn, about never again dragging yourself through two feet of snow to the barn in the predawn dark to chop ice from watering troughs, and you take the money.

But not without regret. I stood with Earl Williams one summer afternoon, next to the sprawling white farmhouse that had been his home and was now labeled the "Clubhouse," or some such, watching a bulldozer tearing a gash of a road across the face of his beautiful farm while real estate agents ran around staking up signs indicating "future swimming pool," "riverside lots," "stable to be

built here," and the like, and Earl's head hung low and swung
from side to side and he said, to no one in particular, just once:
"I never should have sold it."

It's easy to assume he got over it, that he laughed all the way
to the bank, as the saying goes, yet here was the difference between
Earl Williams and Jim Thorsen: one of them loved and respected
the land itself, as some farmers come to love the animals they will
eventually eat; the other cared no more about the land than a
butcher cares about cows, but dreamed the gold-plated dreams of
a John Lewis or a James Patton, of processing thousands of acres
of land and walking away with wealth beyond imagining.

I did not appreciate this difference at the time I first saw
Leisure Point, but I did see a chance for myself in Jim Thorsen's
grandiose plans. On the edge of the river, on the long, south side
of the peninsula, halfway down the drop-off from the level plain
to the riverbank, was an old frame tenant house that was too old,
small, and out of the way to figure in the development plans, but
that occupied a snug and private place on the green quiet river.
I bought it and moved there in the summer of 1970. In December
I held my newborn son in my arms and learned in a staggering,
life-altering minute the nature of unconditional love. I also felt a
sneaky kind of envy that he, and not I, was a native son of the
Shenandoah Valley. When I thought about family, as I did increasingly now that I had one, I saw my nomadic life as a kind of vegetative runner sent out across the continent and of my son as a
new root sent down into the ground of a new place that might
establish a new planting, as it were, of family.

As the months passed, the turmoil of "development" went
on around me, but it was not at all what I had expected. It soon
became obvious on how slender a shoestring Thorsen was operating. The road building stopped soon after it began, because
unless he sold a lot and cleared a profit, he could not afford to pay
the dozer operator to push out a road to the next lot. Often he
accepted a contract on a lot and hired the dozer to extend the

road, only to have the contract fall through because the buyer could not qualify for the financing. Then it would be a matter of holding off the increasingly irate equipment operators while conducting a sweaty search for a lender willing to take the deal. As Thorsen and his small crew lurched from crisis to crisis, there was no money for fitting out the "clubhouse" or installing the swimming pool.

I helped them build a "model home," an A-frame thrown up without benefit of any particular plan, with materials scrounged from woodpiles and fire sales. As we nailed some weathered plywood into place as a subfloor, we joked that if we dropped a marble on the uneven surface we'd be chasing it all day. To my surprise, the structure is still standing. They threw up a crude pole barn to serve as the "stable," and from somewhere Thorsen got a small herd of scrawny horses to give the place the air of a dude ranch. But nobody seemed to know anything about horses, or the containment of horses, and the herd spent a great deal of time wandering the property at large. I was standing with Thorsen one day when one of the few actual property owners came huffing over a slight rise in the ground from where his little cottage stood, surrounded by a patch of fussy landscaping, virtually alone in a large open field. "Your horses," he yelled, red-faced and irate, "are eating my shrubs."

Meanwhile the ads ran in the *Washington Post* (small classifieds, mostly, cash in advance), promising an idyllic location for that "second home" that was becoming the standard of affluence. On the weekends, a steady stream of prospects came onto the property to sample the bucolic lifestyle. Many of the men appeared to be seeking some John Wayne, Old West fantasy, especially the ones who bought one of the nags with their one-acre ranch. I had been around horses much of my life, but I quickly learned not to be helpful. When I saw one dude-rancher plunk a brand-new saddle on his steed and begin lacing the girth strap through whatever hole he could find in the saddle skirt, I was afraid for his life.

If saddle and ride are to stay on a horse, the leather girth strap must be doubled, wrapped, and tied in a specific way. I asked if I could give him a hand. "Never mind," he bristled, "I know what I'm doing." It was a mortal affront to suggest that a guy in a John Wayne fantasy might need some instruction. When they plucked this pilgrim out of a hedgerow a few minutes later, he had suffered only a mild concussion and the loss of his eyeglasses. The horse, on the other hand, suffered long-term harm—he had been encouraged in several bad habits.

For a time all this registered on me as nothing more than a weird business enterprise, from which I enjoyed immunity in my river nook on the sidelines. But the property became increasingly checkered with occupied lots sprouting A-frames and cottages, and the weekend traffic thickened, now a mix of territorial new "owners" and inquisitive lookers who thought nothing of driving into my yard to appraise my house as if it were in a store window marked "Sale." As my personal discomfort increased, I began to hear voices raised against this whole approach to doing business. Some were merely complaining about Thorsen's methods, especially his bill-paying habits. One day in Woodstock I encountered a local businesswoman whose stride and expression telegraphed that she was very upset. To my question, she replied that that blankety-blank Jim Thorsen had come into her store and, while she was trying to collect a huge past-due balance from him, the blankety-blank silver-tongued devil had actually talked her into charging more merchandise to him, and she could not believe she had done that.

Others did not like the look of the landscape that this kind of development was producing, not just at Leisure Point but also on similar tracts all over the valley, and notably on the hills around Front Royal. To those who were not being enriched by it, it was ugly. But most who made this point followed it quickly by saying their esthetic values probably should not be forced on anyone else.

In the argument that began then and continues to this day, those who liked what was happening to the land in the valley—

that is, those who were profiting from it, or might—said that such growth was an inevitable result of the burgeoning population in Washington, D.C., and that nothing could be done to stem the tide of people coming across the Blue Ridge Mountains looking for second homes, retirement homes, or getaway homes. "You can't stop progress," became the refrain of the chambers of commerce. The root of this picture of the future was our shared picture of the past. After all, this had all happened before: hordes of people in need of land had come pouring over the Blue Ridge, and things had turned out all right. It was progress.

Something seemed wrong with it. I did not know what. Increasingly, I was uncomfortable with all sides in the Leisure Point furor: the on-site hucksters, the tire-kickers, the "come-heres" (as some of the locals called the displaced persons who became part-time or full-time residents), and the increasingly hostile local merchants and tradesmen. I was, obviously, no longer a nomad, but a husband, father, homeowner, and community member. What I was also feeling, but had not yet identified, was a connection with the land, a sense that it was being violated, that someone should be speaking up for it. But were not the come-heres responding to the same need I had for reconnection with the land? Were they not members of my own generation, part of its ongoing migration toward a better life? Did I have a right, as developers accused their opponents of wanting, to pull up the drawbridge behind me and deny to those next in line the benefits I was enjoying?

I expressed my inchoate discomfort by leaving Leisure Point for a thirty-acre, isolated farm several miles up the river. But any thought that this move would remove me from the strife caused by the wave of development sweeping over the valley was soon dispelled. I had severed all ties with Washington, D.C., to work happily for much less money, first as the editor of a small weekly newspaper and then as the news director of the valley's only TV station. That work brought me into continual contact with the flashpoints between the "Save-the-Valley" and "You-Can't-Stop-Progress" groups.

My initial inclinations were on the side of progress. Although I was no longer a nomad, had a family, had chosen to limit my income because of the new ways in which I was coming to value the land in this place, I still wanted money. And the people around me who were making substantial amounts of money were doing it by manipulating the land. In a small way, I participated, buying and renovating a few small farms and selling them to the seemingly inexhaustible market of wealthy Washington second-home buyers. I was, to use a word not yet current, recycling farms and not adding to the burden on the land. I still believed that while individual developers might be guilty of poor taste or rapacious tactics, what they were doing, surely, was in the tradition of American enterprise, and those who benefited from it were enjoying the fruits of bedrock American values—the pursuit of happiness, the enjoyment of private property. To oppose such practices, it seemed, would be un-American.

To indulge in such practices, on the other hand, did not assure success. Jim Thorsen's large plans and my small ones came to pretty much the same thing. He eventually left the valley, with the development of Leisure Point little more than begun, trailing a cloud of acrimony and lawsuits. The property became a quiet residential suburb of Woodstock, whose residents tell each other Jim Thorsen stories and never, ever refer to the place as Leisure Point. As for me, in 1979 the second oil shock following the Arab oil embargo of 1973 caught me with three farm properties, all heavily leveraged. As the interest rates on my loans went from 6 to 18 percent, tripling my expenses, the price of gas went to an unheard-of dollar a gallon, and the inexhaustible market of people driving out from Washington drove out no more. I was ruined.

Others weathered the storm, and it was not long before the land sweepstakes resumed, as the evidence mounted that this American enterprise was destroying much more than scenery.

In the 1980s, local politicians who had salivated at the prospect of additional tax revenues from all the new houses found instead that it cost their jurisdictions far more than they collected to provide the schools, fire and police protection, roads, and other services that the come-heres demanded. It soon became apparent that the rising tide of sewage, garbage, lawn chemicals, automobile exhaust, storm runoff, and other effluvia would, if the rate of increase continued, at some point in the future overwhelm the ability of both natural and constructed systems to absorb it. As this information emerged, and the iron logic of destruction became apparent, I became an activist in the cause of containing wholesale development before it was too late.

However convinced I was that my information and logic were correct, it still felt un-American. When I was called a Communist in some heated public debate, it stung, because I harbored the feeling that I was at cross purposes with some of the greatest traditions of American heritage. Then I began to learn the truth about my heritage, and the final piece of the triad of transformation—family, home, and heritage—fell into place.

As great floods do, my awareness of the past began with isolated spatters of information that dropped into my life and invited attention. Many of them came from people I came to know who lived with ghosts: people who never passed the old hotel in New Market without remembering that it used to have a porch, from which Stonewall Jackson once reviewed his Confederate troops; who never passed Round Hill at Toms Brook without remembering, perhaps seeing, General Phil Sheridan sitting his black horse atop it, supervising his Union cavalry as it humiliated the Confederate cavalry at the Battle of Toms Brook; who remembered, perhaps saw, a young George Washington surveying the southern boundary of Shenandoah County, the Fairfax Line (which, in fact, he did not, despite persistent local legend) or an older George Washington striding the streets of Winchester grappling with the stern lessons of military command. I saw John G. Neihardt on television speaking of his book *Black Elk Speaks* and reciting his epic poem "The Death of Crazy Horse," and began to hear the resonance of the Native American way of life and thinking. Bill Gardner summoned me to the Thunderbird Site and confronted me with the story of the First People.

For a time I owned a house that had been home to John Sevier, first governor of Tennessee, and soon I was encountering his shade in my own hallways. He was an associate of John Lewis, of the Irish Tract, whose name of course drew my attention. I was transfixed by a speech made on the floor of the U.S. Senate by John Breckinridge of Tennessee, after Fort Sumter had fallen and the Civil War had begun, in which he, nominally a Southerner, said this war need not be fought, because the slavery the North feared and the South demanded could not expand or indeed sustain itself for reasons of economic and agricultural unsuitability; it would, said Breckinridge, "fall of its own weight" without the agony of a civil war. Breckinridge's grandfather had been an associate of John Lewis, an original grantee on the Irish Tract. Branded a traitor by the federal government, Breckinridge fled the Senate for Tennessee and there, reluctantly, put on the uniform of a Confederate general. He won the Battle of New Market in 1864, eventually became Secretary of War for the Confederate States, and during the final siege of Richmond saved the Confederate archives, for which he should have earned the eternal gratitude of the historians who have for the most part ignored him.

Now the question began to draw me on: what else, and who else, had history ignored? Frequently, that question led me back to the Irish Tract, especially to John and Andrew Lewis. Now their ghosts began to stalk the valley with me, to require me to consider their views, to acknowledge what they had done and left undone. John Lewis, of course, took Jim Thorsen's side, urging the widening of the roads, the sending out of agents to encourage immigration, the swinging of the loans and the platting of the lots with all possible speed. Getting a development loan, it turned out, was not much different from getting a king's grant or colonial patent: write an application, overstate the potential profits, get the right people involved as partners, and suck up to the folks in authority. The recruiting that James Patton had done on the docks of Philadelphia and Belfast was akin to the advertising I had written for Jim Thorsen. In the 1760s, as in the 1970s, an awful lot of these migrating fish were not schooling; they had been hooked and were being landed by anglers with big plans for dinner.

And then there was Andrew Lewis, who did not argue, nor did he spend much time in the valley. He was absent for most of his life, either surveying lots for the land boomers or fighting wars. And why was he so much at war?

The answer to that question completed the lesson, and my transformation.

Part Four

The Wars

The Wars for the Ohio Country

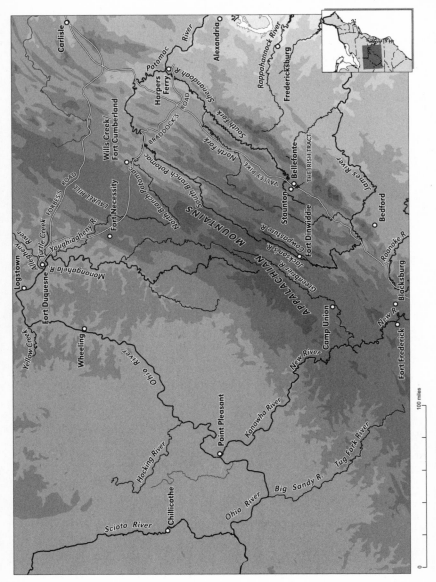

As the land speculators of Virginia, with the Scotch-Irish of the Shenandoah in the lead, mapped out huge tracts of Ohio River country for resale and development, they triggered increasingly desperate responses from the native populations, centered at Logstown and Chillicothe.

Chapter 7

⸺

The French War, 1754-1758

Ordinary people thought the proposed war with France,
Washington wrote, was "a fiction and scheme to promote the
interest of a private company. . . . These unfavorable surmises
caused great delays in raising the first men and money."

AS EARLY AS THE SUMMER OF 1749, when the Virginia land companies first had been choosing their vast acreages to the west of
Shenandoah, a French expeditionary force had traveled down the
Belle Rivière—the French name for the Allegheny and Ohio Rivers—
asserting French sovereignty. This exercise of imperial power was
carried out by a French captain with a squad of men who ceremoniously buried as they went a series of lead plates proclaiming the
sovereignty of France in the region (to the vast amusement of watching warriors). They made the claim by right of discovery of the
Mississippi River system. We found it, the argument went, and
therefore we own it. The rivers were the highways of the day, essential to the fur trade, and the French regarded the Ohio and Mississippi Rivers as the superhighways to the interior. In addition, they
provided an inland connection between the French enclaves in Canada and Louisiana, and described to French satisfaction the western
boundary of English influence on the continent.

As French traders had ranged into the country west and south of the Great Lakes, French officials had been doing what they could to intimidate English competitors and to command the loyalty of the tribes. And French policy toward the Ohio Country became considerably more muscular with the appointment, in July of 1752, just a month after the Logstown conference, of a new governor of New France. Ange de Menneville, the Marquis de Duquesne, came to the office determined to succeed at the task set for him by his monarch: "Drive the English from our territory and prevent them from coming there to trade." In the spring of 1753, he launched an expedition of fifteen hundred armed men to do just that.

This invasion would be portrayed as a sufficient—indeed, an inevitable—cause of war, especially by Governor Dinwiddie. "I hope you will think it necessary to prevent the French taking possession of the lands on the Ohio," he wrote the authorities in London that summer. Yet this invading army was not very large to begin with and, beset by the difficulties of travel, rampant illness, scant supplies, and drought, was soon reduced to a few dozen sick men who, after struggling onward through the summer and fall, staggered to a halt as winter approached a few miles south of Lake Erie. No other colonial government shared Dinwiddie's alarm at this feeble incursion. The western boundaries of the New England colonies were well established, Maryland had pretty much given up on western expansion, the Carolinas were far removed from this conflict, and Pennsylvania's flinty Quakers were determined to avoid armed confrontation at any cost (despite the frantic pleas from their beleaguered fur traders in the Ohio Country).

Even Dinwiddie's own countrymen were far from united in their view of what should be done. The French designs were of little interest to the Virginia Tuckahoes, who felt safe in the world they had created in the Tidewater and whose wildest dreams of westward expansion, when it became necessary to replace their played-out tobacco fields, did not extend beyond the Shenandoah River. Even the settled families of the Shenandoah Valley, for the most part, were far too busy with their farms, mills, and stores to give a thought to the Ohio Country or to geopolitics. And after twenty years of peace in the country, they had little reason to fear the tribes.

But to the land speculators—Dinwiddie of the Ohio Company, John Robinson of the Loyal Company, John and Andrew Lewis of the Greenbrier Company, and their colleagues—the French posed a mortal threat to dreams of great wealth. It was the landmongers, led by Dinwiddie, who now promoted war. And by the fall of 1753, they had the blessing of their sovereign. George II was always ready for war with France, the current excuse being that country's support of Austria in a contest with Prussia (which was allied with George's native Hanover) over possession of Silesia. He was annoyed by French pretensions in India, as well, and North America was just another item on his list of grievances. Warn them off, the king ordered Dinwiddie, and if they don't go, drive them off.

Eagerly, Dinwiddie wrote a threatening letter to the commander of the French expedition, and in haste selected a messenger. His most reliable agent for dealing with aliens in the west, William Trent, was at the Forks of the Ohio building the company's first fort there. It was Trent, in fact, who had alerted Dinwiddie to the approach of the French, and he was having some success in persuading the sachems at Logstown to convene yet another conference, at Winchester, to talk some more about the Ohio lands. These were important matters, so Dinwiddie handed the letter to a brash young man who had just talked his way into an appointment as one of four adjutants of the colony's militia and who was angling for the assignment: George Washington. But Dinwiddie made sure that Christopher Gist went along to make sure the green young adjutant could find his way there and back.

Another who went along on this mission to start a war was Tanacharison, who must have had a great deal to think about while he stared into the campfire at night. The Great Council of the Iroquois League (of which he was most likely a member) had a simple policy with regard to the Ohio Country, and there can be no doubt that he had known what it was even while he had dissembled at Logstown. When the Virginians sent Andrew Montour (he who somehow got the "deed" to the Ohio Country signed) to Onandaga after the conference to see how the council saw the issue, the answer he brought back was painfully clear: "those lands belong to the Indians, and neither the French nor the English should have anything to do with them." The western Iroquois, however, were not entirely of the same mind, and the Mingos, somewhat like the English colonies, were sometimes resentful of the control exerted over them from afar (as were the Shawnees and Delawares, in their roles as conquered subjects of the Iroquois). The Mingos needed reliable trade. An uninterrupted source of powder and shot, cloth, salt, pots, and steel hatchets was no longer a luxury; it was a matter of survival. French trade goods were always in short and uncertain supply, partly because of the long distance they had to be carried overland and partly because of the ability of the British navy to intercept them at sea. The Mingos badly wanted the English to build trading posts in the Ohio Country, and if that meant a few settlers as well, they could live with that. Thus Tanacharison, mindful of all these swirling complexities, was at the moment sticking to the English like a burr, to see what they were actually going to do.

The long and difficult trip up a tributary of the Allegheny River called French Creek to the camp the French named Fort le Boeuf (about twenty miles south of the shore of Lake Erie) proved to be something of an anticlimax. With his worried escorts looking on, Washington delivered his letter, was of course rebuffed, and returned to Williamsburg with a written account of his journey—a stirring account of an intrepid young soldier besting the wilderness to tug the beard of the French king. His journal was widely reprinted and avidly read, not only throughout the colonies, but in London. It helped to set the stage for war and prepare the audience for the war's first hero.

Enthusiasm for war is greatest among those with the least experience of it and the most to gain from it. Governor Dinwiddie, who had spent most of his career as a customs-house clerk and whose hopes for wealth were tied to the fortunes of the Ohio Company, was ardent to get this war under way. He was largely unsuccessful at raising war fever to match his own except at court in London, where war with France was a habit of long standing, and among his fellow land speculators. London sent him three companies of regular troops from New York and South Carolina, a little cash, and a shipment of thirty cannons, which even the inexperienced Dinwiddie recognized as too big to be dragged through woods and over mountains. The speculators set about raising an army.

Dinwiddie soon found, however, that calling out the militia was easier than getting them out. In Augusta County, Colonel James Patton not only ignored Dinwiddie's orders to recruit fifty men and send them north, he condemned the whole enterprise as an attempt by the Ohio Company to save its land grant (his own land speculations were fortunately located farther to the south). But Andrew Lewis, who was interested in contesting the Ohio Company's claims, brought eight men with him to the county courthouse on March 23, 1754, and they all signed up as an independent ranger company. Lord Fairfax had similar recruiting difficulties in Frederick County, as did Washington, who scoured the country between Winchester and Alexandria for volunteers, with scant success. He found that many ordinary people shared Patton's opinion about the declared need for war with France. They thought, Washington wrote, that it was "a fiction and scheme to promote the interest of a private company by any gentlemen that had a share in government. These unfavorable surmises caused great delays in raising the first men and money." Even if there were a real threat, others pointed out, the militia companies had been created and organized to defend their homes, not to leave them without defense in order to undertake some expedition beyond the mountains. For this reason among others, the Virginia Regiment was organized as a colonial army, distinct from the militia companies and, presumably, more willing to fight away from home.

Money could help motivate recruits, but the House of Burgesses proved almost as intractable as the general population. Few of its members were involved with the land speculators, and those few were in competition with Dinwiddie's Ohio Company. The burgesses finally, in February of 1754, agreed to let Dinwiddie spend £10,000 on defense, but it was not an appropriation, merely an authorization to borrow money as needed. More money was needed than could be borrowed for basic supplies—arms, ammunition, food, clothing, shelter, and transport—so Dinwiddie found another way to motivate recruits. He quickly had enacted a proclamation stating that the colony was setting aside 200,000 acres of prime land on the Ohio River to be parceled out at some future date to those who volunteered and served as soldiers in the coming hostilities. Intriguingly, this bounty land sounded like the very same 200,000 acres that the Ohio Company was seeking to patent.

In February, William Trent laid the first logs of a company trading post at the Forks of the Ohio, with the help of the approving and omnipresent Tanacharison. Everyone knew that as soon as spring weather made travel possible, the French would be on the move. Dinwiddie ordered the forces of Virginia out to meet them, under the command of William Fairfax, Lord Fairfax's cousin and land agent. When, in the event, Fairfax was too ill to go, Dinwiddie transferred the command to Joshua Fry, of the Loyal Company. On his way to take up his duties, Fry fell off his horse and suffered injuries that would prove to be fatal. Command of the militia thus devolved to the next ranking officer, the possessor of a freshly minted commission as lieutenant colonel of militia, George Washington.

Seldom has an expeditionary force marched off to start a war with less fervor in the ranks and more ineptitude among its leaders. The principal officers were Washington, Andrew Lewis, and Adam Stephen—a thirty-four-year-old Scot who had been educated as a physician but was more interested in developing his estate in the lower valley (he would lay out the city of Martinsburg nearby) and in various other commercial enterprises, all of which were threatened by this war. This trio of military neophytes made up for their lack of military experience with their enthusiasm for the conquest of the Ohio Country. There was nothing to be done about the reluctance of the privates but threaten them with dire, even capital, punishment should they fail to do their duty.

Washington was at Winchester on April 20 preparing to march west when he received word that, three days before, a French force had arrived at the Forks of the Ohio and had taken the surrender of the company fort there from the crew still struggling to build it. On April 29 Washington led his little army into the wilderness. His orders were to go out and protect the fort at the Forks, but now that it was in French hands he was not sure whether he was expected to attack it. He temporized, awaiting instructions, holding his men at a place called Great Meadows, between the Monongahela and Youghiogheny Rivers about fifteen miles south of Christopher Gist's place and about fifty miles southeast of the Forks of the Ohio. While awaiting clarity, Washington put his men to work improving Ohio Company roads for military purposes.

After weeks of uncertainty, the Virginians received word from Tanacharison that the French had dispatched from Fort Duquesne (as they now called their post at the Forks of the Ohio) a force that intended to attack the first English detachment it came upon. The French would later insist that they had given no such orders and that their soldiers' mission was merely to warn the English to leave the area, much as Washington had done at Fort le Boeuf. Three days later, on May 27, Christopher Gist returned from a scouting trip to say the French had appeared recently at his plantation (where he had left some friendly Indians as guards) and were in the area. That evening the good shepherd Tanacharison sent word that he was camped nearby and that he knew where the French force was.

Washington decided to end weeks of indecision with bold action. He took forty Virginians commanded by Adam Stephen, joined Tanacharison's little band of Mingos, and by shortly before dawn on May 28 had located and surrounded the French force. Whether he intended to ambush the French without warning is unclear; apparently someone in the awakening French camp saw something, yelled a warning, and, as the detachment sprang to arms, the Virginians opened fire. "After an engagement of about 15 minutes," Washington reported, "we killed 10, wounded one and took 21 prisoners." Although Washington would soon proclaim his "engagement" to be a "signal victory," French claims that he had ambushed and murdered an ambassador (the expedition's commander, Lieutenant Joseph Coulon de Villiers de Jumonville, who had been a member of a prominent French family) would cause Washington and Dinwiddie considerable discomfort.

Expecting retribution for his "signal victory," Washington started work on a fort at Great Meadows that he dubbed, with uncharacteristic pungency, "Fort Necessity." More a storehouse than a fort, it consisted of a little log hut, fourteen feet square, covered with deer hides and surrounded by trenches. Its location, at the low point of the swampy meadow, revealed the depth of its builders' military ignorance. Andrew Lewis soon arrived with his Augusta Company, as did Tanacharison, with about eighty Mingo, Delaware, and Shawnee warriors. Some of the warriors reported having seen more than two thousand French fighting men at Fort Duquesne, and after they surveyed the dithering of the little band of Virginians and their forlorn little fort in the middle of Great Meadows, they immediately put as much distance as they could between themselves and the hapless English. Even Tanacharison, who had done his best to forge an alliance with the English, who had tried strenuously to be of help, now gave up and withdrew. Where there had been a steady stream of intelligence and advice, there was now silence. Washington, Tanacharison would later observe, "took upon him to command the Indians as his slaves, but would by no means take advice from the Indians." He was "a good-natured man, but he had no experience."

This was made apparent when a force of six hundred French and Canadian troops with one hundred native allies marched into view of Fort Necessity in heavy rain on July 3. Washington drew his troops up in formation in front of their little fort, apparently expecting an immediate attack and conventional shootout by massed troops. Instead, the French and Indians melted into the woods on the hills overlooking the fort and shot the defenders to pieces. By nightfall, thirty Virginians were dead, seventy wounded, and another hundred disabled by exhaustion, illness, and hunger. Andrew Lewis had been hit twice, but was still on his feet with the aid of a makeshift crutch, and along with Stephen and Washington resolved to die fighting the next day. But the French commander called a parley that night, pronounced himself satisfied, and told Washington that if he struck his flag and signed a surrender, he and his men could leave.

The deal was made, and on the morning of July 4, 1754, the bedraggled force marched away from their fort under the guns of the French and through groups of menacing Indians. One of the warriors snatched up a portmanteau from the mud and started to make off with it, only to be braced by an infuriated Adam Stephen, who owned it. Tempers flared, and the entire truce was about to come unstuck when some French officers came on the scene and took control. They advised Stephen to let the matter go, but he protested that he was an officer, like them, and entitled by the terms of surrender to retain his possessions. Stephen had lost his shoes in the mud, which covered him, his face was black with smoke, his hair in wild disarray, and his claim to be an officer was greeted with some disdain by the correctly uniformed French. Stephen said he would prove his status if he could have his portmanteau, and when the dubious officers allowed him access he whipped out and donned, over the mud and blood and grit and smoke, a clean and braided coat of a captain in the Virginia militia. He left with portmanteau in hand.

Similarly, one of the departing Virginians, later described only as "an Irishman," became enraged at the taunts of one of the hectoring warriors and took aim at the tormentor with his musket. The wounded Andrew Lewis, hobbling along nearby, slapped the man's musket up before he could set off what surely would have been a massacre of the remaining Virginians. Whether it was for this incident, his fortitude under fire despite his wounds, or his steady leadership through it all, Lewis was said to enjoy thereafter Washington's esteem. One wonders: these were two very similar men, both standing a head taller than average height, with auburn hair, imposing physiques, grave manners, and unquestionable courage. It would be hard to imagine two such men working side by side without taking each other's measure. At the moment the chief difference between them was that while Washington spent much of his time cadging for higher rank and more pay, Lewis rather doggedly did what needed to be done without seeking reward.

Washington admirers would assign prescient wisdom and fateful inevitability to his conduct at what would be remembered as the ambush at Jumonville Glen and the Battle of Fort Necessity. George Macaulay Trevelyan, the British chronicler of British achievements, would declare Washington's "victory" at Jumonville Glen "on its own small scale, as complete as that of Wolfe at Quebec." (Assigning supernatural abilities to Washington was perhaps a necessary feature of post-Revolutionary British history; the empire in America, after all, could not have been brought low by a stumblebum.) Similarly, the English earl Horace Walpole saw an omen: "The volley fired by a young Virginian in the backwoods of America set the world on fire." Douglas Southall Freeman, the Southern-gentleman historian of Southern gentlemen, titled the ambush Washington's "First Military Victory," in which he "achieved the ideal of the soldier."

In their straining to find in these events the early signs of Washington's eventual greatness and an iron cause-and-effect relationship with the world war to come, these accounts missed the reality that these backwoods brawls were the products of accident, inexperience, and incompetence and that they were humiliating to their participants. As the kings and potentates lurched toward war—in North America, Europe, India, and on the high seas—there was more embarrassment to come for the ragtag vanguard on the American frontier.

While more experienced hands in London began casting about for someone with actual military experience to deal with the deteriorating situation in the Ohio Country, Dinwiddie and company struggled with a growing welter of problems and fears. They imagined that the French were about to launch a massive invasion of Virginia, and resolved to defend against it with a string of fortifications along the eastern edge of the Allegheny Mountains. That the French had no such intentions, that they did not have the resources to do it if they wanted to, that their tribal allies did not fight that way, or that isolated outposts could do little to stop any invasion—these things did not occur to the Virginians or the British.

In October Washington angrily resigned his commission as colonel of militia when Dinwiddie in effect eliminated the rank by dissolving what had been the Virginia Regiment into independent companies commanded by captains. While Washington sulkily took up residence at Mount Vernon, which he had just leased from his half-brother Lawrence's widow, his officers remained in service. Andrew Lewis, now captain of his Augusta County company, went to work building Fort Dinwiddie, on Jackson's River (in what is today Bath County, Virginia), while Adam Stephen took command of the Frederick County contingent.

While Virginia made ready for invasion, Major General Edward Braddock arrived on the continent from England with orders to take matters in hand, eject the French from the Ohio Country, and then drive them from Canada. Demonstrating that military incompetence was not the exclusive province of inexperienced backwoodsmen, Braddock with his two companies of regular troops (and nine of Virginia militia), with Washington riding along as an aide-de-camp without responsibility, made a ponderous march westward and, approaching Fort Duquesne on July 9, 1755, without deploying scouts, point men, or flank guards, rode into a makeshift ambush that destroyed his army, his ego, and his life. It was little understood or remembered that Braddock was a victim primarily of his own arrogance, that he had led thirteen hundred fighting men with thirteen guns to defeat at the hands of fewer than three hundred soldiers (half of whom were French regulars, the other half French Canadian militia who fled at the first sound of gunfire) augmented by six hundred warriors (who, hours before the engagement began, had not yet decided whether or not to fight). What was understood, and remembered, was that the British Empire had suffered its worst defeat on the North American continent at the hands of France.

Somehow, the debacle enhanced Washington's growing reputation as a military hero, in part by obliterating the short-lived distinction of Fort Necessity as being the worst reversal for British arms in the history of the continent. Andrew Lewis was not part of the Braddock expedition, having been assigned to secure roughly a thousand square miles of Augusta County wilderness. Dinwiddie could not understand why he was not doing a better job of it. "You were ordered to Augusta County to protect the frontiers," the governor complained to Lewis on the day before Braddock's catastrophe. "We have news of barbarous murders on the Holston"—this being a tributary of the Tennessee River, rising in the farthest, southwestern corner of the present state of Virginia. "Colonel Patton has my orders to send for you to assist in defeating the enemy. I order you to obey such orders as he may give you for the protection and defense of the settlers on the frontier and your compliance will be very agreeable."

A few weeks later, toward the end of July 1754, Colonel Patton and his nephew William Preston took time off from their official duties to visit one of Patton's development projects, a settlement on several thousand acres he had patented on the New River. The place was then called Draper's Meadows in honor of one of its first families, and would later be known as Blacksburg. Tired from his journey and recovering from an illness, Patton intended to spend a quiet Sunday at the home of John Draper, who along with his neighbor William Ingles was away from home. Having sent Preston off on some errand, Patton was seated at a table in the Draper house writing letters, perhaps answering some querulous missive from Dinwiddie inquiring as to why the militiamen could not dispatch their enemies in an orderly fashion. Mrs. Draper was in the front yard, and their infant son was asleep in the house. Suddenly, Mrs. Draper emitted a blood-curdling scream, ran into the house, snatched up the baby, and fled out the rear. Through the door behind her burst a party of warriors with their blood up. Patton snatched up his sword—he had laid it on the table in front of him—and cut down two attackers before others shot him down from the doorway. The raiders soon caught up with Mrs. Draper, bashed her infant's brains out, and took her away a prisoner along with the pregnant Mary Ingles and her two children from the next farm, leaving the buildings aflame.

The raid became famous as an example of the barbarity of the Indians, especially after Mrs. Ingles's daring escape from captivity and desperate overland trek back to her home (at heart-wrenching cost; her two eldest children had been taken from her, and she had to abandon her newborn baby in order to get away). Her saga did not end there. On rejoining her husband, she pleaded with him to take her east to safety, real safety, all the way over the Blue Ridge Mountains. Reluctantly, he did so, and on the day they finally departed, the family fort at which they had been staying was overrun and everyone in it killed or captured. Such stories ran among the white settlers like a flame along a fuse, igniting their gratitude for having been spared and their fear of being next. Long after the war was over, such stories of brutal, pitiless slaughter of innocents by heathen red men comforted the victors in the rightness of their cause and the appropriateness of their victory.

Less well known, then and now, were such stories as one set down by James Gilmer, a grandchild of Thomas Lewis, as having happened the previous year, in June of 1754. A dozen warriors returning from a southward foray into Cherokee or Catawba country stopped at John Lewis's place at Staunton, where they were observed by some of Lewis's neighbors "whose families or friends had suffered from attacks of the Indians." If the story puts the correct date on these events—a year before Braddock's defeat—such suffering could not have been very great. The aggrieved neighbors made a great show of hospitality, killing a beef for roasting, lighting a great fire, handing out whiskey, and urging the visitors to perform their sacred dances, described in the story as "their antics." Amicable and rowdy, the party lasted late into the night, whereupon the warriors resumed their journey just long enough to find a barn in which they could take shelter for the night. "As soon as they were sound asleep," James Gilmer recorded many years later, "the whites were upon them with their knives, axes and guns. Only one escaped." Whether or not the story is dated correctly (and such can never be assumed with full confidence when elderly men set down stories about their grandfathers), it made Gilmer think that the barbarity that descended on the western frontier in 1755 was not entirely to be blamed on French incitement of their native allies: "For that night's doings many Virginia wives were made widows, and mothers childless."

Gilmer added to his tale a poignant footnote regarding the cost of brutality to its practitioners. The killers had acted, they thought, on behalf of their community and their race, yet what they did put them beyond the pale of both. "All fled to some distant part of the extended frontier of the colonies," Gilmer wrote, "except one by the name of King, who lived a skulking life for a long time, always keeping his gun near him." Gilmer sketched the pathetic figure lurking outside the old Augusta church during services where, "seated upon the sill of the door with his inseparable companion, the rifle, in his hand, he listened to the words of the preacher, so necessary to the comfort of the Irish spirit, whether Protestant or Catholic. He was suffered to work out his own punishment, avoiding all men, and avoided by all."

Whatever the precise causes of the slaughter, the months after Braddock's 1755 defeat saw enough of it to keep the settlers and their would-be defenders in a constant state of apprehension. In addition to the death of Patton and the capture of Mrs. Draper and Mrs. Ingles, several settlers were killed in a raid on the Greenbrier River settlements in late August and a militiaman was killed and scalped on the Cowpasture River in early October. These incursions caused Dinwiddie intense irritation ("It's a great surprise your militia should be silent and not more active to repel these miscreants," the governor complained), but against such occasional and widely separated strikes, scattered knots of angry armed men had no hope of being effective, either in preventing the strikes or in punishing the perpetrators.

Dinwiddie and Washington piled more responsibility on Andrew Lewis, Dinwiddie rather perfunctorily observing that in the absence of James Patton, Lewis was to command the Augusta militia (doing without the customary rank of lieutenant colonel; Dinwiddie failed to mention any commission) in addition to his company of the Virginia Regiment. Simultaneously, Washington promoted him to major of the regiment (while raising Adam Stephen to lieutenant colonel) and ordered him to turn his company over to Captain Peter Hogg and go to Fredericksburg to train new companies of recruits. "I know your diligence and punctuality require little spur," Washington wrote Lewis, "yet this is an affair that calls for the greatest dispatch." How he was to simultaneously command the defense of Augusta by the militia and train recruits in Fredericksburg, no one explained.

Similar frustrations besieged Adam Stephen, operating out of Fort Cumberland. He and Washington thought the Indian attacks were the beginning of the French invasion, and in October Washington urgently summoned every militiaman under his orders, including Andrew Lewis with his recruits from Fredericksburg, to march with him to "repel those barbarous and insolent invaders of our country." By October 14 Washington, Lewis, and Stephen were ready to head out from Winchester, but when Washington gave the order to march he was dumbfounded to be told that despite the emergency, as he later reported, all but two dozen men "absolutely refused to stir, choosing as they say to die with their wives and families." After three days of threatening and cajoling, he had enough men willing to go, but found they did not have enough equipment and supplies for the mission. When after a few more days they had gathered the necessary supplies, there were not enough horses and wagons to carry them. Fortunately, the invasion never materialized. By the time the men of the Virginia Regiment reinforced Fort Cumberland it was November, and there was nothing for them to do but bury a few mutilated bodies, gather some corn from deserted homesteads, and organize their garrison.

Governor Dinwiddie and his fellow land speculators were finding that despite the depredations against frontier families, almost no one in British America shared their enthusiasm for carrying the battle to the Ohio Country. The other colonies, almost without exception, refused to help. His own House of Burgesses balked at paying for the war effort; the first paltry sum they had approved was merely an authorization to borrow; the second was a loan, to be repaid from the proceeds of a specific tax; and so on. And, except on the very fringes of the frontier, the people of Virginia were massively indifferent to the attempts of the speculators to raise war fever. They resisted recruitment and ignored appeals for horses, wagons, and supplies—to the profound frustration of the hawks. Even in the Shenandoah, where people were anything but indifferent to the threat of attack, they wanted to preserve, protect, and defend their homes, not the colony or England or the Ohio Country. Irate farmers swore out two arrest warrants charging Washington with stealing wagons he appropriated for military use (one of the warrants was returned by the sheriff, not served, he scrawled across its back, because "the within-named George Washington would not be taken. He kept me off by force of arms.") George Fairfax, incredulous that his appeals for military servitude should be ignored, drafted thirty Fairfax County men, then arrested and imprisoned them when they refused to obey. They all escaped.

Governor Dinwiddie, while complaining voluminously of these difficulties, remained at the same time dismissive of them. About some settlers who had fled their Augusta County homes in fear, Dinwiddie wrote, "I wish they had not been seized with such panic as prevented their resisting the few enemies that appeared in your country." Dinwiddie wrote the sentence to James Patton, before receiving news of Patton's death at the hands of his "few enemies." Nor did Dinwiddie allow the realities of the frontier to interfere with his grand strategies. In December of 1755 he ordered Washington to send either Andrew Lewis or Adam Stephen west with a force to destroy a Shawnee village and French trading post on the Ohio River north of its confluence with the Kanawha River. No experienced woodsman would willingly embark on such an expedition in the dead of winter, when the raw weather meant constant worries about shelter and fire, and the lack of forage for the horses and scarcity of game for the men made hunger a constant threat. Washington, unlike Dinwiddie, was learning, and expressed mild objections to the scheme: "I am apprehensive [it] will prove abortive as we are told that those Indians are removed up the river into the neighborhood of Duquesne." But he had already ordered Andrew Lewis to proceed.

Characteristically, Andrew Lewis kept to himself whatever he thought about the wisdom of the orders, and obeyed them. By February 13 he had assembled on the New River at Fort Frederick five companies of militia, numbering about two hundred men. Major Lewis reviewed them, the Reverend Mr. Craig favored them with a martial sermon, and, accompanied by a war party of one hundred thirty Cherokees led by a war chief called Outracité, they marched on February 18. Their intended route to the Ohio River extended across more than two hundred fifty miles of wilderness. They planned to march west a hundred miles or so to strike the serpentine Sandy Creek, then follow it as it became the Big Sandy River and eventually drained into the Ohio. Their supplies consisted of flour, carried by packhorses, and a single wagonload of dried beef.

William Preston was a captain of one of the companies and kept a journal of their progress. He recorded that they reached the head of Sandy Creek on February 28, "where we met with great trouble and fatigue, occasioned by heavy rain, and driving our baggage horses down said creek, which we crossed 20 times that evening." The next day, in order to progress fifteen miles, they had to cross the creek sixty-six times.

Provisions had already run low. On March 2, Preston wrote, they were put on half rations, "each man had but half pound of flour and no meat but what we could kill and that was very scarce." The first crisis came on Sunday, March 7. "The men were faint and weak with hunger," wrote Preston, "and could not travel the mountains and wade the river as formerly, there was no game in the mountains, nor appearance of level country, and their half pound of flour would not support them, and that would soon be gone, and they intended to leave next morning and go home. I proposed to kill the horses to eat, which they refused. They said that might do to support them if they were on the way home, but it was not a diet proper to sustain men on a long march against the enemy. They finally agreed to make one more trial down the river."

And a trial it was: "Proceeded down the river about 3 miles," Preston recorded, "where the mountain closed so nigh the water that we could not pass: went up a branch, crossed a very high mountain, and down another branch to the river, where we met a party of men who had been at the river and could not get down any further." Lewis and the Cherokees lashed together some makeshift canoes with which to try to travel by water. On March 12, "Major Lewis's canoe was sunk in the river," and he and two officers "had to swim for their lives: they lost every thing of value, particularly 5 or 6 guns."

His expedition at the crisis point, Andrew Lewis faced an ultimate test of his leadership. His force was riven by the old animosities rooted in the Lewis-Patton schism; William Preston had been Patton's chief lieutenant, although his regard for Lewis was increasing daily. Others were more like Peter Hogg, a particularly virulent member of the Patton faction, who had pushed his dislike for all things Lewis, and his personal ambition, to the point of mutiny in trying to discredit Lewis and supplant him on this mission. Such discord did nothing for the morale or the resolve of the men, which Lewis now attempted to stiffen by doing something he hated to do; he made a speech.

Lewis was a man of action, not a public speaker. Grave of demeanor and reserved in manner, he was what admirers would call imperturbable and detractors would describe as remote. "In person upwards of six feet high, of uncommon strength and agility, and his form of the most exact symmetry that I ever beheld in human being," a cousin who served with him, Captain John Stuart of Greenbrier County, would write later, "he had a stern and invincible countenance, and was of a reserved and distant deportment, which rendered his presence more awful [meaning awesome] than engaging."

Lewis tried to engage his men with a direct, impassioned appeal. They would soon find better hunting, he said, and in the meantime their horses would feed them adequately. Their duty called them. He stepped forward a few yards, turned, and called dramatically on all who would serve their country and share his fate to step forward. About two hundred men turned around and headed for home. The officers, and perhaps two dozen privates, most of them his relatives, stepped forward. Outracité was willing to continue ("The white men could not bear hunger like the Indians," he would observe later), but the Sandy Creek Expedition was over.

Now the challenge was to get home alive. Not everyone did; many of the men, apparently thinking they would have better luck hunting away from a large body (and no doubt thinking they would have better eating if they did not have to share what they managed to kill), struck off on their own and were not heard from again. In the second week of their two-week return voyage, the men who had stayed with the main party came upon some buffalo hides they had left at the site of a kill on the way out, sliced the hides into narrow strips (tugs, as they were called then), and ate them, bequeathing a name to the Tug River (along today's Virginia-Kentucky border). On the last few days of their odyssey, they were boiling and eating the strings from their moccasins, the belts of their hunting shirts, and slices from the flaps of their ammunition pouches. As the nineteenth-century historian Charles Campbell observed, "the art of extracting nutriment from such articles is now lost."

By this time the sparks struck at Jumonville Glen and Fort Necessity, falling on the dry tinder of Anglo-French animosity, had sent flames around the world, becoming in Europe the Seven Years War and in Asia the Third Carnatic War. After Braddock's defeat, the action in the North American theater, where it was called the French and Indian War, shifted northward to Canada and New England, where it became a struggle for control of the Great Lakes and the St. Lawrence River. The government in London managed to alienate its own subjects in America by heavy-handedly demanding that they pay for their own defense, by insisting that they quarter British regular troops in their homes, and by sending a succession of commanders and governors whose self-regard was better developed than any of their abilities. The Ohio Country was remembered only by the partners in the Virginia land companies.

In the Shenandoah Valley, the pattern set in the fall of 1755 held for three years. Between April and October of each year, small bands of warriors from the Ohio Country, often accompanied by a French or Canadian officer, struck at various isolated settlements, while Washington and his chief lieutenants Andrew Lewis and Adam Stephen marched hither and yon, building forts and abandoning forts, seeking recruits and chasing deserters, dealing with panicky settlers and demoralized militiamen, without ever engaging the enemy (except for one or two occasions when the enemy chose to attack some outpost or patrol). During the four years of the French and Indian War, in all of Augusta County, William Preston would count a total of 298 people killed, wounded, or captured by Indians. From November until March, nothing much would happen, as the warriors who had been raiding all summer instead of hunting had to rely on the French for their winter supplies, and stayed close to Fort Duquesne. Catching on to this rhythm, the settlers gathered in community forts in the summer and during the winter months returned to their homesteads to repair and maintain them. A few, assuming that the first winter weather meant winter had arrived, moved back to their homes prematurely and were attacked by warriors who waited out the first blusters and struck when fair weather returned, as they knew from long experience it would. That time of year would be known thereafter as Indian Summer.

Andrew Lewis spent much of 1756 extending the string of useless western forts southward into North Carolina and trying to recruit Cherokee warriors there to the English cause, without notable success. Adam Stephen spent the year at Fort Cumberland, while Washington tried to get Governor Dinwiddie to resolve a central dilemma; was Washington to use his manpower to man the defensive forts or to try to protect the inhabitants where they lived? He could not do both. He did not know which to do, but was clear on one thing: Fort Cumberland was too far west to be maintained and should be abandoned. Dinwiddie did not know which to do either, and kept trying to insist on a little of both, but was absolutely clear on one thing: Fort Cumberland, key to the plans of the Ohio Company, was not to be abandoned. But Dinwiddie, now sixty-three, was being worn down by the war he had so avidly sought, was plagued by frequent illnesses, was giving up on his dream of a splendid retirement as lord of an Ohio manor, and was talking despondently of returning to England.

Through 1757 nothing broke the sorry pattern of the war in Virginia, although change came to London at midyear when William Pitt came to power as secretary of state for war and foreign affairs. Impatient with the lackluster conduct of the war thus far, Pitt ordered the French Empire attacked everywhere at once, and that included the Ohio Country. Commanders who did not deliver results were quickly replaced, and thus a newly minted brigadier named John Forbes, a fifty-year-old Scot who had been trained as a physician and had been serving as colonel of a regular regiment of foot, was appointed to command of the southern district of the American theater. It was no doubt with great relief that John Blair, of the Blair Company, read to the rest of the governor's council the dispatch from Pitt saying that Forbes would soon arrive and was under orders to move against Fort Duquesne.

It had not been looking good for the land speculators until that point. Robert Dinwiddie had left Virginia forever in January of 1758 and was replaced as governor by Francis Fauquier, who like Pitt and Forbes was, above all else, a competent, no-nonsense administrator. Intelligent, fair, and equable, Fauquier would be remembered as the best-liked royal governor Virginia ever had. But as he had no land interests in the West, and consequently never considered using the powers of his office to benefit the land speculators, it seems likely they did not share in the general good feeling about Fauquier. In fact, it seems likely they were in profound depression until Pitt, for other reasons, sent Forbes to reclaim their Ohio lands.

Avidly, Virginia prepared to do its part in the campaign to end the war. Having learned that trying to recruit soldiers for indefinite service by appealing to their patriotism did not work, the assembly authorized a fat bounty of £10 to anyone who would sign up for duty until the first of December. The terms were attractive enough to double the manpower of the Virginia Regiment to nearly two thousand men. With Washington in overall command, the government created a second regiment and put it under a Tuckahoe— William Byrd III, of Westover, on the Tidewater James River. In the late summer of 1758, Washington assembled both Virginia Regiments at Fort Cumberland (where Byrd immediately fell ill).

Soon after his arrival in Philadelphia to assume his command, Forbes likewise was stricken with an illness that would prove to be mortal, and was seldom well enough to travel with his advance. There was nothing wrong with his mind, however, and for execution of his plans he relied on Colonel Henry Bouquet, a thirty-nine-year-old Swiss officer whose pudgy form and amiable manner belied his keen mind and steely resolve.

Oddly, one of the earliest and thorniest challenges to Forbes and Bouquet came from Washington. Forbes and Bouquet, professional soldiers intent on getting their military job done, attended first to logistics. The situation, in their view, was straightforward: their supplies would come by ship to Philadelphia and then would be hauled by wagon to their army, whose objective was due west of the city. They would use the good existing roads that led from Philadelphia west to Carlisle, they would improve the next seventy-five miles of fair roads to Raystown and then build a road to Fort Duquesne from there. Compared with the road Braddock had built, this route was shorter, easier to defend, and offered much more forage for horses and many more sources of water for men and animals.

Washington was horrified, and resisted this plan to the point of mutiny, for reasons that mystified his military superiors but not his fellow land speculators. Although not a member of the Ohio Company as his half-brother Lawrence had been, Washington had caught the fever. The first land he had bought in his own name was his so-called Bullskin plantation (near present-day Charles Town, West Virginia) on which he never intended to live but from which he intended to profit. It was squarely astride Braddock's Road to the west, which everyone understood would be the primary commercial corridor to the Ohio Country as soon as the war was over. Moreover, that river of commerce would flow directly through the county that had just elected Washington as its representative in the general assembly. Now General Forbes was proposing to build a better, shorter road that would take that commerce through Pennsylvania, away from Washington's property, away from Winchester, and away from the Ohio Company's beloved Fort Cumberland. On this issue Washington, who for the entire war thus far had been a shameless toady to any superior who might conceivably put him in the way of a commission in the regular British army, turned mulish and confrontational.

"All the letters I receive from Virginia," Colonel Bouquet complained to Forbes in the summer of 1758, "are filled with nothing but the impossibility of finding a passage across Laurel Hill, and the ease of going by Braddock's Road. This is a matter of politics between one province and another." Washington protested, in a letter to Bouquet, that he "cannot be supposed to have any private interest" in the matter. Yet on a related issue, writing to fellow land speculator John Robinson, Washington declared that he ought to be listened to, not just because he was a military officer, but also because he was "a man who has property in the country and is unwilling to lose it."

While Washington was banging heads with his superiors over the road issue, he raised another: that of uniforms. In this case, he was tentative and respectful. At Fort Cumberland he was unable to get the coats and buckles and hose and wigs and shoes and straps and buttons required to properly outfit an English soldier. Washington and the Virginia riflemen had learned years ago the many advantages for forest travel and fighting of what they called "Indian" dress: a thigh-length hunting shirt, leggings, and moccasins, with a shot pouch and powder horn on a shoulder strap and a tomahawk and knife on a belt. "Were I left to pursue my own inclinations," he said obliquely in a letter to Bouquet, "I would not only order the men to adopt the Indian dress but cause the officers to do it also. 'Tis an unbecoming dress for an officer," he hastened to add, careful lest he was addressing another English martinet, "but convenience rather than show should be consulted."

In the matter of both the road west and the dress code, Andrew Lewis played a pivotal role. Early in July, Bouquet called on Washington for a detachment to act as an escort for some operations as the army assembled at Raystown. Washington detailed Lewis to take two hundred Virginians to Bouquet, and when they arrived at Raystown on July 10 they created a sensation. These were elite wilderness rangers, hardened by three years of travail, in superb physical condition, completely at home in the woods. General Braddock would have been offended by their casual, Indian-style dress, even more by their insolent, independent manner. But Henry Bouquet was no Braddock; he saw a tough and effective strike force, marvelously suited to the task at hand. "Major Lewis arrived here last night," a British officer recorded. "Colonel Bouquet is mightily pleased with their dress." The wearing of "Indian" dress was approved forthwith.

That Andrew Lewis made a fine impression on the command was confirmed by Adam Stephen's peevishness about it. "I received no orders about the new coats Major Lewis brought with him," he wrote Washington from Raystown with heavy sarcasm, "but I imagine you will have all your regiment dress or undress in the same manner." He whose officer's coat had carried such importance at Fort Necessity soon saw his entire regiment, officers included, authorized and encouraged by General Forbes's orders to dress like Indians. Washington responded smugly to Stephen: "It gives me great pleasure to see this dress, or undress as you justly remark, so pleasing to Colonel Bouquet and that I seem to have anticipated the General's orders." So there.

Although Bouquet for the moment remained coy about what he wanted Andrew Lewis's men to do, it was in fact road building, across Laurel Hill, the mountain barrier to the army's westward progress from Raystown. Bouquet was not yet sure it could be done, and would not rule out using Braddock's Road, as Washington was insisting, until he saw how the work progressed. A few days later

Colonel Bouquet rode up the mountain to find out. To his aston-
ishment and pleasure, he wrote General Forbes, he "found a road
where a six-horse carriage could be taken without difficulty. The
gap is improved and I have seen 20 loaded wagons go up there
without doubling. I have given Major Lewis and Sir Allen MacLean
[probably one of the regular engineers] the thanks which they
deserved for this work." Equally as impressive to Bouquet, the Virginia officers "have kept the troops in a good humor. Everyone is
contented, and believes himself immortalized by having worked to
open this route."

On August 3 Bouquet wrote Washington that the decision was
final. The army would proceed through Pennsylvania (along a route
that would be known to succeeding generations as the National
Road, U.S. Route 40, and Interstate 76).

The main body of the ten-thousand-man army moved out labor-
iously in the last week of August. With a camp and depot securely
fortified at Raystown, a detachment marched about forty miles to
set up the next base at a place called Loyalhannon, beyond Laurel
Hill and about thirty miles from Fort Duquesne. On September 7
Bouquet and most of the remaining troops departed Raystown for
Loyalhannon, now to be known as Fort Ligonier.

While his army was assembling there for the final leg of its
ponderous advance on Fort Duquesne, Forbes authorized a reconnaissance to determine the strength of the enemy. The leader of this
mission was self-selected; Major James Grant of the 77th Highland
Regiment had advocated the mission avidly until Bouquet and
Forbes agreed. Major Grant assembled a substantial force for a scouting mission: 400 regulars and 400 provincials, and the 175 men of
the Virginia Regiment under the command of Andrew Lewis, who
became Grant's second in command despite the fact that Lewis had
gone on record as opposing the whole idea. He had no objection to
a reconnaissance, that is what his men did best, but Major Grant
kept talking about attacking the Indians near Duquesne if the opportunity presented itself. Bouquet was worried about Grant's inten-

tions also, but after instructing him firmly on his limited objective, approved the plan. The force marched on September 9, approaching Fort Duquesne on September 13.

When Major Grant's scouts told him he was within ten miles of Duquesne, he halted his men and issued orders. They confirmed that what Grant had in mind was no reconnaissance. He told Andrew Lewis to take two hundred provincial soldiers, advance five miles, and set up an ambush. Meanwhile Ensign Chew of the Virginia Regiment was to take a small detachment, show themselves to the defenders of the fort, and lead any pursuers into the ambush, which Grant would support with the main force. Grant was seeing himself as the conqueror of Fort Duquesne. Andrew Lewis saw him as an idiot, and began to make haste slowly.

When Grant advanced the main force at three o'clock that afternoon, proceeding four miles to be within supporting range of Lewis, he overtook Lewis, who informed him (no doubt with some satisfaction) that Duquesne was five miles farther away than Grant had thought. Lewis was not in position, and nobody knew where Chew was.

Improvising now, Grant advanced the entire force at 6 P.M. Five miles from the fort, he parked his baggage train and put it under the guard of Captain Thomas Bullett and fifty Virginians. While he was doing this, Ensign Chew and his detachment wandered in, not yet having located the fort. Seething, Grant continued his advance as darkness fell and by about 11 P.M. was within striking distance of the fort, apparently undetected. Grant had liked his original plan and was not about to give it up, even in radically changed circumstances; he ordered Lewis to take half their men, about four hundred, advance through the tangled woods in the dark, fire a volley at the Indian camps around the fort, make one bayonet charge at whatever came out to confront him, then retire, drawing the pursuers into—an ambush. How this complex plan was supposed to work in the woods, in the middle of the night, Grant did not explain, and Lewis most likely did not ask. He simply took his men, disappeared into the night for an appropriate length of time, then returned to Grant to report that it was impossible to advance in the dark. Even after this brief sojourn, lost soldiers were floundering back into ranks for the rest of the night. Disgusted by Lewis's lack of ardor, Grant sent him back to guard the baggage with Bullett—and, of course, to set up an ambush. Grant would handle personally the engaging and enticement of the enemy.

The engaging part was easy. Grant ordered his drummers to sound reveille and his pipers to hit their drones, and marched his Highlanders into the open plain in front of Duquesne. Apparently, and unaccountably, the French and Indians had been unaware until that moment of all the thrashing about in the woods outside their fortification. But now they made up for their lack of vigilance with reflexive speed; eight hundred of them boiled out of the tents and the fort and overwhelmed the astonished Grant and his Highlanders. In minutes they were nearly surrounded, taking heavy fire, dying in droves. Desperately trying to maintain order, Grant directed them to fall back on the baggage—and the ambush. But Lewis, meanwhile, concerned at the volume of firing, concluding correctly that Grant was in serious trouble, advanced to help him. There were two trails between the baggage and the front; Lewis advanced on one, Grant retreated on the other. Their detachments were separately surrounded and shot to pieces, and both officers were taken prisoner.

Captain Bullett got his baggage-guard in hand, counterattacked the advancing French and Indians, organized and covered the retreat of the remains of Grant's force, and managed to get more than five hundred of the men back to Fort Ligonier. Most of the three hundred casualties of the battle were Grant's Highlanders.

For several weeks Majors Lewis and Grant were presumed dead, until Washington received a letter from Andrew Lewis, who was by then in rather genteel confinement in Montreal. He told Washington that he was "as happy, and much more so, than I should have expected under such circumstances." For him, this war was over; he would be exchanged in December of 1759.

Soon the war was over for everyone in Virginia (although it would be another two years before the fighting ended in Canada, five years before the war ended by treaty). On November 24, as Forbes's ponderous march neared Fort Duquesne, in deteriorating weather, with one week to go until the enlistments of his provincial troops expired, his scouts sighted a massive column of smoke ahead. The French had set fire to their fort and fled the scene. Forbes marched (or rather, had himself carried) into the embers, ordered the building of a new and much larger installation, and renamed it Fort Pitt. Then he returned to Philadelphia, and died.

Chapter 8

⸻

The Indian Wars,
1759–1774

These lakes, these woods and mountains were left us by our
ancestors. They are our inheritance, and we will part with them
to no one.

—*Minavavana of the Chippewas*

THE REVEREND ANDREW BARNABY visited the German settlements in the lower Shenandoah Valley in 1759. "If there is such a
thing as happiness in this life," he wrote later, "they enjoy it. Far
from the bustle of the world, they live in the most delightful climate and richest soil imaginable; they are everywhere surrounded
with beautiful prospects and sylvan scenes, lofty mountains, trans-
parent streams, falls of water, rich valleys and majestic woods." Not
only did they live in beauty, the reverend enthused, but they did so
in good health, and without wanting more: "They are subject to
few diseases; are generally robust, and live in perfect liberty; they
are ignorant of want, and acquainted with but few vices; their inexperience of the elegancies of life precludes any regret that they possess not the means of enjoying them; but they possess what many

princes would give their dominions for—health, content and tranquility of mind."

The population of the valley, approaching twenty thousand whites and one thousand black slaves in 1760, was predominantly English and Scotch-Irish in its northern extremity (now Berkeley County), mostly German in its center (today's Frederick, Shenandoah, and Rockingham Counties) and overwhelmingly Scotch-Irish to the south (Augusta, Rockbridge, and Botetourt). Yet throughout there were substantial communities of Mennonites, Quakers, Swiss, Dutch, formerly indentured Irish Catholics, Swedes, and Welsh, accommodating each other's religions, languages, and customs in what James Ireland, a contemporary Baptist circuit rider, described wonderingly as a "common state of sociability." These people remembered, it would seem, the harsh and hopeless conditions in Europe from which they had fled, and remained grateful for the freedom to prosper that this new land offered everyone who came.

As the intermittent butcheries that had marked the four years of the French and Indian War receded into memory, refugee families returned from the eastern side of the Blue Ridge, while the families that had stayed left their communal forts and returned to their farms, whose remarkable fertility yielded up not only plenty of food for those who tilled it, but bounteous surpluses for a growing commerce with the eastern world. By 1760 commodity agriculture was well established throughout the Shenandoah Valley.

The major export crop was hemp. Next to lumber, hemp was the raw material needed most by the imperial British Royal Navy for its global fleet, whose rigging and fittings required endless miles of rope. With the bounties offered by both the royal and colonial governments, hemp was often worth as much as tobacco (in 1759 both were bringing about fifty shillings per hundred pounds). Those who insisted on trying to replicate the past by poking tobacco plants into the soil (such as, for example, George Washington at his Bullskin plantation) could not make a go of it, for all their nursing and weeding and hilling and bug-picking and swearing; tobacco did not like the valley soils and climate, and vice versa. Hemp, on the other hand, grew wild, and under cultivation without much effort the plants reached heights of fifteen feet. During the 1760s Botetourt exported as much as 170,000 pounds of hemp in one year, Augusta averaged 100,000 pounds per year, and Frederick raised around 25,000. Wheat was in second place as an export commodity, although it was the leading crop in the lower valley, where soon after peace returned, scores of mills were steadily grinding out a river of flour that flowed over the eastern mountains.

Livestock flourished, as well, on the valley's luxuriant grasslands. In one year during the Revolution the valley would furnish the Continental armies with a half-million pounds of beef. William Crow of Staunton, second husband of John Lewis's daughter Margaret Lynn, was one of the first major cattle drovers. In his drives of two-hundred-head herds to Winchester, Philadelphia, Fort Pitt, and Alexandria, Crow sometimes accumulated cattle in circumstances that were less than clear. One settler's wife was moved to testify in court that on one occasion, as it passed her husband's property, "Crow's drove increased damnable." Such was his wealth and influence that no one seemed willing to use a word like "rustler" to his face: "I never called you a thief," said one man seeking restitution, "but you took my cow."

In this fertile economic brew, people were free to pursue their interests and specialties. Towns were springing up every ten miles or so along the Valley Pike, and in each there was a profitable place for millers, smiths, the keepers of stores and inns. A few men turned to heavy industry: Isaac Zane's iron works in Frederick County produced several hundred tons of metal a year, sold mostly as plows, cooking utensils, and stoves; Adam Stephen opened a gunnery in northern Frederick (later Berkeley) County that was soon turning out ten to twelve muskets a week. There was even a nascent tourist industry, with people traveling great distances to take the warm and beneficial waters at Bath and Seven Fountains in Frederick County and at Hot Springs and Warm Springs in Augusta County.

All of these activities required market roads, and there was great interest in and activism on behalf of building more and better roads. Almost without exception, the roads wanted and built ran east from the Shenandoah Valley to the markets and ports of Alexandria, Fredericksburg, Williamsburg, and Richmond. There were no markets in the West, and hence little interest in it. Certainly there was no desire, on the part of the busy, flourishing population of the valley, with their blessings of "health, content and tranquility of mind," to reopen the struggle with the western tribes that had brought such gruesome suffering to their homes in the four years just past. Yet within fifteen years they would be embroiled in, and expected to fight, not one but two wars with the tribes, both brought down on them by the frenetic activities of the land speculators in the Ohio Country.

Whatever satisfaction John Lewis may have taken from the knowledge that he had recovered his life and those of his family from disaster, had prevailed in an alien place, and had established a secure and prosperous foundation for his four sons, two daughters, and a growing tribe of grandchildren; whatever goad of ambition he still felt that twitched him to grasp for more western lands, for wealth beyond earthly needs, all became irrelevant when on February 1, 1762, he departed life at the age of eighty-four years. They laid him to rest on a hillside overlooking Bellefonte, under a chiseled slab recalling that he "slew the Irish Lord, settled Augusta County, located the town of Staunton" and that he was remembered as "a brave man, a true patriot and a friend of liberty throughout the world."

Not long after the departure of the French from Fort Duquesne, the surveyors and scouts of the land companies returned to the Ohio Country to perfect their claims and plans, and their numbers increased with every season that passed without hostilities. The attitude of the big thinkers was expressed by a Boston lawyer, James Otis: "The heathen are driven out and the Canadians conquered. British dominion now extends from sea to sea and from the great rivers to the ends of the earth. What God in his Providence has united let no man dare to put asunder." As usual, the heathen— who had not been driven anywhere—were invisible to the white men and were outside the providence of the white men's God.

Throughout the war just ended, the strategy of the Iroquois League had been to maintain a precarious diplomatic balance that would allow them to be on the side of whoever won, and they did not care which side that would be. Tactically, their participation had been as scouts and as conductors of lightning raids, most of them on civilian homes and isolated outposts, intended to inflict a maximum of pain and terror with a minimum of effort and casualties. This was not just a plan to fit the situation, this was the way they had always fought; there was no counterpart in native history for the massed formations and protracted sieges that characterized white warfare of the time.

Now, however, tribal leaders began to come to grips with a new set of realizations: that whatever the outcome of the disputes the whites had with each other, they intended to press westward; that where the whites lived, no tribe could remain; and that no tribe, indeed not even the Iroquois League, had the numbers or organization successfully to resist this rising white tide.

The first tribal leader to express these ideas in the form of a new strategy was a leader of the Ottawas, then living near Detroit, called Pontiac. He, along with most of the Algonquin-speaking tribes of the western Great Lakes area, had been steadfast in his hatred of the English and his friendship for the French; he had personally led his warriors at Braddock's Defeat. With the Iroquois power now divided between the Onandaga Council and the western Mingos, the Algonquins, despite the defeat of their French allies, had the numerical advantage in the area south of the Great Lakes that was now becoming the focus for expansion of English trade. And the

Algonquin tribes were determined to resist the expansion; when the first Englishmen reached Fort Michilimackinac, a Chippewa chief named Minavavana confronted him. "Englishman, although you have conquered the French, you have not yet conquered us! We are not your slaves. These lakes, these woods and mountains were left us by our ancestors. They are our inheritance, and we will part with them to no one."

It was Pontiac of the Ottawas, however, who forged the attitude expressed by Minavavana, along with the numerical advantage of the tribes, into an extraordinary strategic vision that transcended centuries of tradition to propose an alliance of scores of disparate tribes to conduct lengthy, coordinated military operations over an immense territory. As Pontiac traveled from council fire to council fire, urging Wyandots, Chippewas, Potawotamies, Delawares, Mingos, Senecas, and Shawnees to set aside their traditional independence and act in concert, he was helped immeasurably by the avid return of white land speculators to the Ohio Country and by the arrogance of the new commander of British forces in America, General Jeffrey Amherst.

Baron Amherst had presided over the successful sieges of Louisbourg, Fort Ticonderoga, Crown Point, and Montreal. A grateful king had made him governor-general of British North America. Nobility and success, perhaps, had made the baron insensitive to lesser mortals. He withheld permission for trade in powder and lead with the tribes, friends and former foes alike, until they were facing starvation. He quickly hanged any warrior accused of a transgression but neglected to prosecute even the most barbarous white crimes against the tribes. His callous behavior provided a potent, if unwitting, impetus for Pontiac's stratagem.

By May of 1763 Pontiac had put together a grand alliance of tribes from the Great Lakes through the Ohio Country to the Carolinas, focused on a strategy of unprecedented scope. They would attack simultaneously every one of the fourteen British posts along the northwestern frontier, the line anchored on the fortresses of

Mackinaw (on the northern tip of what is now Michigan), Detroit (on the western end of Lake Erie), and Fort Pitt. Pontiac unleashed the first coordinated attacks in May, and by June 22 his alliance had captured every one of the posts but four, including Pitt, against which he mounted a lengthy siege (another tactic unfamiliar to the tribes). As part of the onslaught, a band of Shawnee warriors led by a war chief named Hokoleska, known thereafter to the whites as "Cornstalk," lashed out at white settlements in the Greenbrier Country, along Jackson's River in (present-day) Bath County and into the area around Staunton in Augusta County.

The 250 men at Fort Pitt, although surrounded by increasingly hostile warriors, were not entirely cut off until late in June. Colonel Henry Bouquet, still in service to the British commander, forwarded to the post commander an idea he had cleared with General Amherst and that the post commander, Captain Simeone Ecuyer, promptly executed: to make a gift to the Delawares near the fort of a bundle of blankets deliberately infected with smallpox. When contact with the fort was lost in July, Colonel Bouquet marched 460 men west from Carlisle, Pennsylvania, along Forbes's Road to Fort Ligonier (another of the four frontier posts still in English hands). Bouquet left his wagons there and headed out with about 400 men and a train of 340 packhorses carrying their supplies, including hundreds of bags of flour.

Bouquet was familiar with the details of Braddock's defeat and had marched with Forbes when Major Grant had met disaster, and he fully expected to be attacked. Nevertheless, he left the easier going of Forbes's Road in order to strike a more direct and quicker course to Fort Pitt, one that would take him through a rocky defile along Turtle Creek near its confluence with the Monongahela River ten miles upstream from the fort. It was while avoiding this defile by fording the Monongahela itself that Braddock's army had been destroyed. And it was while approaching the spot, after a march of seventeen miles on August 4, that Bouquet was hit just as his men were preparing to make camp.

A force later estimated to be about a hundred Shawnees, Delawares, and Senecas opened sudden, vicious, and well-directed fire
on the English regulars. Although Bouquet does not seem to have
protected his march with scouts and flankers any better than Braddock had done, he was at least prepared for the attack, and he executed a fighting retreat to a low hill about a mile to his rear, where
he forted up behind stacked bags of flour. From that hill the British
fought through the night and the next day, by the end of which
Bouquet had fifty men dead, sixty wounded, and five missing. "If
we have another action," he wrote in a report to General Amherst
that evening, "we shall hardly be able to carry our wounded." In
the event, there was no more action. The discouraged attackers gave
up and left. Bouquet relieved Fort Pitt on August 10. The siege of
Detroit was lifted a few months later, and Pontiac's War was over.

Late in 1763 the Lewises and others who had fought a war to
secure the land in the Ohio Country, and whose country had just
turned back Pontiac's attempt to reclaim it, learned that their king
had given the land away to their enemies. In an attempt to bring to
an end the constant Indian irruptions in the trans-Allegheny region
and the consequent drain on the royal treasury, King George III, by
proclamation dated October 7, prohibited any and all settlement by
his subjects on any land "beyond the Heads or Sources of any of
the Rivers which fall into the Atlantic Ocean from the West and
North West, or upon any Lands whatever, which, not having been
ceded to or purchased by Us as aforesaid, are reserved to the said
Indians." Moreover, the proclamation directed anyone who had
"either willfully or inadvertently seated themselves upon any Lands
within the Countries above described, or upon any other Lands
which, not having been ceded to or purchased by Us, are still reserved to the said Indians as aforesaid, forthwith to remove themselves from such Settlements."

Everyone involved in the politics of the proclamation understood it was a stopgap measure that would eventually yield to inevitable British expansion, but for the time being all negotiations to that end were to be conducted not by colonial governors, who were always subject to the influence of their leading citizens, but by an imperial supervisor of Indian affairs—Sir William Johnson of New York. The Virginia land speculators were for the moment restrained but far from resigned. Washington called the proclamation "a temporary expedient to quiet the minds of the Indians," and went on another surveying trip along the Kanawha River.

Quieting the minds of the Indians was not a priority for most residents of the frontier. Indeed, ten years of Indian raiding had engendered among some of them a pathological hatred of all red men without regard to tribe, allegiance, or behavior. A prime example of what Benjamin Franklin would call "white savages" was a Pennsylvania gang called the Paxton Boys. Incited by Lazarus Stewart, an elder of the Paxton Presbyterian Church of present-day Harrisburg, the Paxton Boys went on a rampage in December of 1763, murdering six peaceable Indians at Conestoga and then fourteen more at Lancaster, the latter group consisting of old men, women, and children. The Paxton Boys even marched on Philadelphia, intending to dispatch a community of Christian Indians who had been taken there from Bethlehem for protection, but armed Philadelphians faced down the gang.

Their work inspired imitation in Augusta County two years later. Ten Cherokees, English allies on their way to Fort Cumberland, called on Andrew Lewis (now in rank as well as fact the colonel of the Augusta militia) in May of 1765. He acted as their host for two nights and gave them a guarantee of safe conduct to Winchester when they departed on May 7: "I had them provided with proper colors and a pass fastened on the colors," he testified later, "in order to let everybody know they were our brothers the Cherokee and to use them well and allow them to pass." But the next morning, a band of Augusta worthies ambushed the party and killed five of them. The other five vanished into the woods.

Andrew Lewis had been at war for a decade, mostly with Indians; in the course of the war had been wounded and imprisoned; and had suffered deprivation and frustration far beyond the experience of most of his contemporaries. Yet Colonel Lewis refused to practice or tolerate barbarism. He hated neither the victims nor the perpetrators of this crime, calling the latter "poor blinded creatures who have not considered that in consequence of what they have done our frontier inhabitants who are innocent of the crime may be cut to pieces by a nation of Indians who otherwise would have lived in amity with us." Ignorant or not, however, in Lewis's view they were criminals, and he set out to bring them to justice. He quickly found out that about twenty or thirty men had been involved, and he took two of them into custody on the day of the killing.

But in this the longtime defender of Augusta found himself at odds with a significant number of his neighbors. They, like many on the Pennsylvania frontier, blamed their colony's government (of which Andrew Lewis as county lieutenant was a prominent representative) for not protecting them and saw nothing wrong with the Augusta Boys' attempts to exterminate their tormentors. They rescued one of Lewis's prisoners before he could get the man to jail. Two nights later they surrounded the little Staunton jail a hundred strong, and when the terrified jailer refused them the keys they broke open the structure with axes and released the remaining prisoner. They would, the mob announced, "never suffer a man to be confined or brought to justice for killing savages."

When Colonel Lewis informed Governor Fauquier of these events, the governor shared both his fear of a Cherokee response and disgust for the Augusta Boys' actions. "If this is the conduct of your young men," Fauquier asked Lewis, "with what face can they complain of the Indians? Yet I imagine that if any Indian should appear on our frontiers, they would be among the first to call for protection."

What the malefactors did call for, by means of a proclamation posted in the county, was the imprisonment of their tormentor. "We Augusta Boys," the poster claimed, had killed not friendly Cherokees, but hostile Delawares and Shawnees who had been active in Pontiac's War. By giving these hostiles a pass, the tract continued, Colonel Lewis had shown that he "is not attached in heart to his present Majesty or his liege subjects. We therefore do promise a reward of one thousand pounds for the taking of the said Colonel Lewis, that he may be brought to justice." It was, of course, an empty threat. (The Paxton Boys heard of it, though, and sent word of their support.)

In this, too, there was a shadow of the old Patton-Lewis schism. Although most people once involved in the feud, such as William Preston, had gotten over it in the decade since James Patton's death, others had not. "I am told, and I hope I shall be able to prove," Andrew Lewis wrote Governor Fauquier, "that Peter Hogg" (he of the Patton faction, of the near mutiny on the Sandy Creek expedition, whose performance as a captain during the French and Indian War had drawn condemnation from all sides), who "was by the judiciousness of Governor Dinwiddie discarded and who now practices law in this county, Frederick and Hampshire, is the person who wrote this proclamation for the one or two villains who applied to him." To Lewis, such behavior was beneath contempt: "A man who will for fifteen shillings in an underhanded manner, join the Banditti in mockery and disrespect to Your Honor's Proclamation, for the sake of making himself popular with the disaffected . . . ought not to pass unpunished."

Whether or not the ugly reaction to his rectitude was a factor, Andrew Lewis soon moved away from Staunton. It was also, probably, a matter of family geography; his brother William had inherited the home place at Staunton, Thomas was established at Lynnwood to the northeast, and Charles had a place to the west on the Cowpasture River. After 1765 Andrew began acquiring land and preparing a new home on the Roanoke River, where the town of Salem would later be established. In 1769, when the new county of Botetourt was formed, Andrew was named one of its first justices, and in 1772 he was elected its representative in the House of Burgesses.

During the middle part of the 1760s, Britain and her American colonies struggled to come to grips with the aftermath of the French and Indian War. Land speculation in the Ohio Country was crippled, but not forgotten, or even abandoned after the Proclamation of 1763 and the continuing difficulties with the Indian residents. The land speculators of Virginia and Pennsylvania (and the colonial governments they influenced) continued to maneuver for eventual advantage in the area. But the home government could not be as easily manipulated in this regard as before, when opposing the French could be relied on to stir British blood, because the crown was now preoccupied by the crushing debt incurred in the late war. Britain's national debt had doubled. With what seemed to them to be eminent reasonableness, the ministers in London looked for ways the colonies could help pay the annual interest, which was running in the millions of pounds, and indeed help retire the debt, which after all had been incurred in the defense and protection of the colonies. Responsible people in the colonies did not disagree with this idea, and were prepared to ask their legislatures to take steps to accomplish it.

London saw no reason to wait. They were colonies, after all, over which the king had absolute authority. The king had protected them and now the bill was due. A review of the situation revealed a number of taxes and duties that had been on the books for years but had not been collected with sufficient enthusiasm. To these, the parliament added in 1765 something called the Stamp Act. No tax measure could have been designed to be more intrusive into the lives of more people; it provided that henceforward every legal paper— every deed, certificate, commission, degree, will, bond, pleading of any kind in any court, bill of lading, even the pages of a newspaper— must carry a stamp indicating that a tax had been paid in cash. The passage of this odious act, with an effective date of November 1, 1765, ignited a firestorm of opposition in the colonies, most notably in Virginia, so fierce that London was forced to back away from implementing it.

The sputtering dreams of the western land speculators did not flame anew until November of 1768, when Sir William Johnson convened the largest conference of colonial authorities and Iroquois leaders ever held on the frontier. More than three thousand Iroquois gathered at Fort Stanwix, in New York's Mohawk Valley, and Andrew Lewis was there as a representative of Virginia. The colonies were there to acquire the Ohio Country, the Proclamation of 1763 notwithstanding, and of course when the conference was over the English participants declared victory. They had "bought" the Ohio Country yet again from the Iroquois League, with the minor concession of promising to stay south of the Ohio. In this proceeding, the permanent boundary between the two races was not to be the crest of the Alleghenies as King George had decreed, but the meandering Ohio River. The problem soon emerged, predictably, that whatever deal had been struck at Fort Stanwix had not had the participation of the Mingos, Delawares, and Shawnees who actually occupied the ground concerned.

In 1772 a new governor arrived to take charge of the Virginia colony: John Murray, Earl of Dunmore. Dunmore's father had fought with the Highlanders against the troops of King George II at Culloden in 1745 and for his treason had spent the rest of his life in prison. The son, however, was a member of the House of Lords and an avid and loyal supporter of the crown. Dunmore was imperious in manner and rapacious by habit, on fire to make a name and a fortune.

The first session of the elected assembly over which Dunmore presided was a workmanlike one during which not many feathers were

ruffled. A great many road projects, many with a westward compo-
nent, were considered and approved, and two more counties were
carved from Frederick County: Dunmore (later Shenandoah) in the
south and Berkeley in the north. The governor and the assembly
maintained toward each other a veneer of courtesy overlaying deep
suspicion, the assembly worried by Dunmore's aristocratic attitude
and the governor leery of the assembly's seditious tendencies. For a
time the assembly avoided giving him direct affront, and he avoided
to the extent possible calling them into session. And he dismissed
them when they showed signs of veering toward disloyalty, as they did
in the spring of 1773 by creating a committee of correspondence to
coordinate with the other colonies resistance to British taxation.

As soon as he had dispensed with the burgesses, His Lordship
traveled west to Pittsburgh to have a look at the storied country
where so much could be done, and so much money made, if the
troublesome Indian question could just be settled. Dunmore invited
George Washington to travel and speculate with him, but the death
of Washington's stepdaughter intervened.

Whether by design or coincidence, Dunmore's visit to the western frontier marked a year that saw land speculation in the area
erupt with an intensity that had not been seen for a decade. The
previous summer George Rogers Clark had been out surveying tracts
for award to veterans of the French and Indian War. But in this
busy year there was activity from the future state of Kentucky in the
south to the Great Lakes in the north, all the way to the Mississippi
River in the west. Daniel Boone from North Carolina, James Harrod
from the Monongahela, and a man named McAfee from Andrew
Lewis's Botetourt County were laying out potential farms and
towns as fast as they could work in what was to become Kentucky.
Agents of the new Vandalia Company, whose founders included
Benjamin Franklin, were at work throughout the future state of
West Virginia, which, unaccountably, the Privy Council in London
that year granted to them, ignoring Virginia's claim to the region.
In the area around Fort Pitt, Captain Thomas Bullett and a party of

royal surveyors were surveying for Dunmore at the falls of the Ohio and surveyors led by William Preston and John Floyd were working on behalf of Washington, Andrew Lewis, Patrick Henry, and others. Farther west on the Illinois River and the Mississippi, one William Murray, a relative of Dunmore, was dealing for large acreages with the Illinois tribes on behalf of his Illinois Land Company and the affiliated but carefully separate Wabash Land Company, whose principal owner was none other than Dunmore (who forwarded the application of the Illinois Company to London with a bare-faced avowal that he had no personal interest in said application).

The old Ohio Company was still in play, although it had been merged into the Walpole Company; its affairs were represented by the veteran George Croghan, who was in residence at Fort Pitt, but who no longer had as an active partner the governor of Virginia. Apparently, this company had shifted its strategy from land acquisition to the fur trade, as was characteristic of most of the Pennsylvania agents in the Ohio Country; Croghan was desperately trying to assuage the wounded feelings of the tribes in the area, and indeed in 1774 some eleven hundred Indians were in camp near Fort Pitt to see him.

Not surprisingly, this tidal wave of surveyors and speculators— although not yet more than a few dozen actual settlers—raised profound alarm among the again-besieged tribes living in the area. In June the principal Shawnee war chief Hokoleska, or Cornstalk, confronted the Bullett party as it approached the Shawnee town called Chillicothe, on the Scioto River some eighty miles north of its confluence with the Ohio. Hokoleska told Bullett to stop the surveying, which he understood was "designed to deprive us of the hunting of the country, as usual." In October Shawnees attacked Boone's party in the Kentucky country and killed most of them, including his seventeen-year-old son.

In addition to the always-present threat of retaliation by the tribes, the surveyors were distracted by a welter of competitive situations. Those surveying land for awarding to veterans were up against those intent on private profit. The many land companies were in competition with each other, sometimes for the same land, and the Virginia surveyors were at odds with those from Pennsylvania, which was vigorously contesting Virginia's claim to Fort Pitt and the Ohio Country, and who had pulled off a major invasion of Virginia's sphere of influence with the Vandalia project.

Dunmore's official purpose in visiting Fort Pitt was to establish the supremacy in the area of Virginia over Pennsylvania and of England over the native inhabitants. At the same time, he was looking out for his own investment in the region, the existence of which lends clarity to what later became confused in history—Lord Dunmore's subsequent activities and their motivations. His principal move was to place in command of his and Virginia's interests on site one Dr. John Connolly. Although a Pennsylvanian, from Lancaster, and a nephew of George Croghan, Connolly was able immediately to ally with the Virginians and turn his fervid ambitions against Pennsylvanians and Indians alike.

He did so in a manner that made 1774 a memorable year. He and his fellow agents of Virginia confronted the surveyors and officials from Pennsylvania wherever they found them—driving them off, shooting at them, and on a few occasions arresting them and sending them to prison in Staunton or Williamsburg. In January he ordered some henchmen to open fire on a peaceable delegation of Shawnees who were bringing in some fur traders for a conference with Croghan at Fort Pitt. As spring approached, its new growth offering sustenance for long-range travel and cover for fighting, it seemed likely that the tribes would be responding to such unprovoked violence, as well as to the frequent brushes with surveyors throughout the region. The idea of gaining advantage in a squabble at home by finding a common enemy abroad was already well worn, and in April Connolly sent to all the people he knew a circular letter declaring that a state of war with the savages was imminent, that they would no doubt strike as soon as the season permitted, and that all whites in the country should prepare themselves for the onslaught.

But it was not the savages who struck first. Alarmed traders and "land jobbers" as they were called, excitedly reported such incidents as the stealing of some horses from a surveying party on the Ohio (a rumor later determined to be unfounded) and came in from the country, to fort up. The most secure place other than Fort Pitt itself was a new and substantial fort being built under orders from Lord Dunmore at the confluence of Wheeling Creek and the Ohio about fifty miles west of Fort Pitt. The area had been claimed and settled in 1769 by Colonel Ebenezer Zane and his two brothers, who had relocated there from the South Branch of the Potomac. One of the land jobbers who forted up at Wheeling was Captain Michael Cresap, son of the feisty Yorkshireman who had helped organize the Ohio Company and precipitate the French and Indian War. On April 27, when it was reported that a canoe was approaching on the river, carrying two Indians, Cresap immediately proposed to go out and kill them. Colonel Zane argued heatedly that if Cresap did such a thing it would be murder, and would start a war. Nevertheless, Cresap and some fellow hotheads went up the river and after a while returned. Asked what happened to the Indians, Cresap's men said the red men had unfortunately fallen overboard. The bullet-riddled, bloodstained canoe was later found on the riverbank.

Now that the whites had given the Indians even more reason to wage war, the expectation of war increased, although there was still no evidence of hostile action. But a party of thirty-two men led by one Daniel Greathouse, in camp on the river about twenty-five miles north of Wheeling, at Yellow Creek (today Steubenville, Ohio), was suffering from the extremities of war fever when they went to the "defense" of a settler named Baker who had built a house and trading post there, and felt threatened by the presence of a Mingo camp on the other side of the river. Finding the Mingos had not attacked, Greathouse and his men decided it would be a shame to waste a war party. With his confederates hidden from view, Great-house crossed the river for a visit, thus demonstrating his convic-tion that no one was at war yet. While he was in the camp counting warriors, and coming to the conclusion there were too many to attack head on, one of the females in camp warned him, in a friendly way, that some of the braves had heard about the killings downriver and were upset. His reconnaissance finished anyway, he recrossed the river to Baker's cabin.

A short time later six Mingos—five men and a woman carrying a baby—crossed over to visit, three of the braves apparently intent on buying some rum from Baker, who was known to have it for sale. This Greathouse and his lurkers approved, and the three cus-tomers were soon enjoying Baker's product in the cabin, watched over in a friendly way by a big white man with the customary tom-ahawk in his belt. The two warriors who would not drink, and who were thus alert and armed, posed a problem that was soon solved. The vigilantes proposed a friendly contest of marksmanship, set up a target, and graciously allowed the Mingos to go first. As soon as they had fired and their guns were empty, their friendly opponents shot them down. A trader named King shot the first one, leaping forward immediately to cut the dying man's throat, crowing that it was just like dressing a deer. While the worthy in the cabin was clubbing the drunken Indians to death with his tomahawk, one of the others outside took aim at the terrified mother, fleeing toward the canoe in the river, and easily brought her down. Dying as they approached her, she desperately held out her baby to them, implor-ing them not to kill it, as it was "one of yours." Indeed, it was the child of a trader from Carlisle, one Colonel John Gibson, and was eventually returned to him, motherless.

A canoe with two Mingos aboard now approached from the camp across the river, the men calling to know what had happened, and why the gunfire. Greathouse and his boys waited until they were well within range, then shot them out of their canoe. Finally aroused, the remaining Mingos tried to mount an attack, but after losing several more men, gave it up, broke camp, and fled.

While the land jobbers were killing every Indian they saw because they feared war, the tribes were debating their course of action. George Croghan, still laboring to keep the peace, had persuaded the Iroquois and Delawares to remain passive. The Cherokees were restive but not yet hostile. Only the Shawnees and the Mingos were on the verge of taking up the war hatchet, and they were in council struggling to reach consensus on the matter at the very time the Mingo villagers were being massacred. In these deliberations the most powerful voice for war was that of Hokoleska (Cornstalk) of the Shawnees, and for peace that of Taghneghdorus (Branching Oak) of the Mingos, called Logan by the whites. Actually a principal sachem of the Cayugas now living with the western Iroquois tribes, Logan had been a lifelong friend of the whites, had tried to find ways of accommodating their insatiable land lust even after some of his family had been killed by the Conestoga Boys in Pennsylvania in 1763.

Even now, as spring took hold in 1774, he was eloquent in his advocacy of peaceful coexistence. The war hatchet had been struck into the council post by the Shawnees and many of the Mingos, but Logan told them that the Long Knives would come as numerous as the trees in the forest, that war would delay them only a short time at a great cost in lives. Peace was their only chance, said Logan, and he took the war hatchet from the council post and buried it.

His speech was barely done, the hatchet freshly buried, when messengers arrived from Yellow Creek with the fearful news. The first to die, to be bled like a deer by the man named King, had been Logan's brother. The mother who had been shot down was his sister. The town on Yellow Creek had been his town, populated with the people of his clan. Logan reached down into the ground, uncovered the war hatchet he had buried there, shook it over his head, and vowed he would kill ten white men for every relative they had killed that day. Connolly's prophecy of war would be fulfilled.

Other fires were flaring in the American colonies in the spring of 1774, but while vexing they did not distract Lord Dunmore's concentration on his mission of making the Ohio Country safe for people like himself. In the meantime it was his duty to preside over a glittering social season in Williamsburg (Lady Dunmore had decamped to the colonial capital, and there were balls after feasts after parties to be attended in her honor) and a session of the elected assembly.

This assembly was more fractious than ever. The colonies, having faced down their sovereign's government on the Stamp Act and on most of the taxes proposed in the Townshend Act, were intent now on doing the same with respect to the import tax on tea. This the royal government was determined to impose, not merely because of its desperate need for money in the aftermath of the Seven Years' War, but because it badly needed to reestablish the principle of its supremacy over its own colonies, and there were not many taxes left to save. So London held firm on the tea tax, refusing, for example, to allow the return of a shipment of tea to Boston that the colonials refused to unload. Hence the Boston Tea Party, in December of 1773, in which a band of patriotic vandals had broken the deadlock by dumping the tea overboard.

London responded by announcing that it was closing the Port of Boston, effective June 1, 1774. In May the Virginia assembly, including Andrew Lewis representing Botetourt County, approved a resolution declaring June 1 to be a day of fasting, humiliation, and prayer. Lord Dunmore immediately dismissed the legislature. Instead of going home, they reconvened themselves at the Raleigh (their favorite tavern in Williamsburg) and went further; they declared a ban on the consumption of tea and approved the creation later in the year of a Continental Congress of colonies. On this rising tide of sedition, Lord Dunmore turned his back. He had a war to fight in the Ohio Country.

As a preliminary, he sent a party of militia on a raid up the Muskingum River, to destroy the Indian town called Wakatomica and anything else they came across. While this was under way, Dunmore wrote to Andrew Lewis. "I am sorry to find there is so great a probability of your being engaged in a war with the Indians," he began, speaking of the war he had deliberately fomented. He told Lewis not "to wait any longer for them to attack you," but to raise a thousand men and march immediately to the mouth of the Kanawha River, build a fort, and harass the Indian towns in the area. There, or at some place nearby, Lord Dunmore would meet him with another thousand men raised in the northwestern counties, and together they would destroy the troublesome Indian towns on the Ohio River and its tributaries, beginning with Chillicothe on the Scioto River.

Andrew relayed the orders to his brother Charles, who was now the county lieutenant of Augusta, and his old friend William Preston, county lieutenant of Fincastle, telling them to raise the men needed and rendezvous with him at Camp Union (now Lewisburg) for an expedition to, as he phrased it, "bring our inveterate enemies to reason." Preston stated the case more baldly in his circular to raise volunteers, which was immediately successful; they were going, he wrote, to take advantage of "the opportunity we have so long wished for—this useless people may now at last be obliged to abandon their country."

This time, apparently, there were no recruiting problems. Even the private soldiers seemed to understand exactly what was at stake— one of them recorded a bit of popular doggerel in his diary as the expedition began: "The land it is good, it is just to our mind,/Each will have his part if His Lordship be kind./The Ohio once ours, we'll live at our ease,/With a bottle and glass to drink when we please."

Lewis's force assembled on time, early in September at Camp Union, and began its 160-mile march to the Ohio. Dunmore meanwhile got his men together at Fort Pitt and moved down the river.

On October 1 General Lewis reached the rendezvous and went into camp on the site of the proposed capital of the colony of Vandalia, a high promontory bounded by the Kanawha River on the south and the Ohio to the west. The heights formed a blunt wedge, its point facing west, overlooking broad flats along both rivers. A mile north of the Kanawha, a small, marshy creek flowed from the northeast into the Ohio. For its view and amenities, presumably, the place became known as Point Pleasant (see map on page 148).

Lewis was surprised that Dunmore's force had not yet arrived and frustrated as days passed with no word from his commander. He dispatched messengers up the Ohio looking for the rest of the army, and fumed. On October 9 three Indian traders came into Lewis's camp with a message from Dunmore, who had changed his plans: he now thought it better to proceed to Chillicothe by way of the Hocking River, rather than overland from Point Pleasant, and commanded Lewis to join him.

Before dawn the next morning, October 10, two men left Lewis's camp and headed up the bank of the Ohio to get some venison for their cooking pot. The going was far from easy, as Lewis's surgeon, Dr. William Campbell, recalled, through "a heavy growth of timber, with a foliage so dense as in many places to intercept, in great measure, the light of the moon and the stars. Beneath lay many trunks of fallen trees, strewed in different directions, and in many stages of decay. The whole surface of the ground was covered with a luxuriant growth of weeds, interspersed with entangling vines and creepers, and in some places with close-set thickets of spicewood or other undergrowth." They had gone about a mile when they came upon a sight that, in the early gloom and mist, must have defied belief: an enormous assembly of armed Indians who saw them, too, and opened fire. One of the men fell dead, the other ran for his life, all the way back to camp, where he blurted to Captain John Stuart that he had seen "five acres of ground covered with Indians as thick as they could stand."

> Dr. Campbell reported that Colonel Charles Lewis responded to the sudden crisis with due deliberation: he "lit his pipe," wrote Dr. Campbell, "and sent forward the first division." It was hardly a division. Lewis, unable to conceive that this was anything other than a raid, formed two columns of 150 men each to meet the enemy. Colonel William Fleming had the left, and marched along the riverbank. Colonel Lewis kept pace with him, about two hundred yards to the right, or east. They had gone "about half a mile," recalled John Todd, who was there that day, "when on a sudden the enemy lurking behind bushes and trees gave the Augusta line a heavy fire which was briskly followed by a second and third and returned again by our men with much bravery and courage . . . immediately after the fire upon the right line succeeded a heavy one on the left."

Nothing could have prepared the most experienced Indian fighters among them for the ferocity of this onslaught, because it was virtually unprecedented. Pontiac had persuaded warriors of many tribes to fight together, under orders, in a coordinated series of attacks, and to sustain sieges against forts, all tactics that were unfamiliar—indeed, distasteful—to the traditions of the tribes. But no group of warriors had ever fought a battle in the field with the planning, discipline, and skill that was being brought to bear against the Virginians.

Andrew Lewis's principal opponent was the Shawnee war chief Hokoleska, who in preparing for the fight now at hand had pulled together an alliance of Mingo, Delaware, and Wyandot warriors in addition to his own Shawnees. He had made masterful use of intelligence; he knew exactly where the two halves of the Virginia army were. Dunmore, in fact, had sent a request for a peace parley from his camp at the mouth of the Hocking, to which Cornstalk's people replied that he was away, having gone to consult with the Virginians in the south. For this "consultation," Cornstalk applied logistics in a manner uncharacteristic of his people. Using rafts prepared for the purpose, he crossed his entire force of about a thousand warriors over the Ohio to their jump-off position on the night of October 9. Now, with the battle joined, he did not leave its conduct to the individual warriors, but raced from place to place, holding them to his purpose. Survivors of the battle recalled his stentorian voice exhorting his braves: "Lie close, shoot well, be strong, and fight!"

While such supervision in battle was unusual to the point of being unprecedented behavior for a war chief, white officers were expected to give orders, and Colonels Fleming and Charles Lewis coolly deployed their men to face the unexpected severity of the onslaught. These were not British regulars, expected as at Braddock's defeat to remain in formation and take their punishment, but veteran Virginia backwoodsmen who took cover first and then fought. Not so their officers. Within minutes both colonels were severely wounded. Fleming, shot through the shoulder and the body, looked down to see a pink bulge of his own lung protruding from his chest wound. Using the one hand that would still operate, he stuffed the lung back in, while being carried from the field. Charles Lewis, likewise, got off one shot before falling with a terrible wound. Two of his men helped him back into camp, passing his brother Andrew. "I was afraid something fatal would befall you," the general said to his brother. "Fortunes of war," responded the colonel, proceeding to his tent, where he lay down and died.

Disconcerted by the loss of their officers and the sustained ferocity of the attack, the Virginians gave ground, tree by tree, until they had been driven back two hundred yards. At this point Andrew Lewis fed 250 more men into the battle, under Colonel Field, who was almost immediately killed, but whose men strengthened the line and heartened the Virginians, who now, John Todd recalled, "making a fierce onset forced the enemy from their stations and caused them to retreat by degrees about a mile." It was a hard-won mile, and at the end of it the warriors anchored themselves behind good cover along what Todd described as "a fine long ridge," and fought on. Their line extended from the Ohio on their right to a marshy creek on their left that flowed into the Kanawha; with the rivers at their back, the Virginians could not retreat, and the warriors would not. "The confused noise and wild uproar of the battle added greatly to the terror of the scene," recalled a participant. "The shouting of the whites, the continual roar of firearms, the war-whoop and dismal yelling of the Indians, sounds harsh and grating when heard separately, became by mixture and combination highly discordant and terrific."

The veterans among the Virginians must have been astonished that the enemy was sustaining its effort for so long. About one in the afternoon—after six or seven hours of continuous battle—the Virginians gained the ridge, but their enemy simply backed away and continued the fight. Now General Lewis, sensing a slacking in the enemy fire, executed a tactical move designed to press the advantage. He sent three companies out to the right with orders to move stealthily along the bottom of the creek along the east side of the battleground and attack the enemy line from its left rear. They made it into position, charged, and when the warriors saw the assault coming their resistance finally broke. By late afternoon the firing had almost completely stopped, and the Virginians were in possession of the field. During the night the warriors recrossed the river and moved away.

Both sides were stunned by the ferocity, length, and outcome of the battle. The Virginians had not imagined that any Indian force would hit such a large party of armed men so hard, or fight them so long or so effectively. "Never did the Indians stick closer to it, nor behave bolder," wrote Colonel Fleming, who survived his grievous wounds, although with one useless arm. "And let me add I believe that the Indians never had such a scourging from the English before." For their part, the Shawnees and their allies, with total surprise on their side, had expected another Braddock's defeat.

About 75 Virginians died in the fighting, or of their wounds, and another 140 were wounded, included Andrew Lewis's son John, who recovered. Another son, Samuel, fought in the battle, as did a nephew, Thomas's eldest son, John. Colonel Fleming later became a governor of Virginia; other veterans of the battle would serve as governors of Kentucky, Georgia, and the Mississippi Territory. The warriors made every effort to take their dead and wounded with them, or at least throw their dead into the river to deny the whites access to their scalps, but the Virginians counted 33 enemy bodies on the field.

For the rest of his life, despite his victory, Andrew Lewis would be dogged by allegations of cowardice at Point Pleasant. These did not then, and do not now, stand up to analysis, and must have been the product of the remaining pro-Patton, anti-Lewis Augusta Boys; there is simply no other group to which to ascribe the bitterness of the doggerel that later gained currency: "And old Andrew Lewis, in his tent he did set/With his cowards around him, alas he did sweat/His blankets spread over him, and hearing the guns roar/Saying was I at home, I would come here no more." Such criticism is typical, throughout military history, of the private soldier who is ignorant of the requirements of command and resentful of the relative safety of the commanding officer. The fact is that in large-scale battle, it is the duty of the general officer to be in a place where he can collect information, appraise the course of the battle, make tactical decisions, and execute them swiftly. That is exactly what Andrew Lewis did at Point Pleasant, in the face of not only a surprise attack but also unprecedented tactics by the enemy, up to and including the deft flanking movement that decided the outcome.

The next day General Lewis buried his dead, including his youngest brother, the only one of them to have been born in the New World and the first to lie in its soil. He built a shelter for the wounded, left a garrison to take care of them, and marched grimly to the northwest, toward Chillicothe. He and his men were on fire to finish the job they had started.

Hokoleska's warriors were also headed for Chillicothe, where their homes were for the moment, and they, too, were on fire to finish the job they had been unable to do at Point Pleasant. Hoko-leska was no hothead; several times during his exhaustive prepara-tions for giving battle at Point Pleasant he had checked with his people to see if they would not rather sue for peace. Now that they had suffered grievous losses and had been driven from the field they had expected to overrun, scouts came in to report that not only was General Lewis's force in pursuit, but Dunmore's half of the English army was headed for the Chillicothe towns. In council, the hotheads wanted to fight on, until Hokoleska posed a question heavy with irony: "Shall we first kill all our women and children and then fight until we ourselves are slain?" There was silence as the warriors con-templated reality. "No? Then I will go and make peace."

Dunmore went into camp about eight miles east of Chillicothe, accepted Hokoleska's request for a parley, and sent a message to General Lewis, ordering him to halt. Lewis ignored the orders and kept coming. Again Dunmore sent orders that he should stop, and again Lewis ignored them. When he was just three miles from Dun-more's camp, and when Hokoleska's warriors and the residents of the Chillicothe towns had grown distinctly uneasy about Lewis's intentions, Dunmore rode out to confront Lewis personally, accom-panied by one of the Shawnee sachems. It was said by many after-ward that the governor's life was in danger from the excited and vengeful men in Lewis's command, but Lewis kept them in hand, received the governor, and now accepted the orders given him in person: he was to return to Virginia and disband his army while Dunmore negotiated the peace.

With the departure of Lewis's men, Dunmore was outnumbered and surrounded, far from home. Somewhat nervously, he allowed only eighteen warriors at a time to come into his camp to negotiate the peace. One of them, of course, was Hokoleska, who was as dynamic in peace as in war; Dunmore had to listen to a ringing in-dictment of white behavior in bringing on the hostilities, Hoko-leska's powerful voice reported as audible throughout the twelve-acre camp. "I have heard the first orators in Virginia," Colonel Benjamin

Wilson of Dunmore's command recorded later, "Patrick Henry, Richard Henry Lee, but never have I heard one whose powers of delivery surpassed those of Cornstalk on that occasion."

Logan agreed to be bound by the peace, but he refused to come into Dunmore's camp. Instead he sent a speech that he had asked someone to write down for him, and that was to become famous, largely because of Thomas Jefferson's reproduction of it, as Logan's Lament: he had been, he said, an advocate for peace and a friend of the white men until the man he wrongly identified as Colonel Cresap "in cold blood and unprovoked, murdered all the relations of Logan, not even sparing the women and children. There remains not a drop of my blood in the veins of any living creature. This called on me for revenge. I have sought it; I have killed many; I have fully glutted my vengeance: for my country I rejoice at the beams of peace. But do not harbor a thought that mine is the joy of fear. Logan never felt fear. He will not turn on his heel to save his life. Who is there to mourn for Logan? No one."

The peace treaty of Camp Charlotte provided merely for the cessation of hostilities and exchange of prisoners. The land speculators would claim, of course, that it opened the Ohio Country to them, but once again their plans were about to be foiled by events. For one thing, their government had yet again given away most of this troublesome area: by the terms of the Quebec Act of 1774, everything north of the Ohio River went to the province of Quebec, which was to be ruled under the French system of laws and the established Catholic Church.

Conspiracy theories abounded, for many years afterward, about Lord Dunmore's motivation for conducting his little war. Hints, reports, portents, and quotations were produced in support of the persistent suspicion that Dunmore somehow knew the course that history was about to take and had conceived and executed a complex and devious plan to isolate and betray Andrew Lewis's army, thus destroying some of the colony's most experienced fighters and most independent thinkers; to embroil the western frontier in an

Indian war as a debilitating second front for colonial forces in the coming Revolutionary War; and/or to negotiate an alliance between the western Indians and the British with respect to the coming British-American hostilities. Never mind that some of these plots were mutually exclusive, that they required a perpetrator of supernatural prescience and ability, or that they all failed; Dunmore's supposed conniving led many to declare that the Battle of Point Pleasant was in fact the first engagement of the American Revolution. These theories were partly the product of the passions of the times and partly an effort to explain behavior that was, on its face, odd.

Yet it is easily explained. For the fact is that Lord Dunmore was not on the Ohio River in 1774 on behalf of England, or of Virginia, or with any foreknowledge of revolution. He was there to protect, preserve, and defend the land speculators of the Ohio Country. If that required the extinction of the native population, he would do it; if it could more easily be achieved with a peace, he would sign it. The job done, he headed back to Williamsburg, where problems far worse than he had yet imagined awaited him.

Chapter 9

The English War,
1774–1781

Call this war by whatever name you may, only call it not an
American rebellion; it is nothing more or less than a Scotch Irish
Presbyterian rebellion.

—Hessian captain, 1778

THE GENERAL ASSEMBLY that Lord Dunmore had high-handedly
dismissed in May of 1774 before going out west did not stop assembling in his absence. With the declared aim not of rebellion but of
conciliation, the burgesses convened meetings of the freeholders of
their counties to draft resolutions and appoint representatives to a
different kind of assembly (taking a word from the Scotch-Irish Presbyterian church organization, they called it a convention) that would
consider how to preserve the rights and liberties of British Americans. While the Tuckahoes proclaimed their loyalty to the king and
their desire to repair relations with the mother country, the western
Cohees were from the beginning more incendiary. On June 8 the
freeholders of Frederick County meeting at Winchester unanimously
approved resolutions providing for not only a committee of correspondence to coordinate protest with the other colonies, but a ban
on imports of English goods and a threat that if the king enforced

the closing of the Port of Boston, it would "have a necessary tendency to raise a civil war, thereby dissolving that union which has so long happily subsisted between the mother country and her colonies." A week later the new county of Dunmore (named in the governor's honor; it would soon be renamed Shenandoah) passed nearly identical resolutions at a meeting presided over by a martial Lutheran clergyman named Peter Muhlenberg. (Pastor Muhlenberg would earn local immortality by preaching a sermon on the text "Unto every thing there is a season," and on coming to the time for war, throwing off his vestments to reveal the uniform of a colonel of the Continental Army, which he thereafter served with distinction.)

The extralegal convention of Virginia burgesses convened in Williamsburg on August 1, 1774, while Lord Dunmore and Andrew Lewis were preparing for their western war. The convention read, privately approved, published, but did not officially vote on a fiery set of draft resolutions sent to them by a young burgess and lawyer from Albemarle County, Thomas Jefferson, who was too ill to attend. Jefferson, like the Piedmont country that was his home, was neither Tuckahoe nor Cohee, but something in between. His mother was a member of the prestigious Randolph family of the Tidewater, and Jefferson spent much of his childhood on his relative William Randolph's estate, Tuckahoe. Jefferson's father, Peter, on the other hand, was a westerner, surveyor, and would-be land speculator who was thick with the Cohees. Thomas Jefferson adopted the education, mannerisms, and taste of the Tuckahoes but his heart and mind belonged to the Cohees, and he was about to become the leading intellectual of the rebellion. He was, however, a poor speaker, but in this respect he was to get some able help from a neighbor. Not far to the east of his Albemarle estate lived another young lawyer who lacked Jefferson's family connections, wealth, formal education, and style—Jefferson thought him a bit coarse, on first meeting him— and who was not fond of reading or writing, but would give voice to the ideals he shared with Jefferson as could no one else. His name was Patrick Henry.

Among other things, Jefferson on this occasion argued that the British parliament had no right to exercise any authority over the colony of Virginia, that its misdeeds had by default reduced the colony to a state of nature in which it was free to invent its own government. The convention did not want to go that far. Instead, the delegates declared themselves alarmed by events, but still loyal subjects of the king, determined to overcome the difficulties caused by an overzealous parliament that had exceeded its constitutional powers to tax and control the colonies. Because the burgesses had been "deprived of their usual and accustomed mode of making known their grievances"—that is, because Lord Dunmore had dissolved the legislature—they resorted to other means of communication, announcing the appointment of seven representatives to a "General Congress of all the Colonies" in Philadelphia.

That meeting, known thereafter as the First Continental Congress, convened on September 5—while Andrew Lewis was gathering his army at Camp Union—and met for fifty-one days. The delegates were evenly divided between moderates who were intent on repairing relations with Britain and the more radical Patriots, as they were beginning to call themselves, with arguments crafted by Jefferson, oratory declaimed by Patrick Henry, and a block of votes reliably delivered by the Cohees of western Virginia. In the end, the Congress nervously passed a set of resolutions called the Declaration of Rights and Grievances, as drafted by the Patriots. They did not go so far as to declare, or even threaten, independence from Britain, nor did they reflect Thomas Jefferson's argument that the British Parliament had abrogated its authority over the colonies. As a demonstration of its determination, however, the Congress voted to stop the importation and consumption of "any good wares or merchandise" from Great Britain as of the first day of December. And it called for the creation of Committees of Safety in all of the colonies, to organize their armed defense.

In these meetings and procedures the Lewis family took no part. The burgesses Andrew and Charles were, of course, in the field at

Point Pleasant, from which Charles would not return, while Thomas and William were fully occupied with their affairs in Augusta County. Thomas, too nearsighted to fight Indians, had been an active surveyor in the Ohio Country for the Greenbrier and other land companies until the outbreak of the French and Indian War, and had been content for many years to serve as the county surveyor and a magistrate of Augusta County (offices he had held now for thirty years, ever since the organization of the county) and enjoy his estate, Lynnwood, at the southern foot of Massanutten Mountain. William, like Thomas a lover of books and learning, was unlike him in two respects: he had for years served actively as a captain in the Augusta militia, and he had embraced his Presbyterian religion with an ardor that prevented him from taking the oath of conformity with the established Anglican Church that was required for any public service in the colony, an oath that his father and brothers had taken cheerfully with no intention of honoring it.

But in 1775 the lives of these two brothers were transformed. They were the age their father had been at the crisis of his life, in their fifties, when confronted by tyranny in a manner that required their response. Their father, overwhelmed, had fled to a new country. The sons were far from overwhelmed and decided to make a new country where they were. Thomas became deeply involved in the preparations for the second Virginia convention, not only attending the county meeting for that purpose but being elected one of the county's two representatives to the convention. It was unprecedented, however, to find William serving on the committee that drafted the instructions for the delegation. Patriotic ardor had not overcome his religious scruples; no oath of conformity with the English church was required for this work.

When the second Virginia convention assembled in March of 1775, the still-ambivalent Tuckahoes were presented with a western Cohee delegation that was hell-bent for war. One of its first items of business was to receive a letter written and presented by Thomas Lewis, on behalf of Augusta County, expressing support and congratulations for the delegates who had served in the First Continental Congress and declaring, "May our hearts be open to receive and our arms strong to defend that liberty and freedom now being banished from its latest retreat in Europe." The western delegation solidly backed Patrick Henry and Thomas Jefferson, who were advocating calling out and arming the militia to defend Virginia against Britain.

These sentiments were too strong for many of the Tuckahoes—the Blands, Harrisons, Wythes, and others—who still prayed for reconciliation with the mother country. Their pleas for caution were answered on the second day of the session by Patrick Henry, with his famous speech concluding, "Give me liberty, or give me death." With the solid support of the western delegates, Henry carried the day, and the convention leaders appointed a committee to mobilize the military forces of Virginia. Patrick Henry was chairman, and the members included George Washington, Thomas Jefferson of the Piedmont, and three enthusiastic Cohees from beyond the mountains: Adam Stephen, Andrew Lewis, and Isaac Zane.

Now war fever took hold throughout the American colonies. On the night of April 18, the military governor of Massachusetts, General Thomas Gage, marched his troops out to arrest the leaders of that colony's defiant assembly and confiscate the arms being stockpiled by the militia. He was met the next day by the guns of Patriots (warned by Paul Revere) at Lexington and Concord, his troops driven back to Boston in confusion.

Like Gage, Lord Dunmore had been growing ever more fearful about the intentions of his fractious subjects. His imperious orders, such as the decree of March 28 that Virginia would send no delegation to the Second Continental Congress, were having less and less effect. Dunmore's disdain for colonial rowdiness turned to quaking fear of the mob. In the early morning hours of April 20, the day after the clash at Concord (although news of it could not yet have reached anyone in Virginia), Dunmore sent a party of Royal Marines to sneak into the public ammunition magazine in Williamsburg, remove the powder stored there, and take it aboard H.M.S. *Magdalen.* The mob he feared, on learning of the loss of the powder and shot considered to be the property of the people, soon surrounded his residence, its wilder members restrained only with great difficulty by the more responsible leaders from dragging Lord Dunmore out into the street. In a panic, Dunmore released and armed some Shawnee prisoners on condition they defend him, and threatened to free and arm the slaves of the colony and burn Williamsburg to the ground. For the moment, the mob backed off.

In the ensuing days, a substantial army of fourteen companies gathered outside the town, while still more excited militiamen rallied throughout the colony, threatening to join those already at the capital and seize the governor if the gunpowder were not returned. Pitched battle was averted only by the narrowest of margins, because Dunmore said he would return the powder when tempers cooled, and because Washington and others counseled that any action be delayed until the Second Continental Congress had a chance to meet and craft a plan of response. Reluctantly, and for the moment, the army backed off.

But Patrick Henry soon had second thoughts and, at a meeting of the committee of safety and the militia company for Hanover County on May 2, 1775, demanded that Virginia get either the powder back, or the money to pay for it. As usual, his passion and his oratory goaded his audience to action: they made him the captain of their company, and marched for Williamsburg. Word of the challenge spread, and other militiamen joined the Hanover Company by the hundreds. The approach of this rapidly swelling army caused panic not only in Dunmore's counsels, but among the Patriots in Williamsburg, who were afraid Henry was about to ignite a war prematurely. The Patriots sent messengers out to meet him, to ask him to hold off; he arrested the messengers and marched on. Lord Dunmore raged, sent his wife to safety on board a warship off Yorktown, denounced Patrick Henry, and then paid up. Patrick

Henry signed the receipt on May 4 for £330 for the gunpowder. Once again, battle had been narrowly averted.

The Second Continental Congress convened in Philadelphia in May of 1775. The tug-of-war continued between those who wanted to repair relations with the mother country and those who wanted to sever them. Thus while the delegates approved the so-called Olive Branch Resolution, a last-ditch appeal for a peaceful resolution (which King George refused to read), they also created a federal union, an executive council, and a Continental Army. One of Lewis's relatives and biographers, John Stuart, started a story often repeated afterward that Lewis was considered for command of the Continentals, with Washington's approval. No evidence exists to support the story, and it is contradicted by everything known about Washington and the Congress. He had spent his entire life putting himself forward for high command, and while not a voluble participant in the sessions of the Congress, he made a statement loud enough by attending them in the full-dress uniform of a colonel in the Virginia Regiment. Lewis was no doubt qualified by experience and ability for the command, but he was a Cohee, and the worthies of the Congress were having a hard enough time accepting the idea that they should be led by a man of Washington's marginal credentials as a Tuckahoe.

Indeed, Washington had competition for the job, and in a sense it came from the Shenandoah Valley. The candidate was Charles Lee, a minor British officer and dilettante who had served as a lieutenant, and then captain, during the French and Indian War, then had gone off on a series of adventures in Europe. Returning to the colonies in 1773, he became an ardent Patriot, but rebellion was a reflex of his corrosive ego, not a reflection of his convictions. Nevertheless, as a commissioned British officer with European experience who could analyze military history in several languages, and who grandly offered his genius in service to the cause, Lee bedazzled many of the leaders of the Congress. They did not, however, lose sight of the fact that their commander was going to have to inspire immediate and lasting confidence among fighting men throughout the colonies, or he would not have men to command. Only Washington, in their view, had such a reputation. Moreover, General Artemus Ward, already in the field at the head of 16,000 Continentals besieging Boston, might accept Washington as a senior officer, but there was no way he and his New Englanders would take orders from anyone but Washington.

Accordingly, the Congress on June 14 appointed Washington commander in chief and immediately thereafter commissioned Ward and Lee as major generals, with Ward the senior of the two. On confirming his appointment, Lee, although bitterly disappointed at not getting the top command, completed the purchase of an estate in the lower Shenandoah Valley, near the residences of two old friends—Horatio Gates, who had also served as a regular officer at Braddock's defeat and who would join Lee as a major general of the Continental Army, and the Patriot officer Adam Stephen. At the same time, Lee extracted a promise from the Congress to reimburse him immediately for any financial losses he might experience as a result of taking the commission. Then Lee embarked on a course of action that would make the Congress heartily sorry it had ever heard of him.

(Lee sought constantly to supplant Washington, withheld troops contrary to orders during Washington's 1776 retreat through New Jersey, stupidly got himself captured that winter and while in captivity happily advised his former British colleagues on how best they could defeat the Americans, writing a detailed plan for a British expedition into the Chesapeake, which in the event would be conducted by none other than Benedict Arnold. Remarkably, when exchanged in 1778, Lee was welcomed back by Washington and returned to command. But after an astonishingly—some would say traitorously—inept performance at the Battle of Monmouth Courthouse on June 28, a furious Washington had him arrested and tried by court martial. Lee was convicted of disobedience, misbehavior in conducting a disorderly retreat when he was supposed to be attacking, and disrespect to the commanding officer. Lee returned in disgrace to his Shenandoah Valley home, joining his neighbor Adam Stephen, sacked for being drunk at the Battle of Germantown in 1777. They soon had the company of Horatio Gates, relieved after bungling the defense of Charleston, South Carolina, in 1780. The three gathered often for dinner at Gates's home, "Traveler's Rest," near present-day Martinsburg, West Virginia, and it is said that Lee would offer a toast: "To you, General Stephen, who were drunk when you ought to be sober; to you, General Gates, who advanced when you should have retreated; and to you, General Lee, who retreated when you should have advanced.")

On the first of June 1755, Lord Dunmore, desperately trying to preserve his dignity, safety, and an appearance of normality, retrieved his wife from her sanctuary on board the man-of-war H.M.S. *Fowey* and ceremonially convened the House of Burgesses, most of whose members were also delegates to the Continental Congress, and were thus forced to choose between attending to the business of the Patriots or the business of the colony. Peyton Randolph yielded his Congressional presidency to John Hancock and returned to Williamsburg, along with Thomas Jefferson and several others. Dunmore tried to conduct business as usual. But on the night of June 5, a number of citizens seeking to replenish their ammunition, or to arm themselves, went into the public arsenal and set off a booby-trap Dunmore had ordered set; they were seriously wounded, and once again Williamsburg and environs erupted with Patriot fury. With mobs in the streets, Dunmore decamped hastily, this time joining his wife aboard the *Fowey,* sending word to the burgesses that if they wanted to do business with him, they would have to come on board. They did not.

A few days later—June 17, 1775—in Massachusetts, 1,500 Patriots occupied Bunker's and Breed's Hills overlooking Boston Harbor in an attempt to force the British to evacuate. When attacked by British regulars, in the first large-scale engagement between British and American forces, the Patriots managed to inflict an astounding 1,054 casualties on the 2,200-man British before withdrawing.

Yet despite the rising passions, despite all the alarms and rumors of war and the clamorous rhetoric of tyranny and independence, loyalty and rebellion, the potential riches of the Ohio Country were not forgotten. The delegates to the Second Continental Congress from Virginia and Pennsylvania took time from their momentous and historic business to deal with the persistent dispute between their two colonies over which was to rule over the western waters. On July 25 they signed a resolution addressed "To the inhabitants of Pennsylvania and Virginia on the west side of the Laurel Hill." It pleaded with these residents to disband the combatants, and release the prisoners taken, in their ongoing fight for the Ohio Country. This they asked in the name of the defense of "the liberties of America," until "this unfortunate dispute" between the two colonies, "which has produced much mischief and, as far as we can learn, no good, will be peaceably and constitutionally determined."

Nor did the Congress forget the threat posed by the restive tribes along the western borders, whose role in the French and Indian War was well remembered and thoroughly feared. The Congress decided it would not try to use the Indians in any conflict with England, but would strenuously try to keep them neutral. It established, on July 12, 1775, an Indian Department, whose commissioners were to "treat with the Indians in their respective departments, to preserve peace and friendship, and to prevent their taking part in the present commotions."

The land speculators of the Virginia Convention, however, had no intention of being distracted entirely from the Ohio Country. On reconvening in August, the Convention directed one Captain John Neville and a company of one hundred militiamen to take and retain possession of Fort Pitt (which was threatened far more gravely by Pennsylvanians than by Indians or the British). This was but one piece of business in a convention that was trying to come to grips with the realities of rebellion, hearing, for example, vigorous arguments from Thomas Lewis to consider not only "independence" from Britain but a subsequent "federal union." Moreover, the convention was forced to assume more and more of the everyday duties of government as they were relinquished by the governor.

Lord Dunmore in July had decamped to his country seat six miles down the James from Williamsburg and, afraid to return to the capital, did his business from a headquarters in Norfolk that was close enough to his warships that they could either defend him or evacuate him. His business there included rallying the loyalists of the Tidewater and marshaling a defensive force that included not only the British troops and ships available to him, but runaway slaves and hostage Indians. The convention took his absence from the capital as abdication and began to assume the mechanics of government. The delegates elected a committee of safety to wield executive power while the convention set policy for taxation, the collecting and disbursement of public money, and defense. They moved from passing informal resolutions for the information of the people to formal lawmaking under procedures used by the House of Burgesses. As the Congress had done, the Virginia Convention selected its top military commander with a view to his ability to raise troops, which is to say his popularity, and without much concern for military experience or ability. Thus they named Patrick Henry, whose trumpet voice could gather a mob in minutes, to command the Virginia militia.

In the fall of 1775, while Patriot armies were carrying the conflict north into Canada, assailing Montreal successfully and failing to take Quebec, while the Congress was working continuously on a plan of rebellion and a way to pay for it, while the Virginia Convention with Thomas Lewis in prominent attendance met longer and more often to deal with the legal and financial minutiae of insurrection (spending a long time wrangling over what to do about legitimizing those contentious, competitive surveys of western lands), Andrew Lewis was conspicuously absent from the swelling ranks of Virginia regiments that were preparing for the inevitable armed conflict with England. Neither he nor Stephen was considered by the convention for command of the Virginia defenses, possibly because it was assumed they would have larger duties with the Continental Army. Instead, the convention acted as the Congress had, with one eye fixed firmly on the ability of their designated military leader to recruit men into the ranks. The finalists were Hugh Mercer, a Fredericksburg physician who had served as a captain in the French and Indian War and was an active and well-connected member of the Ohio Company; and Patrick Henry, whose fervent oratory had won him such adulation that he was being pushed to the forefront not only in political but in military affairs. After three weeks of rancorous debate, in which the Tuckahoes backed the familiar and reliable Mercer while the Cohees favored the bold and popular Henry, it was Henry who eventually received a slim majority of votes despite his total lack of military knowledge or experience. Andrew Lewis flatly refused to serve under the command of a man, as he put it to Washington "who has never seen any kind of service."

Instead, in October, Andrew Lewis was sent to Fort Pitt to conclude the negotiations with the western tribes that had been started by Lord Dunmore after the Battle of Point Pleasant. In this complex business Lewis was apparently, technically, representing Dunmore as governor of the colony at a conference being conducted by Dunmore's agent John Connolly, whose ostensible purpose had always been to open the Ohio Country to white settlement. Now the competitions among several land companies, between Virginia and Pennsylvania, and between the white and red races were layered over by the additional question of whether possession of the land would be by American Patriots or Englishmen. It is unlikely that Andrew Lewis knew that while he was representing Virginia at the conference, Connolly was distributing to the various chiefs, including Hokoleska, a letter from Dunmore telling them "to rest satisfied that our foolish young men shall never be permitted to have your lands; but on the contrary the great king will protect you, and preserve you in the possession of them." This assurance from a man who had already staked out his own plantation on the Ohio River, and whose agents had platted tens of thousands of acres for their enrichment, could not have been taken seriously by its recipients, who were trying to make sense of the rapidly shifting dynamics among the various white factions. Dunmore's later efforts to raise a regiment of Delawares and Shawnees in the Ohio Country, to be dubbed "Lord Dunmore's Own Regiment of Indians," and to be marched east to help him police the colony, met with no success.

The Fort Pitt conference ended typically, without resolving anything with respect to the land, the parties agreeing only to stop killing each other for the moment. What role Andrew Lewis played in these deliberations, or what he made of them, was not recorded. But Andrew Lewis, Jr., recalled that his father came back from Fort Pitt on this occasion deeply impressed by Hokoleska, whom he had met there for the first time. This was no doubt partly the studied dispassion of the seasoned military man who felt no need to hate the enemy he was required to fight. But this ability to see the natives as human beings—even to find them interesting—set Andrew Lewis apart from many, if not most, of his Scotch-Irish kinsmen, as it had done when he tried to arrest the Augusta Boys.

Virginia's committee of safety now was suffering second thoughts about its commander in chief, Patrick Henry. By November Dunmore's increasing stridency from his Norfolk redoubt (he declared martial law, branded as traitors any men who did not rally to his defense, offered freedom to any slaves or indentured servants who joined him) as well as his frequent, destructive raids into the countryside, goaded the committee into taking action. Further motivation was no doubt provided by Washington's observation, to the president of the Continental Congress, that "the fate of America a good deal depends on his [Dunmore's] being obligated to evacuate Norfolk this winter." The Virginia Convention voted to send the militia to put an end to Dunmore's depredations, but put in command of the enterprise not Patrick Henry but William Woodford, commander of the second of the militia's two regiments. Henry wanted to go; he begged and pleaded to go, and when rebuffed he attempted to at least make Woodford report to him, but Woodford took his orders from the committee and politely but firmly declined to acknowledge Henry's rank.

Norfolk suited Dunmore's purposes well: bounded on the north and east by the Chesapeake Bay and on the south by the broad Elizabeth River, it was accessible to and defensible by his fleet of warships (see map on page 225). To eastward, meanwhile, were swampy adjuncts of the nearby Great Dismal Swamp that were difficult for ground forces to navigate. Woodford, taking the only route available to him, advanced on Norfolk from the southwest with about three hundred men, to find Dunmore defending the north end of the Great Bridge across the Elizabeth River. The Virginia militia was contemptuous of the slight fortifications on the other end of the bridge—some later referred derisively to the British stockade as a "hog-pen"—but they halted nevertheless, because their force was small and had no artillery. They built their own breastworks and awaited inspiration. Weeks passed with the antagonists staring at each other across the bridge while the committee of safety worried about the approach of winter and the additional fortifications and cannons Dunmore was deploying around his Norfolk redoubt.

It was Dunmore who ended the standoff. On learning from a servant who had deserted a Patriot master that there were only three hundred men in Woodford's command, Dunmore ordered out his entire garrison—three hundred runaway slaves he had dubbed his "Ethiopian Corps," another three hundred local loyalists that he grandly called his "Queen's Own Loyal Virginians" regiment, led by sixty British regulars under a Captain Fordyce. The regulars spearheaded the advance at dawn on December 9, 1775, bayonets fixed, confident the rabble would melt away at the fearsome sight. It was a veteran of the western campaigns, the hero of Grant's debacle at Fort Duquesne, Colonel Thomas Bullett, who discovered the threat and gave the alarm; and another, Colonel Adam Stephen, whose riflemen spearheaded the welcoming committee. The Virginians held their fire until the last possible moment, then killed or wounded every one of the British regulars, inflicting more than a hundred casualties on the attacking force and driving it back into its Norfolk fortifications without losing a man. The first armed conflict of the American Revolution in Virginia, called at the time the "Bunker Hill of the South," had ended in an unqualified Patriot victory. Lord Dunmore abandoned his fort and took up residence aboard a British warship offshore.

Patrick Henry, already incensed at being denied a role in the fighting, was beside himself when, after the battle, Woodford turned over command of the militia at Norfolk to Colonel Robert Howe, a Scotch-Irishman from North Carolina, who arrived with five hundred militiamen from that colony too late to get in on the action. But the committee, which apparently wanted Henry's name and voice but not his person at the head of their troops, gave him no satisfaction, leaving him to fume in Williamsburg while they directed affairs at Norfolk.

The momentous year of 1776 opened in Virginia with another offensive move from Lord Dunmore. Vexed by Patriots taking potshots at his ships from the Norfolk waterfront, on January 1 he sent ashore a party of sailors and marines to drive away the harassers and burn the waterfront houses to deny them their cover. Having started a few fires, they retreated to their ships, thus giving the Patriots an opportunity to limit the damage to the town. But the Virginians, having for some time despised Norfolk as a center of Tory sentiment, did nothing to stop the flames. The future justice John Marshall, then a nineteen-year-old member of the Culpeper Militia, remembered that the Patriot soldiers watched the flames spread "with great composure." They did more than watch; according to later calculations, while Dunmore's people burned 51 houses that day, the Patriots torched 863. Moreover, after consulting with the convention, they later set fire to the 400 structures still standing. "Thus was destroyed," wrote Marshall, "the most populous and flourishing town in Virginia." It was, he lamented, "one of those ill-judged measures, of which the consequences are felt long after the motives are forgotten." Andrew Lewis, alone among the delegates, had argued against this act of destruction.

Virginia had meanwhile raised six more regiments of troops, and now offered all eight, as planned, to the Continental Army. But the matter of Patrick Henry's rank remained a problem. "I think my countrymen made a capital mistake," George Washington observed, "when they took Henry out of the senate to place him in the field, and pity it is that he does not see this, and remove every difficulty by a voluntary resignation." But he did not, and so the Continental Army accepted the six new regiments, but not the two original regiments of which Henry was nominally the commander. The Virginia Convention protested this maneuver, not on behalf of Henry but on behalf of the regiments, whose pay and support they wanted the Continental Army to assume. The Continental Congress at length agreed to take the regiments, but while it commissioned Henry as colonel commanding the First Regiment, it sent a brigadier general's commission to Andrew Lewis. This was too much for Henry; he returned the Continental commission and resigned his Virginia rank. He took emotional leave of his distraught men, who thought he had been brought down by the envy of others, and returned to Hanover County, which immediately elected him to the Virginia Convention. And that convention, on approving a Constitution for Virginia in June of 1776, elected Patrick Henry its first republican governor.

While Patrick Henry's efforts were thus redirected to the political realm, General Andrew Lewis took command of Virginia's ragtag volunteer bands and began laboring to turn them into an army. He had very little time: he took command in mid-March and was required to take the field three months later.

During June Lord Dunmore, seeking a safe haven and rallying point, took his fleet of six warships mounting between ten and

The English War

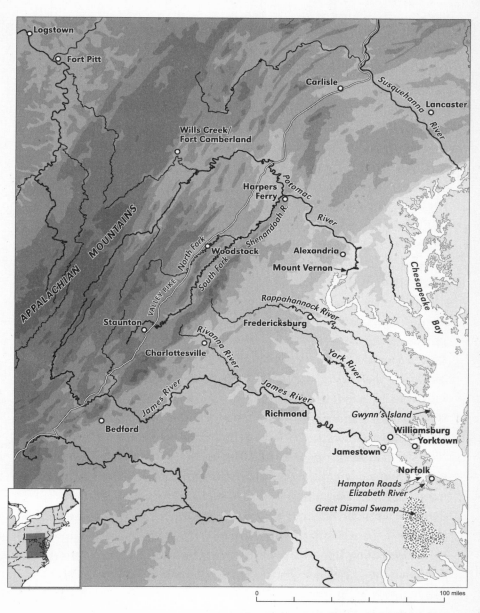

While the principal, early battles of the American Revolution were fought to the north, Virginia and the Shenandoah Valley became important as a source of manpower and materiel. General Andrew Lewis drove the last British governor from the colony and then played a critical role in securing its resources for the Continental Army.

forty-four guns each, along with more than fifty small craft and his five hundred combatants out of Hampton Roads entirely, sailed about thirty-five miles north in the Chesapeake Bay, and landed on Gwynn's Island. This was a four-mile-long spit of land off the end of the peninsula between the Rappahannock and York Rivers, separated from the mainland by as little as two hundred yards of water, which at low tide could be waded. General Lewis went after him.

> With Colonel Adam Stephen at his side, Lewis reached the mainland opposite Gwynn's Island on the evening of July 8, 1776. He deployed his batteries during the night and at first light saw that, inexplicably, Dunmore's flagship (named, of course, H.M.S. *Dunmore*) had moved into the channel between the island and the mainland, under the Patriot guns. With many of his men still out looking for rowboats and canoes with which to launch an assault on the island, Lewis took the opportunity offered and opened fire on the *Dunmore*. In minutes his guns made a dozen direct hits, shredding the cabin, killing the mate, and prompting the dismayed crew to cut the anchor cables and, with no time to raise the sails, try to tow the ship out of range with rowboats. Dunmore, wounded in the leg by a splinter, his crockery in shards around him, wailed, "Good God, that ever I should come to this!" (An echo of General Braddock's final words: "Who would have thought it?")

When H.M.S. *Otter* sailed in to try to give some cover to the fleeing *Dunmore,* Lewis's gunners pounded it until it withdrew, and then destroyed four smaller vessels in the channel. With the fleet damaged and driven out of range, Lewis turned his guns on the island, two batteries dropping converging fire on the Loyalist camp with devastating effect. It took the Virginians all day to round up the boats they needed to ferry a landing force of 250 provincials to the island, and by the time they did so the next day, Dunmore's surviving men had fled from the far side of the island onto the ships of the fleet and had sailed away. The last royal governor of Virginia had been driven from the American continent.

> Dunmore returned to England from whence, safe at last from provincials, he would rail against the American Revolution until it was over. He would be appointed governor of Bermuda in 1786 and would live, stewing in bitter aristocratic juices, to the ripe age of seventy-seven, dying in 1806.

The clearing of British forces from Virginia coincided with the approval of the Declaration of Independence by the Continental Congress and with the first major British offensive of the war—the landing of thirty thousand troops on Staten Island. Washington desperately needed reinforcements, and General Lewis's decisive victory made Virginia troops available. Lewis apparently had learned about motivating others since his disastrous appeal to his men's loyalty on the Sandy Creek expedition; he depicted the plight of Washington's army, of the country, and the glory of the fight to come in such stirring terms that the Virginia regiments almost unanimously renewed their one-year enlistments and marched north to join Washington. Andrew's brother William marched with them, a captain in the First Regiment. And prominent among them was Adam Stephen, who took a few moments to dash off a letter to Richard Henry Lee, who was meeting with the Continental Congress in Philadelphia, to express disdain for the way General Lewis had won the victory at Gwynn's Island.

Lewis wanted to accompany his men, and he pleaded to be allowed to do so. In December he uncharacteristically appealed directly to the president of the Continental Congress, John Hancock, who responded gently but firmly that Lewis was needed most as a recruiter and a defender of Virginia: "Your continuance for the present in Virginia will best promote the interest of American liberty."

In February of 1777, nearly two years after the first fighting at Lexington and Concord and one year after the creation of the Continental Army under Washington, as the struggle with England intensified, the Congress announced the promotion of those officers it deemed worthy. On the list of brigadier generals raised to major generals appeared the name of Adam Stephen (who would later be charged with being drunk during the Battle of Germantown, and relieved in disgrace), but not that of Andrew Lewis.

Lewis was stunned. The previous year, when he had been named brigadier general and ordered to straighten out the mess Virginia's volunteers were in under Henry's inexperienced management, Washington had expressed his pleasure and relief: "I always looked upon him as a man of spirit and a good officer; his experience is equal to anyone we have." When he learned that Lewis had been passed over a year later, Washington wrote to him immediately (having ignored several letters from Lewis in the interval), saying he was "much disappointed" and that he did "most sincerely wish that the neglect may not induce you to abandon the service. Let me beseech you to reflect that the period is now arrived when your most vigorous exertions are wanted."

This was a remarkable communication for several reasons, as Andrew Lewis must have understood. First, its implication that Washington had no influence over the decisions of the Congress in the matter of commissions and promotions was, to say the least, disingenuous. Second, as Lewis well knew, these words came from a man who had resigned his commission (and had threatened to do so countless times) during the worst crisis of the French and Indian War—a few months after Braddock's defeat—because in reorganizing the Virginia forces, the governor had reduced his rank. "If you think me capable of holding a commission that has neither rank nor emolument annexed to it," Washington had said hotly at the time, in response to urgings that he continue to do his duty, "you must entertain a very contemptible opinion of my weakness, and believe me to be more empty than the commission itself."

Andrew Lewis's letter of resignation to the Congress, sent only after he had raised and dispatched to Washington six more battalions of Virginia troops, made it clear that he was taking this step not just because his pride was wounded, although it most certainly was: "It would be very disagreeable to me to be considered as a person standing as a dead weight," he wrote, in a much milder tone than Washington had adopted in his earlier resignation. "I beg leave that I may be suffered to withdraw from an office to which I must be thought unequal." But beyond injuring his pride, the slight had made it impossible for him to function effectively because it altered forever the way he regarded himself and the way the men under his command would regard him: "A man who is not thought worthy of promotion ought to be suffered to withdraw as nothing can lessen a man more or take more from his usefulness than setting persons over him whom he had a right to command." Although he would not serve in the army, Lewis made it clear he was not abandoning the Revolution: "nothing shall ever be able to occasion my withdrawing my utmost exertions in defense of our glorious cause."

It is difficult to understand why the Continental Congress and military command, desperate for manpower and competent officers (the Congress was scouring Europe for them, without success), would thus spurn a man of Lewis's experience and accomplishments. Like any military commander, he had accumulated over the years the barnacles of criticism: that he should somehow have defended Augusta County better, that he should have made a success of the Sandy Creek expedition, that he should have commanded the Battle of Point Pleasant from the front lines, that he should have attacked Gwynn's Island differently. But no one had demonstrated how anyone could have defended Augusta better, made a success of the Sandy Creek expedition, improved on the Point Pleasant victory, or more quickly ejected Dunmore. "Andrew was a man of commanding person and disposition, brave and adventurous, a warm friend to those who gained his favor and haughty towards others," a relative wrote years later. "Hence although a capital officer in many respects he was generally unpopular." This might serve to explain why Lewis, at fifty-seven, was sidelined and going home in the midst of the American Revolution, except for one thing: the description applied as well to George Washington.

At about the time Andrew Lewis left Williamsburg, his old adversary Hokoleska was making a visit to the garrison of Virginia troops at Point Pleasant. His purpose was to tell the commander there, one Captain Arbuckle, about his efforts to keep his Shawnee people out of the confederation being put together by the British to fight the Americans. He did not want to fight the Long Knives, Hokoleska said, but he feared that his people would "float with the stream despite his efforts." Hokoleska's reward for this outreach was to be imprisoned, in a cabin on the fort grounds, along with his two companions, and held there through the summer while Captain Arbuckle awaited instructions, which, when they arrived, directed him to await the arrival of a superior officer.

In September 1777 Hokoleska's son, worried about the long absence of his father (the Shawnee society being patrilineal, unlike most of the neighboring tribes), came into the fort to inquire and not only found his father but was detained with him. The next day, across the river from the fort, two members of the garrison who were hunting deer were fired on by concealed Indians of unknown identity, and one of the hunters was killed. A detachment of militiamen retrieved the body and the survivor, and then stormed toward Hokoleska's cabin, white-faced with rage, weapons in hand. Captain Arbuckle tried to stop them, but they vowed they would shoot him down if he did not stand aside; believing them, he did. They burst into Hokoleska's cabin and riddled him with seven bullets, similarly dispatching his son and two companions. No military or civilian authority took any action against the murderers.

Rage and grief at the murder of their leader, more than any English military design, spurred the Shawnees to a new round of raids along the western frontier in the spring of 1778. To the defense of the settlements, Andrew Lewis, now fifty-eight years old and a veteran of a quarter century of Indian fighting, no doubt contributed advice, but not active service. The torch had passed; when Fort

Donnally, on the Greenbrier River, was attacked and in danger of being overrun in May, it was Andrew's son Samuel who led a rescue mission from Camp Union.

Amid these renewed hostilities, Governor Henry assigned Andrew and his brother Thomas a daunting task: to go to Pittsburgh and persuade the Delawares to allow the passage of a Continental Army through their Ohio River territory for the purpose of attacking the English at Detroit. The Lewis brothers won this concession, which in the event was not used. In addition, they agreed to a proposal made by the Delawares that raised a tantalizing prospect: a commitment to consider the formation of a state, administered by a confederation of tribes convened by the Delawares, to become one of the United States with representation in Congress. But the prospect that the *Lenni Lenape,* the Original People who remembered how their ancestors had come to the land ten thousand years before, might take their place as an equal participant in the United States of America, quickly evaporated. Instead, relations between the tribes and the people now becoming known as Americans would be characterized by what had happened to Hokoleska the previous September, at Point Pleasant. One hundred years later, almost to the day, the Lakota (Sioux) leader Crazy Horse would die in almost identical circumstances.

In 1781 the war came to Virginia, which until then had been a provider of men and supplies for use in other theaters. It was brought by Benedict Arnold, who had been passed over for promotion to major general at the same time as had Andrew Lewis, had acquiesced to Washington's pleading that he remain in the service, and had subsequently turned traitor. He led a British force up the James as the year began, ransacking from Hampton Roads to Richmond, to which the Virginia government had moved to be safe from such raids. The feeble Virginia militia, stripped of its manpower to supply the Continental line, was unable to interfere with Arnold, as it was helpless before the advance of General Charles Cornwallis's army from the south. In response to Governor Jefferson's increasingly frantic pleas,

Washington sent reinforcements: twelve hundred New England and New Jersey troops under the command of one of his staff officers, Major General Gilbert du Montier, Marquis de Lafayette. Although Lafayette was only twenty-four years old (Cornwallis would contemptuously refer to him as "the boy"), he came from a military family, had studied at the military academy in Versailles, and had served as a captain of French cavalry at the age of sixteen.

By now the British had three thousand regular troops based at Portsmouth, from which they probed up the Potomac River, briefly occupying Alexandria and accepting a ransom to leave Washington's beloved Mount Vernon untouched. Then, in April, they once again advanced up the James River, as Cornwallis approached from the south. In May the two forces united, their combined manpower about seven thousand, in front of which Lafayette maneuvered with perhaps three thousand men, two-thirds of them the dregs of the militia. He was, he reported to Washington, "not strong enough even to get beaten." Jefferson and the general assembly relocated to Charlottesville, where the assembly convened on May 28.

On June 3 Cornwallis ordered Colonel Banastre Tarleton to take 250 mounted infantry and dragoons on a secret overnight raid westward to see if they could capture Jefferson and the government of Virginia. As the troopers clanked along the main road from Louisa into Albemarle County late that night, they passed the Cuckoo Tavern. On this mild spring night, a beefy captain of the militia named Jack Jouett was sleeping on the tavern's lawn. Awakened by the clatter, Jouett knew immediately what the riders were after. He saddled up and set off on a wild, forty-mile overnight ride along side roads, back roads, and no roads at all (to the end of his life he bore scars on his face from being lashed by branches that night) to try to beat Tarleton to Charlottesville. It was a close thing; as Jefferson was fleeing from Monticello, Tarleton's men were ascending the slopes of his little mountain.

All but seven of the legislators escaped, and convened on June 7 in the Episcopal Church in Staunton, fearful that Tarleton would keep coming. They were without a governor; Jefferson's term had expired on June 2, and he had seen no need to follow the government west, for which he was suspected of cowardice. William Fleming, who with Andrew Lewis was a member of the governor's council, served as governor until a successor could be chosen. Meanwhile, the old men and boys still at home who were capable of military service were rallied to meet the British advance. William Campbell, grandson of one of the original Irish Tract settlers, would lead them. Andrew's son Samuel Lewis, now a colonel of the militia, galloped up to his uncle William Lewis's house in Staunton late one night shortly thereafter (William had been captured at the siege of Charleston, along with most of the Virginia Continental line, and was a prisoner for the duration). "Where are the boys, Aunt?" called Samuel, referring probably to William's sons Alexander, eighteen, and William, fifteen. She told him they were asleep. "Call them up, Tarleton is coming."

In fact, Tarleton was not coming. It was worse than that. Tarleton had retired, but only to join Cornwallis and the British infantry, and they were all coming, inching their way up the Rivanna River toward Charlottesville. Lafayette managed to get in front of them, about ten miles east of Charlottesville, but with an inferior force. On June 10 General Anthony Wayne (with William Lewis's son Thomas serving as a major on his staff) joined Lafayette with eight hundred reinforcements from the Continental Army, bringing the opposing forces into approximate parity. But the arrival two days later of William Campbell with six hundred militiamen—who had been rousted from their western county homes at the gallop by Samuel Lewis and others—disheartened Cornwallis, who there began a retreat that ended at Yorktown, and surrender, in October.

The whereabouts and activities of Andrew Lewis during these stirring events are not known. In mid-September he was back in Richmond at a meeting of the governor's council, at the behest of the new governor, Thomas Nelson. Lewis began to feel ill, from what William Preston described as a "bilious fever," and he decided to go home. But when he reached Bedford, with twenty miles to go, he was unable to continue, and was put to bed in the home of a Captain Talbot. A messenger was sent to his home, and his old friend and doctor William Fleming responded along with Andrew's sons Thomas and Andrew. They hurried to Talbot's, Preston wrote, "and found him speechless and in the agonies of death a few hours before he breathed his last."

It was September 26, 1781. On October 19, at Yorktown, General Cornwallis surrendered his army to General Washington. (Among those who watched the seven thousand British prisoners march out of their fortifications was fourteen-year-old Ensign Thomas Lewis, Jr.) The independence of the United States of America had been won.

———

Andrew Lewis was buried on a hill overlooking the curve of the Roanoke River, near the commodious Botetourt County home where he had spent so little time in the ten years since it had been built. Part of the two-thousand-acre estate was soon sold to Nathaniel Burwell, and in 1800 more of it was sold off to provide land for a town to be called Salem. The house burned to the ground and was not replaced. The town boomed after the Civil War, doubling its population in the first nine months of 1890 as promoters advertised it as the "Switzerland of the South." In 1897 Andrew's body was moved to East Hill Cemetery in the town, making way for a sprawling industrial district. Meanwhile, back in Staunton, the stone house where Andrew and Elizabeth had lived for twenty years, where all of their seven children had been born, was obliterated. Few physical traces remained of the dispensable man of the American Revolution.

Of the three sons of John Lewis alive when the Revolution began, two served in the Continental Army and one in the political leadership of Virginia. Ten of his grandsons saw service, eight of them as officers. After the war, the grandchildren, eventually numbering 43, and about 220 great-grandchildren, began dispersing across the new country.

The landmongers and the frontiersmen had fought the French and won, fought the Indians and won, now had defeated the British and were starting their own country, and still they could not close the big deals they had been pursuing for four decades. As the British government repeatedly had snatched the Ohio Country from corporate hands, giving it to the Indians, then to the province of Quebec, so now the new national government of the United States imposed its will. Mired in debt, the new government saw the Ohio Country as a source of wealth for itself. As soon as the 1783 Treaty of Paris with Britain conveyed ownership of the territory, the Confederation Congress required the existing states, including Virginia, to relinquish their claims to the West in favor of the national government. The Congress then divided the area north and west of the Ohio River, all the way to the Mississippi, into ten territories, each a grid of six-mile by six-mile townships. Five square miles, or sections, of each township were reserved; one for a school and four for land bounties owed Revolutionary soldiers. The other thirty-one sections were for sale for a minimum of one dollar per acre. There would be no Vandalia (although its agents had struggled to keep the deal alive throughout the Revolution), no Ohio Company or Loyal Company empire established by Virginians.

There would be another century of difficulty in forcing the resident natives, whether tribes or pre-Revolutionary settlers, into or out of the neat grids of the new maps. But within a year after the procedures were made final by the Land Ordinance of 1787, a large tract of land was sold to, and a substantial settlement started by, a group of Massachusetts businessmen calling themselves the Ohio Company Associates. They started a town called Marietta and in just fifteen years appended to the United States of America the first post-Revolutionary state—Ohio.

History had moved west from Shenandoah, but it was still about the land.

Journal

—

The Legacy

After the American Revolution, the Scotch-Irish for all practical purposes ceased to be the Scotch-Irish. They were prominent among the tide of settlers heading west from Shenandoah, of course, because they had long experience on the frontier and because so many of them were, as veterans of the Revolution, entitled to free western land. But they traveled as Virginians, Pennsylvanians, and North Carolinians who easily became Kentuckians, Georgians, Missourians, and Texans. They mingled freely with their fellow pioneers, whether Germans or English, Quaker or Catholic, and never again sought to establish enclaves of their own kind to the exclusion of others. Before and more completely than any other ethnic group, they became unhyphenated Americans. Yet their contributions were massive, and are, with some effort, identifiable.

Descendants of John Lewis became mayors and governors, legislators (legendary Speaker of the House of Representatives Nicholas Longworth was a descendant of William Lewis; governor and U.S. Senator Charles Robb of Virginia descended from Thomas), soldiers in every American war, and explorers of new frontiers—the first American to walk in space, Edward H. White II, was a descendant of Andrew.

Scotch-Irish songs and stories were the raw material for what became American country music, and many of their expressions became part of the American language. Because of their allegiance while in Ulster to the Protestant William, Prince of Orange, the Scotch-Irish carried various appellations with them as memorials of that great conflict. Two of them became iconic in Appalachia: "Billy Boys," as they were known in Ulster, was transmuted to "hillbillies" in America; and the habit of the Presbyterian Covenanters of wearing a red scarf earned them the name "rednecks." A descendant of Andrew Lewis married Samuel Augustus Maverick, the largest landowner in Texas in the mid-nineteenth century whose lust for land made him inattentive to his cattle, contributing his name to the language as a word denoting an unbranded stray. His grandson Maury Maverick was a prominent New Deal congressman in the 1930s who gave the word maverick political expression and invented another word for bureaucratic jargon: gobbledygook.

Many people of Scotch-Irish heritage have become famous, not as Scotch-Irish, but for their achievements. Here is a gallery, by no means complete, of the more prominent among them.

- Music: Burl Ives, Reba McEntire, Dolly Parton, Elvis Presley
- Films: Walter, John, and Anjelica Huston; Robert Mitchum; Elizabeth Taylor; John Wayne
- Finance: J. P. Getty, Andrew Mellon, John D. Rockefeller
- Technology: Thomas Edison, Cyrus McCormick (who invented the mechanical reaper, and transformed agriculture in the Shenandoah Valley)
- Art and Letters: Annie Dillard, Washington Irving, David McCullough, Margaret Mitchell, Edgar Allan Poe, Jackson Pollock, John Steinbeck, Mark Twain, Thomas Wolfe
- Television: Johnny Carson, Fred Rogers
- Sports: Jack Dempsey, Arnold Palmer

- Government: Jefferson Davis, Sam Houston, Andrew Jackson, Richard Nixon, Theodore Roosevelt, Adlai Stevenson, Woodrow Wilson
- Explorers: Daniel Boone, George Rogers Clark, David (Davey) Crockett
- Civil War generals: Ulysses S. Grant, Thomas J. "Stonewall" Jackson, George B. McClellan, J.E.B. Stuart
- Civil Rights: Rosa Parks (yes, that Rosa Parks; she was the granddaughter of a Scotch-Irish indentured servant); Lola Maverick Lloyd, a founder (with Jane Addams) in 1915 of the Women's International League for Peace and Freedom and a driving force in the National Woman's Party, which won the vote for women in 1920

This catalog of Scotch-Irish achievements is submitted with no claim of determinism; these people and ideas did not succeed *because* they were Scotch-Irish in origin, rather they succeeded *and* they are Scotch-Irish. No doubt anyone who wanted to do the work could compile a list, for example, of Scotch-Irish serial killers. A list of the contributions made to America during three centuries by any other ethnic group would be equally impressive.

The problem is the extent to which the Scotch-Irish have been forgotten, and have forgotten themselves. There is a profound difference between sailing turbulent seas before a hard wind alone and traveling in the company of a vast fleet with long experience of troubled waters—even when the other ships are mostly hidden from our view.

———

During the decades that this story has beguiled me and the Shenandoah Valley has claimed me, my life has been transformed from that of a rootless nomad to that of an awed participant in a vast and magnificent story that did not begin with me and will not end with me, but to which I am bound by myriad living sinews. I live now with many ghosts. When I encounter them in the places where they lived, or they come to me where I live, they offer counsel and commentary like some Greek chorus expounding on the events of a play. Like the living members of a family, they are not always right and can often be irritating, but their perspectives shine light into places that I alone would never see.

These visitors are not limited to those with whom I share a blood connection. In fact, I do not know for sure, as this is written, whether I am directly descended from the Lewises of this story. It does not matter. I am connected to them, I bear their name and receive their legacy whether or not one of them specifically begat one of mine. I am likewise connected with the First People; I see their shadows along the primeval waters and think often of the song of their lives and how it contrasts with mine.

I am grateful for the fact that my grown children have not joined any new migration in search of gratification, but are building their lives here in the Shenandoah Valley, and feel rooted in and nourished by this place. As for me, every molecule of my physical being is made of Shenandoah water, earth, and air; every thought I have is framed by these old mountains and watered by this ancient river; and my spirit seems to have lost the knack of feeling elation anywhere but here. I regret that this is not the place of my parents or grandparents, that it is not shared by uncles and aunts and cousins-once-removed, but this family has sent down a taproot into the ground once more, and is better for it.

I have presumed to present here these personal reflections as an invitation to join me in connecting with the past, so that our history—including the troublesome, contradictory, embarrassing, and forgotten parts of it—can function in the present. Awareness of the past does not simplify life, but enriches it; does not solve problems, but gives us many more places to stand while we are taking their measure.

When we are connected with our heritage, we are not easily misled about the nature of the world. Thus, for example, when desperate natives of other lands attack us, and politicians bellow that such a thing has never happened to Americans before, we remember the hundreds and thousands of American pioneers who died in their homes and fields at the hands of desperate natives, and we marvel at what can be forgotten. When our leaders urge us to send our children to war in a distant place to prevent some future harm, we remember the governors Dinwiddie and Dunmore, and how they got their wars, and why. When we are urged to revile the people of a country, a race, or a religion because they have harmed us, we think of Andrew Lewis insisting, at the price of the goodwill of his neighbors, on holding out dignity and justice to a race of people with whom he spent most of his life at war.

And when I see the land around me being ravaged to satisfy unquenchable greed, I reflect that this, too, is part of my heritage, a practice of which my ancestors would heartily approve. Knowing when they were wrong is as important as honoring them for what they achieved. Cultural amnesia is not cured by remembering only the good parts of the story.

Bibliography

In the slender literature of the Scotch-Irish, James Leyburn's *The Scotch-Irish: A Social History* (see complete citation below) stands as the definitive work. Scholarly and objective, it is at the same time a good read. Henry Jones Ford's 1915 book *The Scotch-Irish in America* is wide in scope and useful, but dated. Wayland Dunaway has added rich detail, with the focus on Pennsylvania, with his excellent *The Scotch-Irish of Colonial Pennsylvania*.

The written history of the Shenandoah Valley rests on the twin pillars of Samuel Kercheval and John W. Wayland. Kercheval published his works in the mid-nineteenth century, Wayland in early twentieth. While invaluable for preserving a large quantity of valley lore, and as precious as they are to genealogists and researchers of structures, their works consist in the main of anecdotes collected from "respectable" elders, all accepted at face value. Their books suffer from a distressing lack of organization and verification, but are useful as raw material. Julia Davis wrote a poetic book in 1945 for an "American Rivers" series—*The Shenandoah*—that gives a nice overview of the sweep of Shenandoah Valley history, notwithstanding some flights of romantic fancy, most especially in its embroidery of the John Lewis story.

Two books have come to hand that have as their focus the Lewises of Augusta County. *The Family of John Lewis, Pioneer* contains genealogical data compiled by Irvin Frazier and a historical text written by Mark W. Cowell Jr., the whole edited by Lewis Fisher, all Lewis descendants. Although it is primarily an exhaustive genealogy, the introductory chapters by Cowell offer a reliable basic history of the family. Patricia Givens Johnson's biography of Andrew Lewis, *General Andrew Lewis of Roanoke and Greenbriar,* is very well done and deserves a much larger audience than its limited printing can reach. Beware of the much-circulated "Common-Place

Book of Me," printed in a North Carolina magazine in 1869 and purporting to be a diary kept by Margaret Lynn Lewis: It is bogus.

A word about the Internet: Although one must guard against genealogical and ideological gibberish, an ever-increasing number of primary-source documents and serious manuscripts are available on the Web. I have recently been surprised by the high-quality material a search engine can produce in response to a query. Given the evanescence of Web sites, it would not be useful to print a list of current resources here, but I want to acknowledge my indebtedness to the libraries and private collectors around the world who are electronically publishing important documents.

Abbot, W. W., ed. *The Papers of George Washington,* Colonial Series, Vols. I–V. Charlottesville: University Press of Virginia, 1983.

Alden, John R. *Robert Dinwiddie, Servant of the Crown.* Williamsburg, Virginia: Colonial Williamsburg Foundation, 1973.

Ambler, Charles H. *George Washington and the West.* (Reprint) New York: Russell and Russell, 1971.

Aquila, Richard. *The Iroquois Restoration: Iroquois Diplomacy on the Colonial Frontier, 1701–1754.* Detroit: Wayne State University Press, 1983.

————— . "The Iroquois as 'Geographic' Middlemen: A Research Note." *Indiana Magazine of History* 1984 80(1): 51–60.

Bailey, Kenneth P. *Christopher Gist: Colonial Frontiersman, Explorer, and Indian Agent.* Hamden, Connecticut: Shoe String Press, 1976.

Baker-Crothers, Hayes. *Virginia and the French and Indian War.* Chicago: University of Chicago Press, 1928.

Boucher, John N. *History of Westmoreland County Volume I.* New York: The Lewis Publishing Company, 1906.

Brown, Stuart E. Jr. *Virginia Baron: The Story of Thomas 6th Lord Fairfax.* Berryville, Virginia: Chesapeake Book Company, 1965.

Campbell, Charles. *History of the Colony and Ancient Dominion of Virginia.* (Reprint) Spartanburg, South Carolina: The Reprint Company, 1965.

Chalkley, Judge Lyman. "Before the Gates of the Wilderness Road." *Virginia Historical Magazine* 30: 190.

Cleland, Hugh. *George Washington in the Ohio Valley.* Pittsburgh: University of Pittsburgh Press, 1955.

Colden, Cadwallader. *The History of the Five Indian Nations.* Ithaca, New York: Cornell University Press, 1964.

Cooper, Jerry. *The Militia and the National Guard Since Colonial Times.* Westport, Connecticut: Greenwood Press, 1993.

Craven, Wesley Frank. "Indian Policy in Early Virginia." *William and Mary Quarterly,* Third Series, 1(1): 65–76.

Darlington, Mary C., ed. *History of Colonel Henry Bouquet and the Western Frontiers of Pennsylvania.* Pittsburgh: University of Pittsburgh Press, 1920.

Darlington, William M. *Christopher Gist's Journals: with Historical, Geographical and Ethnological Notes.* Pittsburgh: J. R. Weldin & Co., 1893.

Davis, Julia. *The Shenandoah.* New York: Farrar & Rhinehart, Inc., 1945.

Downes, Randolph C. *Council Fires on the Upper Ohio: A Narrative of Indian Affairs in the Upper Ohio Valley until 1795.* Pittsburgh: University of Pittsburgh Press, 1969.

Dunaway, Wayland F. *The Scotch-Irish of Colonial Pennsylvania.* Baltimore: Genealogical Publishing Company, 1981.

Every, Dale Van. *Forth to the Wilderness: The First American Frontier 1754–1774.* New York: Mentor Books, 1962.

Ferling, John. "Soldiers for Virginia: Who Served in the French and Indian War?" *Virginia Magazine of History and Biography* 1986 94(3): 307–328.

Fisher, Lewis F., ed. *The Family of John Lewis, Pioneer.* San Antonio, Texas: Fisher Publications, Inc., 1985.

Fitzpatrick, John C., ed. *The Writings of George Washington.* Washington: United States Government Printing Office, 1931.

———. *The Diaries of George Washington 1748–1799* Vol. I. New York: Houghton Mifflin Company, 1925.

Flexner, James T. *George Washington.* 4 vols. Boston: Little, Brown, 1965–1972.

———. *Lord of the Mohawks: A Biography of Sir William Johnson.* (rev. ed.) New York: Little, Brown, 1979.

Foote, Rev. William Henry. "Cornstalk, the Shawanee Chief," *The Southern Literary Messenger* 16(9): 533–540.

Ford, Henry Jones. *The Scotch-Irish in America.* Princeton, New Jersey: Princeton University Press, 1915.

Freeman, Douglas Southall. *George Washington: A Biography.* Vols. 1–2. New York: Charles Scribner's Sons, 1948.

Friedenberg, Daniel M. *Life, Liberty and the Pursuit of Land.* Buffalo, New York: Prometheus Books, 1992.

Gardner, William M. *Lost Arrowheads and Broken Pottery: Traces of Indians in the Shenandoah Valley.* Front Royal, Virginia: Thunderbird Publications, 1986.

Gipson, Lawrence Henry. *The British Empire Before the American Revolution.* Vol. IV. New York: Knopf, 1939.

Gist, Christopher. *Christopher Gist's Journals.* Wm. Darlington, ed. Cleveland, Ohio: Arthur H. Clark & Co., 1893.

Graymont, Barbara. *The Iroquois in the American Revolution.* Syracuse, New York: Syracuse University Press, 1972.

Greene, Jack P. "The Seven Years' War and the American Revolution: The Causal Relationship Reconsidered." *Journal of Imperial and Commonwealth History* (Great Britain) 1980 8(2): 85–105.

Greiert, Steven G. "The Board of Trade and Defense of the Ohio Valley, 1748–1753." *Western Pennsylvania Historical Magazine* 1981 64(1): 1–32.

Guy, Louis L., Jr., "Norfolk's Worst Nightmare." *The Norfolk Historical Society Courier,* Spring/Summer 2000.

Gwathmey, John H. *Twelve Virginia Counties: Where the Western Migration Began.* (Reprint) Baltimore: Genealogical Publishing Co., Inc., 1981.

Hamilton, Charles, ed. *Braddock's Defeat.* Norman: University of Oklahoma Press, 1959.

Hanna, Charles A. *The Wilderness Trail: Or, The Ventures and Adventures of the Pennsylvania Traders on the Allegheny Path, etc.* 2 vols. New York: G. P. Putnam's Sons, 1911.

Hart, Freeman H. *The Valley of Virginia in the American Revolution 1763–1789.* New York: Russell & Russell, 1971.

Heckewelder, John. *A Narrative of the Mission of the United Brethren Among the Delaware and Mohegan Indians, from Its Commencement, in the Year 1740, to the Close of the Year 1808.* Philadelphia: McCarty & Davis, 1820. Reprinted 1971 by Arno Press.

Henderson, Archibald. *The Conquest of the Old Southwest.* (Reprint) Spartanburg, South Carolina: The Reprint Company, 1974.

Hofstra, Warren R. *A Separate Place: The Formation of Clarke County, Virginia.* White Post, Virginia: The Clarke County Sesquicentennial Committee, 1986.

Holiday, Carl. *Woman's Life in Colonial Days.* Williamstown, Massachusetts: Corner House Publishers, 1982.

Hough, Walter F. *Braddock's Road Through the Virginia Colony.* Winchester, Virginia: Winchester–Frederick County Historical Society, 1970.

Howard, James H. *Shawnee!: The Ceremonialism of a Native Indian Tribe and Its Cultural Background.* Athens: Ohio University Press, 1981.

Jacobs, Wilbur R., ed. *The Appalachian Indian Frontier: The Edmond Atkin Report and Plan of 1755.* Lincoln: University of Nebraska Press, 1967.

James, Alfred Proctor. *The Ohio Company: Its Inner History.* Pittsburgh: University of Pittsburgh Press, 1959.

Jennings, Francis. *Empire of Fortune: Crowns, Colonies, & Tribes in the Seven Years War in America.* New York: W. W. Norton, 1988.

Jennings, Francis, et al., eds. *The History and Culture of Iroquois Diplomacy: An Interdisciplinary Guide to the Treaties of the Six Nations and Their League.* Syracuse, New York: Syracuse University Press, 1983.

Johnson, Patricia Givens. *General Andrew Lewis of Roanoke and Greenbriar.* Christiansburg, Virginia: Patricia Givens Johnson, 1980.

——————. *James Patton and the Appalachian Colonists.* Verona, Virginia: McClure Press, 1973.

Johnston, David E. *A History of the Middle New River Settlements and Contiguous Territory.* (Reprint) Radford, Virginia: Commonwealth Press, 1969.

Journals of the Continental Congress, 1774–1789, Vol I. Washington: Library of Congress, 1904.

Kemper, Charles E., ed. "The Early Westward Movement of Virginia, 1722–1734." *Virginia Magazine of History and Biography,* 9(2): 113–174.

Kent, Donald H. *The French Invasion of Western Pennsylvania.* Harrisburg: Pennsylvania Historical and Museum Commission, 1954.

Kercheval, Samuel. *A History of the Valley of Virginia.* Harrisonburg, Virginia: C. J. Carrier Company, 1981.

Knollenberg, Bernhard. *George Washington: The Virginia Period, 1732–1775.* Durham, North Carolina: Duke University Press, 1964.

Koontz, Louis Knott. *Robert Dinwiddie: His Career in American Colonial Government and Westward Expansion.* Glendale, California: The Arthur H. Clark Company, 1941.

Kopperman, Paul E., and Russell S. Nelson. *Braddock at the Monongahela.* Pittsburgh: University of Pittsburgh Press, 1977.

Lewis, Virgil A. *Soldiery of West Virginia in the French & Indian War . . . to the War with Mexico.* (Reprint) Baltimore: Genealogical Publishing Co., 1978.

Leyburn, James G. *The Scotch-Irish: A Social History.* Chapel Hill: The University of North Carolina Press, 1962.

Lowdermilk, Will H. *History of Cumberland, Md.* (Reprint) Baltimore: Regional Publishing Co., 1971.

Mayer, Henry. *A Son of Thunder: Patrick Henry and the American Republic.* New York: Grove Press, 1991.

Mulkearn, Lois, ed. *George Mercer Papers Relating to the Ohio Company of Virginia.* Pittsburgh: University of Pittsburgh Press, 1954.

Pargellis, Stanley, ed. *Military Affairs in North America 1748–1765.* (Reprint) Hamden, Connecticut: Archon Books, 1969.

Parker, Arthur C. *The Constitution of the Five Nations.* (Reprint) Oshweken, Ontario, Canada: Iroqrafts, Ltd., 1984.

————. *Parker on the Iroquois.* W. N. Fenton, ed. Syracuse, New York: Syracuse University Press, 1968.

Peyton, J. Lewis. *History of Augusta County, Virginia.* Harrisonburg, Virginia: C. R. Carrier Company, 1985.

Rogers, Alan. *Empire & Liberty: American Resistance to British Authority, 1755–1763.* Berkeley: University of California Press, 1974.

Seaver, James E. *A Narrative of the Life of Mrs. Mary Jemison.* (Reprint) Syracuse, New York: Syracuse University Press, 1990.

Sipe, C. Hale. *Indian Wars of Pennsylvania.* (Reprint) Salem, Massachusetts: Ayer Company, 1971.

Skinner, Constance. *Pioneers of the Old Southwest.* New Haven, Connecticut: Yale University Press, 1919.

Slick, Sewell Elias. *William Trent and the West.* Harrisburg, Pennsylvania: Archives Publishing Co., 1947.

Stone, William L. *Border Wars of the American Revolution* Vol. I. New York: Harper & Brothers, 1843.

Stuart, Col. John. "Narrative of Col. John Stuart of Greenbrier." *William and Mary College Quarterly*, 22(4): 229–234.

Titus, James Russell Wade. *Soldiers When They Chose to Be So: Virginians at War, 1754–1763*. New Brunswick, New Jersey: Rutgers University Press, 1983.

Waddell, Jos. A. *Annals of Augusta County, Virginia from 1726 to 1871*. (Reprint) Harrisonburg, Virginia: C. J. Carrier Company, 1979.

Wallace, Paul A. *Indians in Pennsylvania*. Harrisburg: Pennsylvania Historical and Museum Commission, 1989.

Wilson, Howard McKnight. *The Tinkling Spring, Headwater of Freedom: A Study of the Church and Her People*. Fishersville, Virginia: The Tinkling Spring and Hermitage Presbyterian Churches, 1954.

Withers, Alexander Scott. *Chronicles of Border Warfare: A History of the Settlement by the Whites of Northwestern Virginia, and of the Indian Wars and Massacres in That Section of the State*. (Reprint) Parsons, West Virginia: McClain Printing Company, 1980.

Index

Otis, James, 183
Ottawa River, 68
Ottawas, 183
Outracité, 165, 167

Paleo-Indians, 78, 79–80
patent fees, disputes over, 123–24
patents, delays in recording, 123
patrilineal tradition, 64–65, 71
Patton, James, 108, 109, 112, 124, 130,
    146, 153
  desire for wealth, 117
  high sheriff of August County, 114
  land deal with Lewis, 111, 112–13
  named lieutenant colonel of militia
    for Augusta County, 113
Patton, John, 27, 128
Patton-Lewis schism, 113–14, 189,
    204
Paxton Boys, 187
pedology, 79
Penn, William, 29, 31, 32, 33, 73, 99
Pennsylvania
  immigrant destination, 29–30
  land disputes with Virginia, 126–27,
    218
People of the Longhouse. *See* Iroquois
pistole controversy, 123–24
Pitt, William, 170
plantation, change in meaning of term,
    96
plantation economy, 100–101
planting (English system of plantation
    agriculture), 15
Plymouth Company, 93
Polk, James, 28
Polk, Leonidas, 28
Pontiac, 183, 184–86
Potomac River, 97
predation, 55
Presbyterians, 16–17, 19–21
Preston, John, 108–9
Preston, William, 160–61, 166–67,
    169, 189, 193, 199, 233
Proclamation on 1763, 186–87, 190

Protestants of Ulster, migrating to New
    World, 24–26
Puritanism, 17
Puritans, 19

Quakers (Society of Friends), 30
  approach to land settlement, 33
  determined to avoid armed conflict
    with French, 150
  reaction to Scotch-Irish immigrants,
    105
Quebec Act of 1774, 206
Queen Anne's War, 69
quitrents, 98, 123

Rafinesque, Constantine, 72
Raleigh, Walter, 15, 93
Randolph, John, 106
Randolph, Peyton, 217
Randolph, Richard, 106–7
Randolph, William, 210
Rappahannock River, 96, 97
Rattlesnake People. *See* Iroquois
Reformation, 19
Revere, Paul, 213
River of Wild Geese, 34
Roanoke Island, 15
Robb, Charles, 237
Robinson, Henry, 111
Robinson, John, 107, 111, 121, 151, 172
Rodgers, Lanier, 77–78
Rolfe, John, 95
Ross, Alexander, 99, 101
Roundheads, 20–21, 97
royal charters, rules for settling, 31–32

sachems, 65
Salem, 189-90, 234
Sandy Creek Expedition (1756), 165–68
Scaroyady, 130
Scotch-Irish, 3, 4
  identity, 5
  immersion into America, 237–39
  origins of term, 30
  settling west of Appalachians, 31–32